Attorney Fee Awards:
a Handbook for Attorneys

By Leonard Bucklin

This is a Trial Lawyer Forms book
"Making Good Lawyers Better"

Published and printed in the United States of America.
Booklocker.com, Inc.
2006

ISBN 1-60145-086-9

This is a LawyerTrialForms™ book.
"Making Good Lawyers Better"

LawyerTrialForms™ is a provider of legal forms and texts designed for the lawyer who wants quickly read summaries, clearly stated direct advice, and easy-to-use forms that are immediately useful in litigation. This Attorney Fee Award Handbook is another of our products that give you valuable original ideas and solid insights expressed in the text and in the forms, by an experienced trial attorney.

Visit us on the Internet at www.LawyerTrialForms.com

Foreword

The intention of this book is simply stated. I want you to have a compact and powerful handbook, ready to guide and support you throughout the entire course of litigation, not just at the last moment of trial. I intend to give you the confidence, knowledge, and tools to efficiently and effectively recover, or defend against, an attorney fee award.

This handbook gives you the practical knowledge and advice you need as you handle civil litigation. It tells you, compactly, the essential information. It gives you proven advice, tools and forms, in down to earth direct language. You can, and should, and probably will, read through this entire compact handbook. You will thus start your attorney fee award recovery or defense confidently and in the right way, with the understanding to guide you in your local jurisdiction legal research.

This handbook is aimed at civil litigation, not at criminal cases, and not at domestic relations cases. Attorney fee awards in criminal cases or domestic relations cases have many different rules regarding when attorney's fees may be awarded and to whom, varying widely among the states. Those two areas of litigation are beyond the scope of this compact handbook (although Chapters 03 - 11 of this handbook do have much information that will help you in those two areas).

Inevitably, in short instructions and commentaries of this kind, the author must appear dogmatic. I confess to the use of unqualified summations and assertions, designed to give you quick compact information.

The scheduled periodic updates of this handbook give me the opportunity to incorporate your suggested changes. Send suggestions to me though the contact page on the internet at www.LawyerTrialForms.com. I make the same request of you that was made five centuries ago by an outstanding legal scholar, who was known for his wisdom in dispensing useful advice to lawyers.

.

> "I ask the reader, if he finds in this work anything superfluous or erroneous, to correct and amend it, or pass it over with eyes half closed, for to keep all in mind and err in nothing is divine rather than human."
>
> William Hudson, *A Treatise of the Court of Star Chamber*, 239 (Originally wrote in 1621). Printed at *A Treatise of the Court of Star Chamber by William Hudson*, in Volume 2 of *Collectanea Juridica, consisting of tracts relative to the law and constitution of England*, at pp 52-115. (ed. Francis Hargrave 2 vols., London, 1791-2).

I am grateful to those trial lawyers or legal assistants who have taken the time to express their comments and tell me of the use they have made of my various texts and forms. It affords me a compounded pleasure of authorship. Thank you.

Leonard Bucklin

Copyright, License, Disclaimers and Limitations

Contents at a Glance

[Detailed Table of Contents begins on next page.]

Detailed Table of Contents

Conventions Used in This Book

☞ **TIP** This icon indicates a special tip, suggestion, or note that is associated with the subject under discussion.

◀)) **WARNING** This icon indicates a warning or caution associated with the subject under discussion.

Forms in this book have two special characteristics: [Text withing square brackets] and left justification. Square brackets signal instructions for using the form. The forms are left justified, not full justified, to make it easier for those of you buying the electronic version of this book (or those of you scanning a printed form into your computer) to use your word processor to copy, paste, and edit the form for your own case.

Attorney Fee Awards

Attorney fee awards are an important part of lawsuits. This handbook is designed to be read, and it is designed to be used. It brings law, ethics, and practical advice together, for the prevailing attorney to win an attorney fee award, and for the defending attorney to attack the request for an attorney fee award.

If you want to recover an attorney fee award, you need to know what will be required to prove up an attorney fee. As this Attorney Fee Awards handbook points out, you need to know what is required *before* you make that first time slip recording your attorney time. As you proceed in the litigation, you need to know how to ask the court to grant you an attorney fee award, and you should have some tools and checklists to guide you in making the request. On the other side of the table, if you are defending a request for an award of attorney fees, you need solid ideas and checklists to defeat the request, including ideas to use in deposing the billing attorney and a deposition outline to attack the adverse expert.

In law school they probably did not teach you much about the subject of attorney fee awards. Yet attorney fee awards are now an important part of litigation. In some cases, the amount of the attorney fee award exceeds the amount of the underlying judgment. That is why you need to have compact, essential, fundamental, core information about attorney fee awards.

This is a handbook to be read and keep you on track. It is not intended as a comprehensive multi-volume work. The subject of court-awarded attorney fees has inspired multi-volume treatises, and thick books on specialized aspects of attorney fee awards.[1] If you want all the case and statute law in all jurisdictions, with extended discussion, that is, if you want to purchase a multi-volume work[2]: do so, but don't expect to read it before you have a problem. Thick multi-volume works are designed to help you out of a problem. You won't read through the multi volume treatises before you have a problem.

In contrast, as stated in the Forward to this Attorney Fee Award handbook, "You can, and should, and probably will, read through this entire compact handbook." I want you to know the concepts and tips that will keep you out of problems. This handbook brings law and practical advice together to teach you — before you get into a problem — how to claim, or defend against, an attorney fee award.

The practical lawyering of litigation requires you to have at hand, to be read right at the outset of litigation, a compact handbook of law, advice, and practical tools to help you in your lawsuit and settlement. It is to those needs that this handbook is addressed.

---

[1] See, e.g., Schwartz and Kirklin, 2 Section 1983 Litigation, "Statutory Attorney Fees," (3d ed. 1997); *Bennet, Winning Attorney Fees from the U.S. Government* (19th ed. 2003)

[2] If you do not want a compact handbook in the $70 range (i.e., this handbook), there is a four volume set by Alba Conte, *Attorney Fee Awards*, with annual supplements, published by Thompson-West in the $500 range, and a three volume work by Mary Derfner et *al, Court Awarded Attorney Fees*, published by Matthew Bender, with annual supplements, in the $1000 range.

Chapter 01   Attorneys Fees as a Damage Element

§ 01.01   Importance of attorney fee awards in today's litigation

Today, an important consideration in many litigated cases is whether you can recover your attorney's fees from the opposing party. Attorney firms of even a half dozen attorneys are today what the man on the street would call "Big Bucks Business." Attorney fees can be tens of thousands or even hundreds of thousands of dollars for one case. The importance of recovering an attorney's fee is based on the simple, undisputable fact that the attorney's fees for litigation have taken off on a skyrocket, pricing some litigants out of the market. The size of attorney fees is a large part of why for the client recovering (or defeating) an attorney fee award is important.

There is a cottage industry of attorneys seeking cases solely for the amount of attorneys' fees involved.[3] Pursuant to a statute or a contract between the parties, it is not unusual for a court to approve a fee-shifting award that exceeds the damages recovered by the client. See, e. g., *Hruska v. First State Bank of Deanville*, 747 S.W.2d 783, 785, 31 Tex. Sup. Ct. J. 292 (Tex. 1988) (upholding a $13,000 fee to recover $3,000); *Sibley v. RMA Partners, L. P.*, 138 S.W. 3d 455, 458-59 (Tex. App.--Beaumont 2004, no pet.) (upholding $ 83,000 fee on a recovery of $ 43,000). Hence, for the plaintiff's attorney, the attorney fee itself may become the incentive for undertaking cases that otherwise would be turned down as unprofitable.

This 21st century starts with the awarding of attorney fees having an important financial effect in many cases. This is a fact of the business world today, a fact of which your corporate clients are aware. Further, the award, going to a party prevailing in a matter, drives home a psychological gain or loss that can cement or disrupt an attorney - client

---

[3] The most noted example is that of class action lawsuits brought where the successful plaintiffs each only get a certificate (which they probably will never use) good for a nominal rebate if they purchase more of the product involved, but the plaintiffs' class lawyers get a multi-million dollar fee. *In re Bristol-Myers Squibb Securities Litigation*, No. 02 Civ. 2251(LAP) Slip Copy, 2005 WL 447189 (S.D.N.Y.,2005) has a wonderful footnote that "...plaintiffs in common fund cases [generally remain] mere 'figureheads,' and the real reason for bringing such actions [remains] 'the quest for attorneys' fees." ' *Goldberger v. Integrated Resources, Inc.*, 209 F.3d 43 at 53 (2d Cir.2000) quoting Ralph K. Wittler, *Paying Lawyers, Empowering Prosecutors, and Protecting Managers: Raising the Cost of Capital in America*, 42 Duke L.J. 945, 984 (1993)"

relationship. Attorney fee awards can no longer be viewed simply as an afterthought in your litigation work.

§ 01.02   Availability of attorney fee awards in today's litigation

The importance of attorney fees in modern litigation is increasing not only because of the large size of attorney fees in dispute, but also because the categories of litigation where attorney's fees are recoverable are increasing. Attorney fee awards are more available than they were a generation (20 years) ago.

Indeed the difference between the last quarter of the 20th century and the first quarter of the 21st century is striking. Beginning with the civil rights and employment era of the late 20th century, legislatures began authorizing attorney fees in many types of cases where the actual compensatory damages are often small. Court-awarded attorney fees were considered critical in preserving access to the courts for poor people's survival, and that, without attorney fees awards to plaintiffs, numerous federal laws protecting rights to housing, health care, and other necessities would remain unenforced.

Further, in the last 25 years the judiciary of states courts have joined their legislative brethren in creating entire categories of cases for the recovery of attorney's fees. A good example of that is of late 20th century courts awarding attorneys fees to plaintiffs suing their insurers for contract breach. In 1985, California pronounced, and other states echoed California's pronouncement, that

> When an insurer's tortuous conduct reasonably compels the insured to retain an attorney to obtain the benefits due under a policy, it follows that the insurer should be liable in a tort action for that expense. The attorney's fees are an economic loss – damages – proximately caused by the tort . . . What we consider here is attorney's fees that are recoverable as damages resulting from a tort in the same way that medical fees would be part of the damages in a personal injury action.
>
> *Brandt v. Superior Court of San Diego County,* 37 Cal. 3d 813, and 693 P.2d 796, 210 Cal. Rptr. 211 (1985).

Commentators have suggested that "an argument can be made that the court's decision [in *Brandt*] portends the end of the traditional American rule that the parties to a lawsuit must bear their own attorney's fees."[4]. As we suggest elsewhere in this book, if we look at the cases actually tried, the exceptions to non-taxability of attorney fees are starting to swallow up the rule. For example, contract cases have become the majority filed in federal courts; federal courts use state law in awarding damages; states like Texas

---

[4] Litigation Research Group, *"Attorney's Fees as an Element of Damages"*, Insurance Litigation Reporter, at 7 (March, 1985)

provide for attorney's fees as part of the substantive law[5] of damages in contract cases. *Ergo*, in most of your commercial litigation you'd better be prepared on the issue of attorney fees.

There are many areas of the law other than insurance and contract cases where special statutes or court decisions have directed that the attorney's fees in the litigation are substantive damages, at least for the claimant. For example, the substantive law theory that plaintiff's damages include the attorney's fees needed to recover from the defendant something deliberately or negligently withheld underlies statutes such as the 1985 Texas statute[6] that provides:

> A person may recover reasonable attorney's fees from an individual or
> corporation, in addition to the amount of a valid claim and costs, if the claim is for:
> (1) rendered services;
> (2) performed labor;
> (3) furnished material;
> (4) freight or express overcharges;
> (5) lost or damaged freight or express;
> (6) killed or injured stock;
> (7) a sworn account; or
> (8) an oral or written contract.

This Texas statute is not unusual. Running a computer search on almost any state will show dozens of statutes for recovery of attorney fees when something should have been furnished or paid and was not. Indeed if you represent a plaintiff and fail to research whether attorney fees are recoverable (relying on your law school training that the general rule is that attorney's fees are not recoverable), you may face a malpractice complaint.

Alert plaintiff's counsel can capitalize on the growing opportunities to collect attorney fees for their clients. An injury at the hands of a police officer can become a civil rights violation case as well as a pure personal injury case, and thus allow the recovery of attorneys fees. Viewing the recovery under its different aspects may provide an avenue of recovery to alert counsel. An example is found in the district court decision to award about two million dollars as attorney fees in *Hooven v. Exxon Mobil Corp.*[7] The trial

---

[5] Thus the Texas statute providing for attorney's fees to get your money after furnishing goods or services has been construed also to allow recovery of fees in a suit for quantum merit. See *Olivacea v. Porter Poultry & Egg Co.*, 523 S.W.2d 726 (Tex.Civ.App.--San Antonio 1975, no writ)(involving a quantum merit claim for materials furnished)

[6] § 38.001 *Civil Practice and Procedure Code*, Texas Statutes, Acts 1985, 69th Leg., ch. 959, § 1, eff. Sept. 1, 1985.

[7] *Hooven v. Exxon Mobil Corp.*, Slip Copy, 2005 WL 417416, E.D.Pa.,2005., Feb 14, 2005.

court there found that although the plaintiffs did not recover under their ERISA claim and so were not entitled to an award of attorney fees under ERISA's discretionary fee-shifting provision, they did recover under another theory on the same facts. Hence, the plaintiffs' employment contract which promised attorney fees to any worker who "prevails in any material respect" in an ERISA claim was applicable.

The increase in the number of categories in which attorneys fees may be recovered has coincided with the rise in absolute numbers of cases within those categories. Civil rights and employment cases in the courts are the most significant in the changes in absolute numbers. The makeup of tort trials in the federal courts has shifted from a predominance of bodily injury torts to a predominance of civil rights cases.[8] In the same era, in the federal courts, contract cases now comprise a majority of cases filed (although not of cases tried).[9] State court studies, although not so extensive, indicate the same trends as the federal courts. Contract writers have generated more clauses providing for an award of attorney fees to a prevailing party in any dispute over the contract, and legislatures have authorized attorney fee awards in more contract cases. So both personal injury and commercial litigators more and more often are involved with attorney fee awards.

§ 01.03   Failure to consider attorney fee awards as a damage element

An attorney's failure to consider the possibility that attorney's fees might be recovered for the client can hurt the plaintiff in the pocketbook. E.g., a statute may allow recovery of attorneys fees in an action for conversion, but be silent about unlawful taking of the property under a sales contract, typically a fact situation which supports a conversion theory complaint.[10] Absent the award of attorney fees, counsel might have little care whether the complaint is phrased one way or the other, but with the award possible only under one of the alternative theories, pleading choices can be significant.

---

[8] See the epic studies of Marc Galanter, *The Vanishing Trial: An examination of Trials and Related Matters in Federal and State Courts*, 1 Journal of Empirical Legal Studies 459 (2004) and also Marc Galanter, *Contract in Court, or Almost Everything You May or May Not Want to Know About Contract Litigation*, 2001 Wis. L. Rev. 577 (2001). Other studies show the same.

[9] Ibid.

[10] "Respondents in their notice of appeal argue that they should recover attorney fees . Respondents rely upon *Gits v. Norwest Bank Minneapolis,* 390 N.W.2d 835 (Minn. Ct. App. 1986) to support the argument for an award of attorney fees. We conclude that respondents' reliance upon Gits is misplaced. Gits was a conversion action under article 5, whereas this case is a claim for wrongful repossession under article 9." *Robinson v. Mack Trucks*, 1988. MN. 418, 426 N.W.2d 220

On the other side of the table, alert defense counsel can capitalize on the carelessness of a plaintiff's attorney who fails to prove the attorney fees as he/she would for the other damage elements in the case. For examples, one needs only to look at the reported cases in which an attorney sought attorney fees but failed to provide the court with records containing what we call "The Four Most Important Elements in Time Records." The growing judicial disenchantment with atrocious record keeping and star-status billing rates for average-quality legal work in unexceptional cases can be used by defense counsel to sometimes win the financial war although losing the liability battle. The case of *Role Models America, Inc. v. Brownlee*,[11] is a good recent example of bad plaintiff presentation attacked by an alert defense.

> Insisting that Role Models's request is 'clearly unreasonable,' the government urges us to reduce it drastically....In view of all this -- inadequate documentation, failure to justify the number of hours sought, inconsistencies, and improper billing entries -- we will allow reimbursement for only fifty percent of the [more than 800] attorney hours that Role Models requests.

So whichever side of the counsel table you sit on, it will be wise for you to consider the subject of attorney fees seriously, and decide at the outset of the litigation what you are going to do about litigating attorney fees. This Attorney Fee Award Handbook is devoted to helping you recognize *when* attorney fees can be an important part of your litigation tactics, then show you *how* to secure (or defend against) an award of attorney's fees.

Justice Brennan was right, when he said in ascorbic language:

> Regular appellate scrutiny of [attorney fee awards]....generates a steady stream of opinions, each requiring yet another to harmonize it with the one before or the one after. Ultimately, §1988's straightforward command [to award a reasonable attorney fee] is replaced by a vast body of artificial, judge made doctrine, with its own arcane procedures, which like a Frankenstein's monster meanders its well-intentioned way through the legal landscape leaving waste and confusion (not to mention circuit splits) in its wake.

> *Hensley v. Eckerhart*, 103 S. Ct. 1933, 461 U.S. 424 (1983) (concurrence in part).

Our purpose now, with this Attorney Fee Award Handbook, is to arm you to battle the monster that Justice Brennan has described.

---

[11] 353 F.3d 962 (D.C.Cir., 2004)

Chapter 02　When Attorney's Fees Can be Obtained

§ 02.01　Black letter law is a poor guide

The general black letter rule, learned by generations of law students, is that attorney's fees cannot be recovered by the prevailing party in a lawsuit. The black letter law is supported by court statements such as the following, which abound.

> It is an elemental principle of law in this State that attorney's fees may be awarded a prevailing party only under three circumstances, viz: (1) where authorized by contract; (2) where authorized by a constitutional legislative enactment; and (3) where awarded for services performed by an attorney in creating or bringing into the court a fund or other property."[12]
>
> "[W]e must consider the fundamental principle that attorney's fees are not awarded unless expressly provided for by statute or rule.
>
> *Village Market, Inc. v. State Farm Gen. Ins. Co.*, 970 S.W.2d 243 (Ark. 1998).

Such statements give the wrong impression today. Today, the more accurate impression is given by a statement that: In many types of cases attorney fees can be awarded, although there has to be specific statutory or case law authorizing the award. Statutes controlling numerous cases, such as state and federal civil rights, employment cases, and contract breach cases, allow the prevailing party to recover reasonable attorney's fees and costs. Various court doctrines of fairness allow the recovery of attorney fees. Contract provisions frequently give a prevailing party the right to collect attorney fees. Arbitration is common, and arbitrators have the right to award attorney fees. In short, today in the federal system and in every state court system there are a plethora of statutes, several case law doctrines, and several routes for awarding attorney fees.

§ 02.02　Attorney fee awards in federal courts

In England since 1607, the courts have been authorized by the King and Parliament to award counsel fees to prevailing parties in litigation. It is customary in England, after the litigation of the substantive claims has concluded, to conduct separate hearings before

---

[12] *Kittel v. Kittel*, 210 So. 2d 1, 3 (Fla.1967)

special Taxing Masters to determine the amount of counsel fees to be awarded to the prevailing parties.[13]

In the United States, during the first years of the federal-court system, Congress provided through legislation that in awarding attorney fees the federal courts were to follow the practice of the courts of the states in which the federal courts were located. However, in 1796, the United States Supreme Court, seeking to unify the federal system, took the position that the federal judiciary branch itself would create a general rule for the "United States," as opposed to the Congressional scheme which would produce different results in the sundry federal courts. In those days of the quill pen, before the invention of the typewriter and copying machines, a short opinion was written. The entire text of the opinion follows.

> By The Court:
>
> We do not think that this charge ought to be allowed. The general practice of the United States is in opposition to it; and even if that practice were not strictly correct in principle, it is entitled to the respect of the court, till it is changed, or modified, by statute.
>
> There are several ways in which the charge may be expunged: but we recommend, as, perhaps, the easiest way, that the counsel for the Defendant in error, should enter a remittitur for the amount.
>
> *Arcambel v. Wiseman*, 3 U.S. 306, 3 Dall. 306, 1796 WL 896 (U.S.R.I.), 1 L.Ed. 613.

To the present day the United States federal courts have adhered to that holding: the federal *general* rule is that attorney fees are not allowed – unless there is a federal statute modifying the court's rule and specifying the recovery of attorney fees.[14]

Congress has stepped into the gap created by the Supreme Court. Congress has supplied more than three dozen statutes which do authorize attorney fees. Because these statutes supply the substantive basis for a majority of federal cases actually tried nationwide, an award of attorney's fees in federal courts is common. A partial list of the many federal statues authorizing counsel fee awards follows. Read this partial list to enjoy the variety of federal claims involving attorney fee award litigation.

---

[13] See generally Goodhart, *Costs,* 38 Yale L.J. 849 (1929); C. McCormick, *Law of Damages* 234-236 (1935). Several pre-Revolutionary American colonies forbid attorney-client fee contracts for litigation, instead using fee awards in litigation as part of a system of regulating attorney fees, and they continued to do so after the Revolution. By 1796, attorneys had won the right to have fee contracts to handle litigation. Hence, the general practice of clients and attorneys was to use fee-contracts, rather than fee awards to pay attorneys. Note the *Arcambel* opinion in the text, regarding "general practice."

[14] The case most often cited for the proposition that attorney fees are not allowed in federal courts is *Alyeska Pipeline Service Co. v. Wilderness Society,* 95 S. Ct. 1612, 421 U.S. 240 (1975).

Administrative Procedure Act, 5 U. S. C. § 504(b)(1)(A)

Childhood Vaccine Injury Act, 42 U. S. C. § 300aa-31©

Civil Rights Act, 42 U. S. C. § 1998

Clean Air Amendments of 1970, 42 U. S. C. §§ 7413b, 7604(d), 7607(f) and 42 U. S. C. § 7622(b)(2)(B)

Comprehensive Environmental Response, Compensation, and Liability Act, 42 U. S. C. § 9659(f)

Deep Seabed Hard Mineral Resources Act, 30 U. S. C. § 1427©

Deepwater Port Act, 33 U. S. C. § 1515(d)

Emergency Planning and Community Right-to-Know, 42 U. S. C. § 11046(f)

Employee Retirement Income Security Act ("ERISA"), 29 U.S.C. § 1132(g)

Endangered Species Act, 16 U. S. C. § 1540(g)(4)

Energy Policy and Conservation Act, 42 U. S. C. § 6305(d)

Energy Reorganization Act of 1974, 42 U. S. C. § 5851(e)(2)

Equal Access to Justice Act (EAJA) 28 U.S.C. § 2412(d)(2)(A)

Equal Employment Opportunity Act, 42 U. S. C. § 2000e-1(k)

Federal Oil and Gas Royalty Management Act, 30 U. S. C. § 1734(a)(4)

Federal Water Pollution Control Act, 33 U. S. C. §§ 1365(d), 1369(b)(3)

Federal Power Act, 16 U. S. C. § 825q-1(b)(2)

Federal Trade Commission Act, 15 U. S. C. § 57a(h)(1)

Hazardous Liquid Pipeline Safety Act, 49 U. S. C. App. § 2014(e)

Historic Preservation Act, 16 U. S. C. § 470w-4

Longshoremen's and Harbor Workers' Compensation Act, 33 U. S. C. § 928(d)

Marine Protection, Research, and Sanctuaries Act, 33 U. S. C. § 1415(g)(4)

Noise Control Act, 42 U. S. C. § 4911(d)

Ocean Thermal Energy Conversion Act of 1980, 42 U. S. C. § 9124(d)

Oil Pollution Act, 33 U. S. C. § 2706(g) (1988 ed., Supp. II)

Outer Continental Shelf Lands Act Amendments, 43 U. S. C. § 1349(a)(5)

Petroleum Marketing Practices Act, 15 U. S. C. §§ 2805(d)(1)©, 2805(d)(3)

Powerplant and Industrial Fuel Use Act of 1978, 42 U. S. C. § 8435(d)

Public Utility Regulatory Policies Act, 16 U. S. C. § 2632 (a)(1)

Safe Drinking Water Act, 42 U. S. C. § 300j-8(d)

Surface Mining Control and Reclamation Act, 30 U. S. C. § 1270(d)

Tax Equity and Fiscal Responsibility Act, 26 U. S. C. § 7430(c)(1)

Truth in Lending, 15 U.S.C.A. § 1640(a)(2)

Removal to Federal Court, Remand Orders, 28 U. S. C. §1447 (c) [15]

After reading the above illustrative list, your mandate is clear: if federal law is involved, use the electronic search means available to you to scan the statutory chapter involved for "attorney fee."[16]

---

[15] Although 28 U. S. C. §1447 (c) provides that a remand order sending a case back to state court "may require payment of just costs and any actual expenses, including attorney fees," improper removal of a state cause of action to a federal court does not automatically authorize award of attorney fees. In *Martin v. Franklin Capital Corp.*, 126 S.Ct. 704, 163 L.Ed.2d 547 (2005) the Supreme Court ruled that, attorney fees should not be awarded when the party who sought removal had an objectively reasonable basis for doing so, but only where no absolutely no objectively reasonable basis for removal existed can fees awarded. This is not the first time that, when applying fee-shifting statutes, the Supreme Court has found "just limits" to "the large objectives" of the relevant act. E.g., *Zipes*, 491 U.S., at 759.

[16] The statutory grant of an attorney fee as part of the cause of action or procedure involved in the cause of action sometimes is buried under an unlikely section title that includes other items, so merely scanning a table of contents of section titles may not lead you to the attorney fee award provision.

Aside from the abundant statutory authorizations, the federal courts, handling federal litigation, recognize only three[17] common law reasons for awarding attorney fees.

A federal court may award attorney's fees to a party whose litigation efforts directly benefit others.[18] This is the so-called "common fund exception," which derives from a historic exercise of equity jurisdiction.

A federal court may assess attorney's fees as a sanction for the willful disobedience of a court order.[19] This is really part of the court's range of authority to punish for contempt of court.

A federal court may assess attorney's fees when a party has "'acted in bad faith, vexatiously, wantonly, or for oppressive reasons," or when a court finds that fraud has been practiced upon it, or when a party shows bad faith by delaying or disrupting the litigation or by hampering enforcement of a court order.[20] This bad faith exception to the non-awarding of attorney's fees is premised on the court's inherent power to protect the integrity of the judicial process. An oft-coted enunciation of that theory is in *Alyeska Pipeline Service Co. v. Wilderness Society.*[21] There, the U.S. Supreme Court asserted that a federal court can assess attorney's fees when a party has "acted in bad faith, vexatiously, wantonly, or for oppressive reasons."

In addition to statutory authorizations and the three common law reasons, the federal courts use one other authority for the award of attorney fees, to wit: the Federal Rules of Civil Procedure. A federal court has powers under Rules 11 and 37 to assess

---

[17] A fourth doctrine, the private attorney general doctrine used in state courts, was explicitly disavowed for use in the federal courts by *Alyeska Pipeline Service Co. v. Wilderness Society,* 95 S. Ct. 1612, 421 U.S. 240 (1975).

[18] See *Sprague v. Ticonic National Bank*, 307 U.S. 161, 164 (1939).

[19] See *Fleischmann Distilling Corp. v. Maier Brewing Co.*, 386 U.S. 714, 718 (1967); and *Toledo Scale Co. v. Computing Scale Co.*, 261 U.S. 399, 428 (1923).

[20] See, e.g., *F. D. Rich Co. v. United States ex rel. Industrial Lumber Co.*, 417 U.S. 116, 129 1974); and *Hall v. Cole*, 412 U.S. 1, 5 (1973)

[21] 421 US 240 at 258-259 (1975). Further examples of a federal court awarding attorney's fees as a part of its power to protect the integrity of the judicial process are *Caspe v. Aacon Auto Transport, Inc.*, 658 F2d 613 (8th Clr 1981) (conduct in failing to comply with court discovery order, abusing discovery requests, being obstructive at trial); *Obin v. District 9 of the International Association of Machinists*, 651 F2d 574 (8th Cir 1981) (plaintiff sued defendant against whom there was little evidence); *Coleman v. General Motors Corp.*, 27 Fair Employment Practice Cases 1009 (8th Clr 1981) (employee who sued a union for failure to raise a particular argument in a discharge proceeding could not reasonably have believed that the union had a discriminatory motive).

attorney's fees for misuse of the court's rules, or for causing expense by creating improper discovery or substantive problems for adversaries.

Yet one more source of fee awards in federal court exists — an award of attorney's fees when a state cause of action allowing attorney fees is being tried in federal courts. State claims can be brought in federal court where there is diversity of state citizenship of the parties.[22] In addition, state claims may be litigated in federal court where the claims are pendant or ancillary to a cause of action for which there is federal jurisdiction.[23]

The question the federal court is faced with is: what happens to a state law providing for recovery of attorney fees when the case is removed to federal court (or is started in federal court on diversity grounds)? In diversity cases *Erie Railroad v. Tompkins*[24] requires federal courts to apply substantive state law to substantive questions. Likewise, when a state law cause of action is being tried in federal court only because of pendant jurisdiction, then *Erie Railroad v. Tompkins* requires federal courts to apply substantive state law to substantive questions.

There is a well-developed body of federal case law holding that when various fee-shifting statutes are part of a particular state's substantive law they can be applied by the federal court in the state cause of action before it. The federal court will investigate whether the state law is substantive or "merely procedural in determining damages." Then it will apply the state fee-shifting if the state law is substantive and not procedural. *Hinde v. Provident Life and Accident Insurance Company*[25] illustrates the point nicely. In the federal district court, Provident was awarded attorney fees as the prevailing party, under Alaska state law, because the Alaska fee-shifting law was considered substantive by the district judge. But — when there was an appeal, the federal appeals judges decided that the Alaska rules providing for fee-shifting of attorneys fees on appeal was only procedural, not substantive. The net effect was fee-shifting of the prevailing party's attorney fees before the appeal, but not of the attorney fees for the successful appeal.

If you are arguing that state law on attorney's fees applies in your federal court case, the place from which you start your brief is the *Rules of Decision Act*.[26] That Act was originally adopted as a provision of the Judiciary Act of 1789, and has remained largely unchanged to this day. The *Rules of Decision Act* states that "the laws of the several

---

[22] 28 U.S.C. sec. 1332(a)(1)

[23] 28 U.S.C. sec. 1367.

[24] 304 U.S. 64 (1938).

[25] No. 95-35463 (9th Cir. 04/25/1997)(Unpublished).

[26] : 28 U.S.C. Section 1652.

states, except where the Constitution, treaties or statutes of the United States will otherwise require or provide, shall be regarded as rules of decisions in trials at common law in the courts of the United States in cases where they apply. Then you point to *Erie Railroad v. Tompkins.*[27]   Until the *Erie* decision, the federal courts were construing "laws of the several states" in the Rules of Decision Act to only mean statutory law. The significance of *Erie* was that the meaning of "the laws of the several states" was expanded to include all substantive law including state common law. *Erie* had a significant effect on the federal/state judicial dynamic. Essentially, Erie requires that unless there is an applicable federal law, state law applies if the state law is a "rule of decision," not a mere procedural rule. Your job in arguing that state law applies to allow fee awards to your client in federal court is to convince the federal court that the award of attorneys' fees to the prevailing party is not just a matter of state procedure, convenience, or making the state court run smoothly. To do this, you should specifically make the argument that there is an important substantive public policy behind the state decision to award of attorney's fees to the prevailing party.

§ 02.03   Attorney fee awards in state courts

In state courts, the classes of cases in which attorney's fees may be recovered as damages are a bewildering array. Each state seems to have had legislatures with their own pet ideas of what is a substantial injury that some rascals are creating and only lawsuits can stop. For example, in Texas, the legislature has tender concern for those seeking remedies for "...(5) lost or damaged freight or express; (6) killed or injured stock."[28] In North Dakota, legislative concern is for cruelly caged animals, but not if the animal mistreatment involves "agricultural display of caged animals by any political subdivision."[29] In Arizona, where residential construction is a main industry, rental disputes get attorney fee awards.[30] In Vermont, when an "injury was caused by the driving or floating of lumber" then a reasonable attorney fee may be recovered.[31]

However, among the various state statues, there are some common threads on the award of attorney fees. Here following, as an example, is a list of some of the statutes and case law that exists generally in the various states. I repeat: each state is unique.

---

[27] Is 304 U.S. 64 (1938)

[28] *Tex.Civ.Prac.& Rem.Code Ann.* § 38.001 (Vernon 1997).

[29] NDCC 36-21.1-02

[30] ARS 33-2105.

[31] Vermont Statutes: Title 25, Chp 5., Subchapter 2, § 243.

The legislatures sometimes even may adopt a Uniform Act but specially inject or remove attorney's fees as damages. Because this book is not a multi volume text devoted only to attorney's fees, we are *not* going to give you a list of every attorney fee statute or attorney fee case in every state.[32] What we do want to point out to you here is that a prevailing party in many states can often recover attorney's fees in more types of cases and more types of situations that most attorneys appreciate.

Pay particular attention to the possibility of an award of attorney fees in cases litigated in state courts when:

✓   **An award of attorney's fees is provided for in the contract being enforced.** Although a contract typically calls for attorney fees if there is a breach of a contract, a suit seeking a declaratory judgement or an injunction (instead of damages for breach) does not eliminate an award of fees. E.g., see *Texas Commerce Bank v. Garamendi*, 28 Cal.App.4th 1234, 34 Cal. Rptr. 2d 155 (1994). In many states, such as Florida, attorney fee provisions are, as a matter of law, interpreted to be reciprocal even if the language appears to be one sided.

✓   **The suit is to enforce a contract.** Even though the contract does not speak of attorney fees or indemnity, in a number of states the entire category of contract cases is subject to statutory provisions authorizing attorney fee awards. Indeed, contract suits probably are the most common subject of state statutes authorizing an award of attorney fees.

✓   **The suit is to enforce civil rights or antidiscrimination protections.** Almost always the legislature includes a provision for attorney fees on the theory that private attorney generals do more than the state attorney general. In short, the legislatures passing civil rights litigation disregards the argument that there will be numerous "frivolous lawsuits" and considers it necessary to utilize private civil suits and private attorneys to uphold the public interest in these sensitive fields of legal enforcement.

✓   **The suit is one brought under a "public nuisance" or "private attorney general" concept.** Somewhat akin to the "common fund creation" theory, in the state courts there are cases holding that common law allows an award of attorney fees to secure benefits for a broad class of persons by effectuating a strong public policy, whether or not there is a statute authorizing a fee award. *Serrano v. Priest*, 20 Cal. 3d 25,141 Cal. Rptr. 315, 569 P.2d 1303 (1977) is a good

---

[32] Furthermore, we exclude from this handbook the subject of attorney fee awards in domestic relations cases. An award of legal fees and costs in a marital dissolution is considered essential to the proper assertion of marital rights to which the less financially favored party might be entitled. Like so much in the domestic relations and marital dissolution field, entitlement to attorney fees and the procedures governing such awards are determined in accordance with local law, which are considerably varied by state.

illustration of a state award if fees under the concept of private enforcement of public rights, especially since *Serrano* had neither the authority of a statute nor contract that authorized fee-shifting, and indeed California had a statute (§ 1021 of the Code of Civil Procedure) which provided that "each party is to bear his own attorney fees unless a statute or the agreement of the parties provides otherwise."

But to the contrary in the federal courts, no such theory is available after *Alyeska Pipeline Service Co. v. Wilderness Society*, 95 S. Ct. 1612, 421 U.S. 240, 44 L. Ed. 2d 141 (1975). Although lower federal courts had made attorney fee awards under a private attorney general concept, the majority *Alyeska* opinion stated, at 44 L. Ed. Page 269: "[C]ourts are not free to fashion drastic new rules . . . in Federal litigation or to pick and choose among plaintiffs and the statutes under which they sue and to award fees in some cases but not in others, depending upon the courts' assessment of the importance of the public policies involved in particular cases. Nor should the Federal courts purport to adopt on their own initiative a rule awarding attorneys' fees based on the private-attorney-general approach when such judicial rule will operate only against private parties and not against the Government." The *Alyeska* case majority opinion, dissent, and counsel notes in the Lawyer's Edition contain many helpful arguments and citations to authority on both sides of the question of a "private attorney general" concept of fee awards.

✓ **The wrongful acts of the defendant caused the plaintiff to become involved in litigation with a third party.** This "third party exception" rule, sometimes called the "tort of another exception" is embodied in the *Restatement of Torts* and is generally followed in the United States. See *Rest.2d Torts*, § 914, subd. (2), and appendix; *Annot.*, 45 A.L.R. 2d 1183 (1956); 22 Am. Jur. 2d *Damages* § 618 and 621(1988). The plaintiff must show that: (1) he became involved in a legal dispute because of the defendant's tortious conduct; (2) the dispute was with a third party; (3) the plaintiff incurred attorneys' fees in connection with that suit; (4) the expenditure of attorneys' fees was a foreseeable or necessary result of the tortious conduct; and (5) the claimed fees are reasonable. Sample cases are *Collins v. First Financial Services Inc.*, 815 P.2d 411, 168 Ariz. 484 (Ariz. App., 1991); *Blair v. Boulger*, 336 NW2d 337 (ND, 1983); *Prentice v. North Amer. Title Guar. Corp.*, 59 Cal. 2d 618, 620-621, 30 Cal. Rptr. 821, 381 P.2d 645 (1963). The courts classifying the cost of litigation with third parties as "substantive damages," hence compensatory, instead of as "attorney fees" hence not compensatory, are growing in number.

✓ **It is a will contest or some other probate transaction or litigation.** The trial court may award attorney fees for legal services in a will contest if the proceedings benefit the estate as a whole. Attorneys often overlook the possibility of recovering fees if more than their specific client will benefit from the result. A North Dakota case correctly sums up the doctrine.

> In Estate of Rohrich, 496 N.W.2d 566, 570 (N.D. 1993), this Court ....recognized the trial court may award attorney fees, as a matter of equity, for legal services benefitting the estate as a whole. It has been held that the equitable power of a court authorizes an award of attorney fees in an action by one person which benefits a class of persons, thus making it equitable to spread the costs of the action among the members of the benefitted class. More specifically,...when, at their own expense and not for their sole benefit, their attorney's services benefitted the estate as a whole by increasing a common fund in which other beneficiaries might share.

> *In Estate of Hass*, 2002 ND 82.

An increase in money in the estate is not required to permit the award of an attorney fee, if there is some other substantial benefit.

> To be beneficial, it need not be shown that net tangible monetary advantage was realized or that a money loss was avoided. The administration of trust property does not permit so simplified a test of 'benefit.' The word applies to every aspect of administration which sound judgment would approve. If in the carrying on of such an administration legal services are required either in defense or in attack, the fiduciary may contract for or may pay and receive allowance for reasonable fees.

> *In re Pelgram's Estate,* 146 Misc. 750, 262 N.Y.S. 848, 854 (1933).

✓   **The suit is with the government about taxes.** The revenue code involved most often has a provision for limited attorney fees on a successful suit against the government — if the suit followed various conditions precedent to suit.

✓   **The suit is by an insured against the insurance company to collect benefits.** Generally the insured can collect attorney fees if they win; the insurer cannot. For the insurer to collect, the statute or case law must be specific.[33]

✓   **The suit is one to secure employee benefits**. Statutes, group benefit contracts, and employee contracts frequently provide for attorney fees on an employee benefit suit.

✓   **The action is to enforce a construction lien or to enforce a claim against a construction bond**. Statutes often so provide.

---

[33] E.g., see Village Market, Inc. v. State Farm Gen. Ins. Co., 970 S.W.2d 243 (Ark. 1998).

✓ **The dispute is referred to arbitration.** In some states attorney fees may be awarded in arbitration if requested by the parties during the arbitration process.[34] Almost always, each side inserts a boilerplate request for attorney fees in their arbitration pleadings, leading to someone getting attorney fees awarded. In other states, "arbitrators, unless expressly restricted by the agreement of the parties, enjoy the authority to fashion relief they consider just and fair under the circumstances existing at the time of arbitration"[35] which power includes the power to award attorney fees unless contractually prohibited by the arbitration agreement or contract.

✓ **The action is to collect a worthless check.** Statutes often so provide.

✓ **The suit involves protecting a trade secret, or a copyright, or trademark, or patent**. The Uniform Trade Secrets Act, adopted in some states, provides that courts may award reasonable attorneys' fees to a prevailing party (1) if an opposing party in bad faith (a) claimed misappropriation of trade secrets, (2) moved to terminate an injunction, or (3) resisted a motion to terminate an injunction, or (2) or if the opposing party willfully and maliciously misappropriated a trade secret.

Under 17 U.S.C. § 505, a court may award reasonable attorneys' fees to the prevailing party in copyright litigation, but in the federal courts 35 U.S.C. § 285 allows the fees only if the case is "exceptional." However, federal intellectual property rights can be enforced in state court. State copyright, trademark and intellectual property statutes frequently provide for attorney fees.[36]

✓ **It is an action for a declaratory judgment.** The Uniform Declaratory Judgments Act §8 only allows the court to award "costs," not attorney fees. But some states have modified the uniform statute to provide the court also may award attorneys fees.[37] Other states' case law suggests that if the declaratory judgment action

---

[34] E.g., *Emery Roth & Sons v M & B Oxford 41*, 298 AD2d 320, 321 [2002], leave denied 99 NY2d 509 [2003]).

[35] *Advanced Micro Devices, Inc. v. Intel Corp.*, 9 Cal.4th 362, at 383 (1994)

[36] E.g., in Texas obtaining a trademark by a false representation that is only ignorant, not fraudulent, subjects you to "damages . . . , plus costs of suit, including attorneys' fees". §16.27, *Business and Commerce Code*, Texas Statutes

[37] E.g., § 37.009, *Civil Practice and Procedure Code*, Texas Statutes

involves an underlying subject where attorney's fees might be awarded, attorney's fees are likewise appropriate in the declaratory judgment action.[38]

✓   **The suit is for legal malpractice, and the underlying case was one in which attorney's fees could have been recovered by a prevailing party.** See, e.g.:

> If Fulton had been required to prove his underlying discrimination claim, he may have been entitled to attorney fees incurred as a result of proving up his underlying claim in the malpractice action. See *Lorenzetti v. Jolles*, 120 F. Supp. 2d 181, 190 (D. Conn. 2000) (permitting a prevailing party to recover those attorney fees incurred as a result of proving an underlying claim in a legal malpractice claim); *Fitzgerald v. Walker*, 121 Idaho 589, 594, 826 P.2d 1301, 1306 (1992) (affirming denial of attorney fees in malpractice case involving underlying antitrust claim because an attorney tried to prove his fees by post-trial affidavit; held: fees to prove underlying claim are part of measure of damages and must be submitted at trial as part of proof of damages); *Admiral Merchs. Motor Freight, Inc. v. O'Connor & Hannan*, 494 N.W.2d 261, 267 (Minn. 1992) ("In Minnesota malpractice cases, attorney fees incurred in the underlying dispute constituting the alleged malpractice may be recovered."); *Glamann v. St. Paul Fire and Marine Ins. Co.*, 424 N.W.2d 924, 927 (Wis. 1988) (awarding attorney fees to prevailing party in legal malpractice action for portion of claim that went to proving underlying employment discrimination claim).
>
> *Fulton v. Schermer*, No. C7-01-1449 (Minn.App. 04/02/2002).

✓   **The case involves a claim for indemnity though either an indemnity contract or an indemnity provision.** What if the indemnity contract is silent on the subject of attorney fees? The state law is rapidly changing on this subject. At one time attorney's fees were not allowed to the plaintiff, but now the cases talk of the intent of indemnity being that the injured person should not have to bear any cost, including attorney's fees to collect the indemnity due them. An illustrative case is *Hoge v. Burleigh County Water Management District,* 311 NW2d 23 (ND 1981). The court allowed recovery of attorney fees where there was an agreement between the parties for "indemnity" but attorney's fees were not specified to be recovered. This case overruled without mentioning the doctrine expressed 20 years earlier in *Hartford Accident & Indemnity Company v. Anderson,* 155NW 728 (ND. 1968) (which forbade recovery of attorney's fees, even if specifically a part of the indemnity contract, as contrary to public policy).

✓   **The suit is for unfair and deceptive trade practices.** Statutes often so provide.

---

[38] E.g., *Farmland Mut Ins. Co. v. Farmers Elevator Ins.*, 404 NW2d 473 at 478,footnote 1 (ND, 1987).

✓ **The suit is for anti-trust or monopoly statute violations.** Statutes often so provide.

✓ **The suit is by a limited partner required to sue on behalf of the partnership, or a derivative suit by a stockholder.** Partner suits to force general partners to act, or a derivative suit by a stockholder against the corporation to force the corporation to act, are treated akin to common fund cases. If a judgment in such a suit confers a substantial benefit on a corporate or partnership defendant, the defendant may be required to pay the attorney fees incurred by the plaintiff.[39]

✓ **The state law or rule of civil procedure allows parties to litigation to make offers of judgment or proposals of settlement.** Such offers if not accepted by a party may require payment of attorney's fees, depending upon the ultimate result in the litigation.

✓ **A statute which provides for an award of attorney fees to the prevailing party in the specific claim in litigation.** Because there will be times when statutes give you a surprise, we call this "The all-too-often-overlooked statute." For example, commercial printed contracts frequently provide that the seller can recover attorney's fees if the contract needs to be enforced. The defendant may automatically assume that a successful defense does not entitle the defendant to attorney fees, because the contract does not so provide. Yet your state may have a hidden statute like Florida, which has tucked contract attorney fees into *Florida Stautes* 57.105, which is misleadingly headed ".... sanctions for raising unsupported claims or defenses; service of motions; damages for delay of litigation."

> (7) If a contract contains a provision allowing attorney's fees to a party when he or she is required to take any action to enforce the contract, the court may also allow reasonable attorney's fees to the other party when that party prevails.

The moral to this example of a hidden statutory provision is that a computer search of your state statutes for "attorney's fees" may produce more than will browsing the likely subject topic headings in the statutes.

Do not do only a computer search for "attorney's fees" generally in the statutes, Read the entire specific statutory chapter involved with the claim in litigation; it may give you (or take away from you) attorney fee rights treated otherwise in a general statute. For example, earlier in this text we mentioned Texas Article 2226 of the *Civil Practice and Remedies Code* as a general statute governing the

---

[39] E.g., *Fletcher v. A. J. Industries, Inc.*, 266 Cal. App. 2d 313, 323-325, [72 Cal. Rptr. 146 (1968).

recovery of attorney's fees. The general areas of cases in this Texas statute are broad and several.[40]   Yet the Texas statutes and case law contain tens of additional special statutes providing for attorney fees. E.g., in Texas if you stopped after reading the general attorney fee statute in the *Civil Practice and Remedies Code*, you would have missed additional items such as:

> Failing to pay a salesperson a commission results in a "plus reasonable attorney's fees and costs" award.[41]

> Mere mental anguish without economic loss results in a plus "reasonable attorney fees" award, if the mental anguish arose because a mental health provider engaged in sex with the patient.[42]

> Using water that someone else rightfully was entitled to will results in some plus "reasonable attorney fees and expert costs" award.[43]

Texas is not alone in having a slew of specific statutes on attorney fees. These examples now should have convinced you to start looking for such statutes anytime you start a case. Do not stop when you read a state's general statute on attorney fees or general case law. Research statutes and case law specifically on your cause of action, and you may be surprised to find an award of attorney's fee possible.

§ 02.04   Carefully choose among alternative theories of recovery

The language you use in your complaint may determine whether or not you have a right to recover an award for attorneys fees. For example, a common statute in various states is one that allows an award of attorneys fees on a suit for breach of contract. That does not necessarily mean that if you pick only one aspect of the contract breach as the basis of your claim that you can recover the attorney fee. For example, in *Carlisle Corp. v.*

---

[40] Originally, the provisions of Article 2226 were strictly construed. However, strict construction is not required since Article 2226 was amended in 1979 to provide for liberal construction to promote its underlying purpose. *McKinley v. Drozd*, 685 S.W.2d 7 (Tex. 1985).

[41] § 35.84, *Business and Commerce Code*, Texas Statutes.

[42] § 81.004, *Civil Practice and Remedies Code*, Texas Statutes.

[43] § 11.0841, *Water Code*, Texas Statutes.

Medial City Dallas, LTD.,[44] suit was maintained not broadly as a breach of contract, but rather specifically as a breach of an express warranty that was a part of the contract. Plaintiffs pointed out the "the universal rule that a warranty, either express or implied, must grow out of contractual relations between the parties," and sought recovery of an attorney fee under a statute providing for attorney fees in contract cases. Nevertheless, the court denied an attorney fee award on the reasoning that there was not a recovery a on breach of contract claim because a breach of warranty claim "is distinct from a breach of contract claim." The moral here is that on the plaintiff's side of the case you must be alert to the possibility that by being too specific you may be excluding the attorney fee as a part of the recovery. For another example, in *Robinson v. Mack Trucks,*[45] phrasing a complaint as one for wrongful repossession, instead of wrongful conversion of property, was all that prevented plaintiffs' recovery of an attorney fee.

§ 02.05   Attorney fees as substantive damages.

On the plaintiff's side, an attorney should consider advancing the theory of attorney fees as *expected* substantive damages inherent in the civil wrong. Try to use an argument like the California court used in finding attorney's fees as common law damages in insurance policy holder litigation. The language of the *Brandt* court reflects the common law idea that for an expected injury, a tortfeasor should be held liable. The *Brandt* court simply *added* the idea that the defendant would *expect* the policyholder to be injured by the incurrence of attorney fees needed to collect insurance proceeds.

> When an insurer's tortuous conduct reasonably compels the insured to retain an attorney to obtain the benefits due under a policy, it follows that the insurer should be liable in a tort action for that expense. The attorney's fees are an economic loss -- damages -- proximately caused by the tort. . . . What we consider here is attorney's fees that are recoverable as damages resulting from a tort in the same way that medical fees would be part of the damages in a personal injury action.
>
> *Brandt v. Superior Court of San Diego County*, 37 Cal. 3d 813, and 693 P.2d 796, 210 Cal. Rptr. 211 (1985).

Although there are special fiduciary duties of an insurer, the Brandt theory of attorney fees as *expected damages* can be applied to many other classes of civil wrong.

---

[44] 2006 Tex. App. LEXIS 576.

[45] 1988 MN.418, 426 N.W.2d 220

§ 02.06   Equitable power of the court

If you cannot find specific statutes or case law for an award of attorney's fees for your case, check to see if the general equitable power of the court that may be invoked. The United States Supreme Court has phrased that equitable power thus:

Limited exceptions to the American rule have, of course, developed. They have been sanctioned by this Court when overriding considerations of justice seemed to compel such a result. In appropriate circumstances, we have held, an admiralty plaintiff may be awarded counsel fees as an item of compensatory damages (not as a separate cost to be taxed). *Vaughan v. Atkinson,* 369 U.S. 527 (1962). . . . . Sprague   v. Ticonic National Bank, 307 U.S. 161 (1939) involved yet another exception. That exception had previously been applied in cases where a plaintiff traced or created a common fund for the benefit of others as well as himself. *Central Railroad & Banking Co. v. Pettus,* 113 U.S. 116 (1885); *Trustees v. Greenough,* 105 U.S. 527 (1882). In that situation to have allowed the others to obtain full benefit from the plaintiff's efforts without requiring contribution or charging the common fund for attorney's fees would have been to enrich the others unjustly at the expense of the plaintiff. Sprague itself involved a variation of the common-fund situation where, although the plaintiff had not in a technical sense sued for the benefit of others or to create a common fund, the stare decisis effect of the judgment obtained by the plaintiff established as a matter of law the right of a discernible class of persons to collect upon similar claims. The Court held that the general equity power "to do equity in a particular situation" supported an award of attorney's fees under such circumstances for the same reasons that underlay the common-fund decisions"

Fleischmann Distilling Corp. v. Maier Brewing Co, 87 S. Ct. 1404, 386 U.S. 714 (1967).

Of course, if you are defending, resist the imposition of attorney fees under the rubric of equitable power by finding the oversimplified legal thinking probably found in at least one of your state's cases that will read something like the following.

It is an elemental principle of law in this State that attorney's fees may be awarded a prevailing party only (1) where authorized by contract, or (2) where authorized by a specific statute.

In fact, you might even put it in bold black letters (it looks so impressive!) and point out that it is black letter law that we all learned in law school. Some states may agree with you (e.g., see the assertion of the Illinois court in *People ex rel. Henderson v. Redfern*[46] "... The assessing of attorneys' fees against the losing party rests wholly upon statutory or contractual authority.....There is no common law or equitable principle allowing attorneys' fees either as costs or damages." The language expresses bad law, but the language is there for you to use.

---

[46] 104 Ill.App.2d 132, 243 N.E.2d 252, 254 (1968).

§ 02.07   Prevailing party

To recover attorney's fees, generally your client must be a "prevailing party." There is much case law defining who is a prevailing party in various circumstances. But 99 times out of 100 it boils down to the following items # 1 and # 2. This is all you need to know if you want a compact definition of who is a "prevailing party."

 # 1. Defendant. A defendant must win totally on all the claims involved in the subject matter to be a prevailing party.

A defendant faces another hurdle if the fee-shifting statute is deemed one arising form a public policy to encourage plaintiffs to bring suits needed for a public purpose. The following quotation is often used in these instances of public policy.

> The fee provisions of the civil rights laws are acutely sensitive to the merits of an action and to antidiscrimination policy. Unlike § 1927, both § 1988 and § 2000e-5 (k) restrict recovery to prevailing parties. In addition, those provisions have been construed to treat plaintiffs and defendants somewhat differently. Prevailing plaintiffs in civil rights cases win fee awards unless "special circumstances would render such an award unjust," *Newman v. Piggie Park Enterprises,* 390 U.S. 400, 402 (1968) (per curiam), but a prevailing defendant may be awarded counsel fees only when the plaintiff's underlying claim is "frivolous, unreasonable, or groundless." *Christiansburg Garment Co. v. EEOC,* 434 U.S. 412, 422 (1978). This distinction advances the congressional purpose to encourage suits by victims of discrimination while deterring frivolous litigation.
>
> *Roadway Express v. Piper,* 100 S. Ct. 2455, 447 U.S. 752 (1980).

 # 2. Plaintiff. Two issues for the plaintiff seeking an attorney fee award are (A) how much the litigant has to win and (B) what form the victory must take. The United States Supreme Court holds that a plaintiff need not win every single issue or even the central issue to obtain prevailing party status. A prevailing party is "one who has succeeded on any significant claim affording it some of the relief sought . . . ." [47] Losing on some issues does not affect "the availability of a fee award *vel non.*"[48]

> A typical formulation is that "plaintiffs may be considered `prevailing parties' for attorney's fees purposes if they succeed on any significant issue in litigation which achieves some of the benefit the parties sought in bringing suit.
>
> *Hensley v. Eckerhart,* 461 U.S. 424 (1983)

The second question for the plaintiff —what form the victory must be take—became clearer after *Buckhannon Board v. West Virginia Department of Health and Human*

---

[47] *Texas Teachers Association. v. Garland School District,* 489 U.S. 782, 791 (1989).

[48] *Texas Teachers Association,* 489 U.S. at 793.

Resources.[49] *Buckhannon* held that voluntary change in behavior by a defendant caused by a pending lawsuit does not qualify the plaintiff as a prevailing party for fee purposes. There must be a "judicially sanctioned change in the legal relationship of the parties." To put it another way: there must be a judicial order that can be called upon for enforcement, or there is no prevailing party. For there to be a "prevailing party" in a settlement, the settlement terms must be incorporated into a court order in the format of a consent decree, and the court must retain jurisdiction to enforce the agreement.[50]

In general, state courts tend to the same conclusions as the United States Supreme Court when defining who is the prevailing party.

§ 02.08   Litigation in bad faith

Even without statutes the federal courts can award attorney's fees to the prevailing party when the adverse party has been guilty of conspicuously bad or offensive conduct. In the federal system, the original version of 28 U.S.C. §1927 allowed recovery of "costs" against a lawyer who "so multiplies the proceeding ... as to increase costs unreasonably and vexatiously." In *Roadway Express, Inc. v. Piper*, 447 U.S. 572 (1980), the Court held that §1927 would not support an award of attorney's fees outside statutory costs. Congress responded to the decision by amending §1927 in 1980 to include "attorney's fees" as well as "costs." This amendment made it possible to tax attorneys' fees to counsel in two ways: under the §1927 "unreasonable and vexatious" test, or under an inherent court power to punish for "a bad faith" litigation test.

In the seminal case of Alyeska Pipeline Service Co. v. Wilderness Society the Supreme Court established the inherent court power, pointing out that a court has a foundational power to assess attorney's fees "when the losing party has acted in bad faith, vexatiously, wantonly, or for oppressive reasons." This bad faith exception to the non-awarding of attorney's fees is premised on the court's inherent power to protect the integrity of the judicial process.

The statutory power of §1927 to punish under an "unreasonable and vexatious" test, and the inherent court power to punish under "a bad faith" litigation test, are separate powers, phrased in different words. Although there is a split of authority, some courts

---

[49] *Buckhannon Board v.West Virginia Department of Health and Human Resources,* 532 U.S. 603 (2001).

[50] E.g., *Roberson v. Giuliani*, 346 F.3d 75 (2d Cir. 2003); *American Disability Association v. Chmielarz*, 289 F.3d 1315, 1320 (11th Cir. 2002); *Smyth v. Rivero*, 282 F.3d 268, 278–81 (4th Cir. 2002); Barrios, 277 F.3d at 1135 n.5; *Truesdell v. Philadelphia Housing Authority*, 290 F.3d 159, 165 (3d Cir. 2002).

have concluded that the "unreasonable and vexatious" language of §1927 sets a lower threshold than that of the "bad faith" language of the inherent power to punish conduct.[51]

In like manner, state courts have the inherent power to assess attorney's fees against counsel for litigating in bad faith. However, most state courts will take note of the United States Supreme Court's admonition in *Chambers v. NASCO,* 501 U.S. 32, 50 (1991), that a court must exercise caution in invoking its inherent power, and it must comply with the mandates of due process, both in determining that the requisite bad faith exists and in assessing fees. Some courts will not exercise their "inherent" power, if a state statute provides for penalties for bad faith litigation

§ 02.09   Attorney's fees in frivolous lawsuits

There is one other large category of cases in which attorney's fees can be awarded in state cases.[52] That is the category of "frivolous lawsuits." As we explain below: a pleading can be frivolous without necessarily being made in bad faith. The award against an offending party or attorney bringing a frivolous suit, may be based on a Rule 11 type sanction, or on one of the many statutes, or on the court's own inherent powers to police its system and prevent injustice.

Many states not only have Rule 11 type rules that allow assessment of attorney's fees for pleadings not well grounded in fact or not warranted by law, but also the states have multiple statutes that provide for punishing those who bring claims "without reasonable cause," that are "brought in bad faith," or that are "frivolous claims."[53] The distinction, between a claim brought without reasonable case and a frivolous claim, if there is one, seems to be that a frivolous claim is which lacks substance to a reasonable person trained in the law, whereas a claim brought without reasonable cause doesn't need legal knowledge to make it so. As an example, see *Bellon v. Bellon.*[54] The appeal involved was deemed "frivolous" because (1) the appeal was a mere collateral attack on a judgment' and (2) the bar against collateral attacks on a judgment is so well known that no attorney could reasonably advise his client to try it; so (3) such an attempt must be "frivolous." Another example is New Jersey, which had a separate statute for frivolous

---

[51] E.g., *Louis v. Brown & Route, Inc.,* 711 F.2d 1287 (8th Cir. 1983).

[52] The federal courts handle these as "unreasonable and vexatious," as described in the preceding section of this handbook.

[53] E.g., North Dakota's NDCC 28-26-31 ("Allegations and denials in any pleadings in court made without reasonable cause and not in good faith, and found to be untrue") versus NDCC 28-26-01 ("frivolous pleadings").

[54] 237 NW2d 163 (ND, 1976).

pleadings and one for sham pleadings. *Holdman v. Tansey*[55] interpreted the difference to be that frivolous means legally insufficient, whereas sham means legally good on its face but without reasonable cause or factual substance.[56] Texas wraps two concepts into one statute and imposes a penalty of attorney's fees on anyone who brings a "complaint that is groundless *and* brought in bad faith."[57] In Indiana in a civil action, the court may award attorneys' fees, as part of the court costs, to the prevailing party, if the court finds that either party brought the action or asserted a defense which is frivolous, unreasonable, or groundless.[58] That statute was dissected and interpreted by the Indiana court[59] to mean that (1) a claim is "unreasonable" if, based on the totality of circumstances, including the law and facts known at the time of filing, no reasonable attorney would consider that the claim or defense was worthy of litigation or justified; (2) a claim is "groundless" if no facts exist which support the legal claim relied upon and presented by the losing party; and (3) a claim is "frivolous" if (A) litigated with an improper motive in bad faith, or (B) even without improper motive, if litigated without good faith and rational argument in support of the claim.

In short, in your state there probably is a statute dealing with frivolity, unreasonableness, groundlessness, shamness,[60] or bad faith in pleadings and motion papers; the statute may well be hidden in an odd place in the statutes; and you will need a dictionary to decide when it/they can be used. Once you have found one such statute, keep going; there may be multiple statutes. Legislatures have a penchant to deal with the perceived multiple lawsuits and claims involving lawyers given to frivolity, unreasonableness, groundlessness, shamness, and bad faith.

---

[55]   151 A. 873, 107 N.J.L. 378, 1930.NJ.40016.

[56]   Cf., the U.S. Supreme Court definition of sham found four footnotes later in this text.

[57]   § 571.176, *Government Code*, Texas Statutes. [emphasis supplied.]

[58]   Indiana Code § 34-52-1-1.

[59]   *Greg Allen Construction Co., Inc. v. Estelle*, 762 N.E.2d 760 (Ind. App. 2002)

[60]   For those of you who think there is no word "shamness," I refer you to the United States Supreme Court which set out a two-part test for shamness. "First, the lawsuit must be objectively baseless in the sense that no reasonable litigant could realistically expect success on the merits. . . . Only if challenged litigation is objectively meritless may a court examine the litigant's subjective motivation. Under this second part of our definition of sham, the court should focus on whether the baseless lawsuit conceals 'an attempt to interfere directly with [other parties] . . . through the 'use [of] the governmental process -- as opposed to the outcome of that process . . . ." *Professional Real Estate Investors, Inc. v. Columbia Pictures Industries, Inc.*, 508 U.S. at pp. 60-61 [113 S. Ct. at p. 1928, 123 L. Ed. 2d at p. 624,

§ 02.10   Attorneys who have been discharged by client.

The main use of this handbook arises when the recovery in the case involves the setting of a "reasonable attorney fee." However, there is a small subset of attorney fee award cases we should also discuss, to wit: cases involving an attorney who has been discharged by the prevailing party before the case he/she is handling has been completed.

In most states, if an attorney hired on a contingent-fee basis is discharged without cause before the representation is completed, then the attorney may seek compensation in *quantum meruit* or in a suit to enforce the contract by collecting the fee from any damages the client subsequently recovers.[61]

When enforcing or resisting attorney-client contractual fee agreements it is not enough to simply say that a contract is a contract. "There are ethical considerations overlaying the contractual relationship." *Lopez v. Munoz, Hockema & Reed, L.L. P.*, 22 S.W. 3d 857, 868, 43 Tex. Sup. Ct. J. 806 (Tex. 2000).[62] When the attorney initially contracts with his/her client the lawyer is held to something stricter than the morals of the marketplace. Not honesty alone is to be the standard of the attorney's behavior, but in addition the lawyer's behavior is mandated to always keep the client's best interest in mind.

Therefore, both the remedy of *quantum meruit* and also the remedy of contractual enforcement are subject to the ethical prohibition against an attorney-client contract which charges an unconscionable fee. A court will not be party to an unethical proceeding; hence a contract that is unethical for an attorney will not be enforced by the courts, as a matter of public policy. Whether a specific fee amount or contingency percentage charged by the attorney is unconscionable can be an issue for the fact finder[63]. On the other hand, whether a contract, including a fee agreement between

---

[61] E.g., in Texas, see Mandell & Wright v. Thomas, 441 S.W.2d 841, 847, 12 Tex. Sup. Ct. J. 346 (Tex. 1969) (citing Myers v. Crockett, 14 Tex. 257 (1855).

[62] Texas law on this subject is representative of most states, so is used for the examples in this secdtion of the text.

[63] See, e. g., Curtis v. Comm'n for Lawyer Discipline, 20 S.W. 3d 227, 233 (Tex. App.--Houston [14th Dist.] 2000, no pet.) (evidence supported a finding that a contingent fee equaling 70% to 100% of the client's recovery was unconscionable).

attorney and client, is contrary to public policy and unconscionable at the time it is formed can be a question of law.[64]

---

[64] See, e. g., *Ski River Dev., Inc. v. McCalla*, 167 S.W. 3d 121, 136 (Tex. App.--Waco 2005, pet. denied) ("The ultimate question of unconscionability of a contract is one of law, to be decided by the court."); *Pony Express Courier Corp. v. Morris*, 921 S.W.2d 817, 821 (Tex. App.--San Antonio 1996, no writ) (distinguishing procedural and substantive aspects of unconscionability).

Chapter 03 Definition of a "Reasonable" Attorney Fee

[A] 'reasonable attorney's fee" cannot have been meant to compensate only work performed personally by members of the bar. Rather the term must refer to a reasonable fee for the work product of an attorney. Thus the fee must take into account the work not only of attorneys, but also of secretaries, messengers, librarians, janitors, and others whose labor contributes to the work product for which an attorney bills her client; and it must also take into account other expenses and profit.

Missouri v. Jenkins, 491 U.S. 274, 105 L.Ed.2d 229, 241 (1989).

§ 03.01 Federal criteria of a reasonable attorney fee

In the federal courts, "reasonable attorney's fee" means a fee which is appropriate for the work performed after considering a specific twelve-point criteria list. A federal trial court setting the "reasonable attorney's fee" must consider individually each of the twelve points. Failure to do so may result in an appeals court sending the case back to the trial court.

The federal court twelve-point criterion for determining what constitutes a reasonable attorney's fee was first set out in *Johnson v. Georgia Highway Express, Inc.*[65] These twelve points were derived from the criteria found in the then American Bar Association *Code of Professional Responsibility*, Disciplinary Rule 2-106. The *Johnson* case achieved landmark status two years later when Congress enacted the Civil Rights Attorney's Fees Awards Act of 1976,[66] authorizing the award of a reasonable attorney's fee. This landmark status came about because the *Johnson* opinion's twelve factors were noted by the House Report discussing the new act's provision for an "attorney's fee," and then the twelve-factor list of *Johnson* was specifically approved by the U.S. Supreme Court in *Hensley v. Eckerhart.* Thereafter the *Johnson* case with its twelve-point list has been cited as the prime authority by federal courts whenever they set a "reasonable attorney fee" amount for any type of case or for reason.

The *Johnson* case twelve-point criterion list is:

---

[65] , 8 F.2d 714 (5th Cir. 1974)(criteria specifically approved in *Hensley v. Eckerhart*, 103 S. Ct. 1933, 461 U.S. 424 (1983).

[66] 42 U. S. C. §1988.

(1) the time and labor required;

(2) the novelty and difficulty of the question;

(3) the skill requisite to perform the legal service properly;

(4) the preclusion of other employment by the attorney accepting the case;

(5) the customary fee;

(6) whether the fee is fixed or contingent;

(7) time limitations imposed by the client on the circumstances;

(8) the amount involved and the results obtained;

(9) the experience, reputation and ability of the attorneys;

(10) the "undesirability" of the case;

(11) the nature and length of the professional relationship with the client; and

(12) awards in similar cases.

§ 03.02   State criteria of a reasonable attorney fee

In the state courts, "reasonable attorneys' fee" means a fee which is appropriate for the work performed after considering the factors (usually eight in number) contained in the specific state's rules of professional conduct at the point where a reasonable attorney fee is defined. For example, in Texas the list of required factors to be considered is at their Rule 1.04,[67] and in North Dakota it is at their rule 1.5(a).[68] Whatever the ethics rule number, all the states have taken the substance of their ethics rule defining "reasonable fee" from either the American Bar Association *Code of Professional Responsibility*, Disciplinary Rule 2-106 or the ABA *Model Rules of Professional Responsibility*, Rule 1.05(a). The *Model Code* and the *Model Rules* now both contain the same statement of factors, to wit:

---

[67] *Discussed in Bocquet v. Herring*, 972 SW2d 19 (Tex. 1998); and *Arthur Anderson & Co. v. Perry Equipment Corp.*, 945 SW2d 812 (Tex. 1997).

[68] Discussed in *T.F. James Co. v. Vakoch*, 2001 ND 112, 628 N.W.2d.

(a) A lawyer shall not make an agreement for, charge, or collect an unreasonable fee or an unreasonable amount for expenses. The factors to be considered in determining the reasonableness of a fee include the following:

> (1) the time and labor required, the novelty and difficulty of the questions involved, and the skill requisite to perform the legal service properly;

> (2) the likelihood, if apparent to the client, that the acceptance of the particular employment will preclude other employment by the lawyer;

> (3) the fee customarily charged in the locality for similar legal services;

> (4) the amount involved and the results obtained;

> (5) the time limitations imposed by the client or by the circumstances;

> (6) the nature and length of the professional relationship with the client; and;

> (7) whether the fee is fixed or contingent.

As can be seen from comparison, the twelve-point list used by the federal courts and the eight-point list used by the state courts are substantially the same. This is not surprising, since as earlier noted, the state and federal sets of factors are built from the same ABA foundation. (The first three separate items in the federal list are combined into one as the first item in the state list.) The sole exception is that the 12th federal standard of "awards in similar cases" is not found often in a state court analysis. This is probably both because of the lack of "similar cases" in most states and also because in state courts juries are often involved in setting the amount. However, because the standards in federal and state courts are so similar, the state court judges often quote from federal cases on the subject when determining a "reasonable fee" in a state case. In like manner, we will merge our discussion of these various factors in later sections of this text, using both state and federal law to illustrate the point as necessary.

§ 03.03   Where all courts start from: the lodestar amount

In both the state and federal courts, the determination of what is a reasonable fee starts with fact finding to determine:

> (1) the number of hours of time reasonably spent on the matter, and

> (2) the customary hourly fee for similar work, done in the geographical area of the work performed, by attorneys of the skill reasonably needed to do the job.

This fact finding is then followed by mechanically multiplying those factors together to produce the "lodestar amount." After the lodestar amount is determined, than other factors are examined to determine if the lodestar amount should be adjusted upward or downward to yield the "reasonable attorney fee" for the job.

Fact finding the number of hours "reasonably expended" is the bedrock of the fact finders' decision on fees. For the next few chapters we will lay out for you the core elements in the fact finding the number of hours reasonably spent on the matter. Then, when we get to Chapter 07, we will turn our attention to the other items that need to be addressed in asking for, or defending against, an award for an attorney's fee.

§ 03.04   Percentage method in large common fund cases

There is only one class of cases in which the federal twelve-point or the state eight-point criterion lists frequently are not used as a *primary* basis for defining/computing a "reasonable fee."[69] That class of cases is the large common fund cases. When the attorney's efforts have created a common fund which is large either because of the number of participants or the large amount of the recovery for the class, the courts frequently use the opportunity to escape the task[70] that the tedious accounting that the lodestar method and the twelve or eight-criteria list would entail. They use a percentage of recovery as to determine a reasonable fee dollar amount, and only quickly cross-check the percentage with a rough lodestar computation to ensure that the hourly rate given the attorneys is not so much as would shock the conscience or cause undue news media attention to the judge's decision.

The awarding of the attorney fee from the common fund depletes the amount available for distribution among the class of persons benefitted by the successful lawsuit. However, neither the plaintiffs named as parties nor the defendants have any incentive to expend resources to object to a fee request. The plaintiff class members--the intended beneficiaries of the suit--rarely object to the attorney fee request, no matter how outrageous. They have no real incentive to hire expensive lawyers to engage in an expensive contest that at best would result in only a tiny pro rata gain to them personally from a fee reduction. On the other side of the table, once the total settlement amount has been agreed upon, the defendants have no interest in how the total amount is

---

[69] But note: unlike the federal courts and many state courts, some state courts absolutely mandate the eight point method, starting with the lodestar amount, as the only method the trial court can use to calculate a "reasonable fee."

[70] A task that a process the opinion in *Goldberger v. Integrated Resources, Inc.*, 209 F.3d 43(2d Cir.2000) likened to "resurrect[ing] the ghost of Ebenezer Scrooge, compelling district courts to engage in a gimlet-eyed review of line-item fee audits."

distributed. The defense has no financial incentive to spend more money to oppose whatever fee award the successful attorneys request. Unfortunately, that simple fact creates a temptation for the defense to offer, and the plaintiffs' lawyers to agree upon, a less-than-optimal settlement for the plaintiffs in exchange for a nominally negotiated large attorney fee to go to the plaintiffs' attorney.

Only the court stands in the way of the plaintiffs' attorneys gathering an unconscionable windfall in fees. The judges are mindful of their responsibility. I have included in the Appendices *In re Bristol-Myers Squibb*[71], an excellent case discussing the awarding of common fund attorney fees. It can be read with profit by any attorney seeking to convince the court to award a percentage of the recovery. The case highlights the sort of reasoning that will, or will not, be successful in prosecuting the petition for attorney fees so based.

The *Goldberger*[72] decision of the Second Federal Circuit sanctioning both the lodestar and also the percentage methods for calculating reasonable attorneys' fees in class actions is representative of court decisions generally.   The percentage method is far easier for the trial court. In determining what percentage to award, courts consider

(1) the risks of pursuing a case;
(2) the complexity and uniqueness of the litigation;
(3) the quality of representation;
(4) counsel's time and effort;
(5) the requested fee in relation to the settlement; and
(6) public policy considerations

Courts typically reduce the percentage of the fee as the size of the recovery increases and only utilize the lodestar method to confirm that the percentage amount does not award counsel an exorbitant hourly rate[73]. When the lodestar amount is used merely as a cross-check, the hours documented by counsel are not thoroughly scrutinized.

---

[71] *In re Bristol-Myers Squibb,* 2005 WL 447189 (S.D.N.Y.,2005).

[72] *Goldberger v. Integrated Resources, Inc.*, 209 F.3d 43(2d Cir.2000)

[73] See, e.g., *In re NASDAQ Market-Makers Antitrust Litig.*, 187 F .R.D. 465, 486, 489 n. 24 (S.D.N.Y.1998); *Roberts v. Texaco,* 979 F.Supp. 185, 195 (S.D.N.Y.1997)

Chapter 04   The Ethics of Attorney's Fees.

§ 04.01   Ethics and the attorney's bill to the client

The relationship of the attorney to their client is of the highest fiduciary character. Because of that high fiduciary character, attorney fee agreements and attorney fee bills must be fair, reasonable, and fully understood by the client.

> The falsification *in any manner* of legal bills to clients is unethical and reprehensible. Billing practices, like every other aspect of client dealing, should be conducted in a scrupulously honest manner.[74]

The ethical prohibition against falsification *in any manner*, means there is no room in the fiduciary relationship for padded bills, unnecessary work, or excessive work that produces income for the attorney but no corresponding benefit to the client. The attorney's fiduciary obligation to the client is a relationship of trust. Thus, as a fiduciary a lawyer is ethically obligated to exercise billing judgment and make a good-faith effort to exclude from his fee bill submission any charge for hours that are excessive, redundant, or otherwise unnecessary

The fiduciary relationship also mandates that although the work is legitimately billed, it should not be billed in vague or misleading words which cannot be understood and evaluated. An attorney may not recover a fee in excess of that which was explained to the client, and to which the client has consented. [75] Attorneys have a professional, ethical, duty to render bills the client both can understand and also can use to evaluate whether the services are worth the fee amount claimed.

§ 04.02   Ethics and the attorney's submission to the court

Courts assume that attorneys do not state a falsehood to the court. A relationship of trust exists between the lawyer and the court when the lawyer submits a bill to the court for payment under court rules or under statutes.   A lawyer's actions in court are

---

[74] *Florida Bar v Herzog*, 521 So.2d 1118 (Fla. 1988) [Emphasis supplied.]

[75] E.g., see State Bar of California Standing Committee on Professional Responsibility and Conduct, *Formal Opinion No. 1996-147.*

supposed to be trustworthy, without guile causing the court to err. An assertion purporting to be on the lawyer's own knowledge, as in an affidavit or testimony by the lawyer regarding the time spent by the lawyer or his/her firm in litigation before the court, may properly be made only when the lawyer *knows* the assertion is true or believes it to be true *on the basis of a diligent inquiry.*[76] I've emphasized "knows" and "on the basis of a diligent inquiry" in that last sentence --- an attorney cannot claim ignorance of what is in his/her bills submitted as evidence to the court. The legal reason is that an attorney has an ethical obligation to introduce only valid evidence to the court. The practical reason is that to make a claim of ignorance or negligence of what is in the bill (evidence) submitted to the court is to invite the judge's ire. If the jury is the fact-finder, claiming ignorance of one's one bill invites suspicion.

In addition to an assumption of no-falsehood by attorneys, courts assume that attorneys routinely exercise billing judgment[77] and good ethics in presenting bills to their client Courts assume that attorneys use that same billing judgment and good ethics in presenting legal bills for payment to the courts and one's adversary.[78]

The Hensley case opinion used the term "billing judgment," and courts ever since have picked up the term in testing the reasonableness of an asserted fee.

> [A]ttorneys seeking court-awarded fees are expected to exercise voluntary 'billing judgment' excluding from a fee request 'hours that are excessive, redundant, or otherwise unnecessary.'[79]

☞ **TIP.** If you are the fee-requesting attorney, with particular items in the bills that either are vulnerable as excessive in time spent or are vulnerable as not needed for the successful prosecution of the successful cause of action, then — make discrete reductions as "billing judgement." Announce that you have done so "as a matter of billing judgment to avoid any unnecessary charge." Your reduction may be made either by deducting a stated percentage of the total time expressed in the bill, or by deducting or reducing some specific time entries. The voluntary deduction, by either method, has the dual advantage of preventing a few entries making the entire bill seem suspect, and rendering ineffective any attack on your total bill by attacking a few entries.

---

[76] *ABA Model Rules of Professional Conduct,* Rule 3.3 Candor Toward the Tribunal, Rule 3.3, Comment, at [3].

[77] *Hensley v. Eckerhart,* 461 U.S. 424, 434, 103 S. Ct. 1933 (1983).

[78] *Hensley, supra; Ecos, Inc. v. Brinegan* 671 F. Supp. 381 (M.D.N.C. 1987); *LeRoy v. City of Houston*, 906 F.2d 1068 (5th Cir. 1990)

[79] *Hensley, supra*, at 435 and 434.

§ 04.03   Presumptively unreasonable fee contract arrangements

An attorney cannot contract to receive both a contingency fee and also the amount of an attorney fee award. The attorney fee award is adjudged payable to the client, not to the attorney; hence the attorney ethically must seek an award of attorney fees to benefit the client. The basic ethics rule on fees is expressed in *Model Rule* 1.5(a), which says a lawyer's fee shall be reasonable. The American Law Institute's *Restatement (Third) of the Law Governing Lawyers*, §34, reflects case law that a contract granting the attorney both a standard contractual fee and also the client's attorney fee award, without crediting the award against the contractual fee, is unreasonable and unenforceable.

§ 04.04   Ethics standards for billing judgment and billing entries

Ethics standards for billing can be found in the applicable ethics rules and opinions:

> the American Bar Association *Model Rules of Professional Conduct* (and the earlier ABA *Model Code of Professional Responsibility*),

> ABA ethics opinions,

> state rules governing professional conduct (often derived from the ABA *Model Rules* or *Model Code*),

> state bar ethics opinions, and

> state disciplinary cases.

Statutory and case law concerning attorney's fees and billing, billing guidelines adopted by sophisticated consumers of legal services, custom and practice of attorneys also bear upon the determination of what is ethically correct for the attorney to charge. We will discuss those factors, which are not directly within the sphere of legal ethics, at Chapter 07 of this text. Let's now turn our attention to the directly applicable ethics standards for billing which can be found in the ethics rules and opinions: .

Several of the ABA *Model Rules* are applicable especially to billing and timekeeping.

> Rule 1.5 provides that a lawyer's fee "shall be reasonable." One — but only one — of the factors listed in Rule 1.5 for determining the reasonableness of a fee is "the time and labor required."

> Rule 7.1 provides that a lawyer "shall not make a false or misleading communication about...the lawyer's services."

Rule 8.4 provides that "it is professional misconduct for a lawyer to engage in conduct involving dishonesty, fraud, deceit, or misrepresentation."

There are three major American Bar Association statements on the subject of the ethics of lawyers' fees. The first is the *Model Rules* and its official comments. The rules themselves offered little guidance on how the enumerated factors were to be determined or applied. The official comments to the Rules are not particularly helpful to a person who is not an expert ethicist.

The lacks of help in the Model Rule or its official comments eventually lead to the second major ABA statement on the ethics of lawyers' fees — the 1993 opinion of the ABA's Standing Committee on Ethics and Professional Responsibility, to wit: Formal Opinion 93-379, "*Billing for Professional Fees, Disbursements and Other Expenses*." That formal opinion interpreted in some detail the meaning and limits imposed by Rule 1.5 of the *Model Rules* on billing for legal services and disbursements. While Model Rule 1.5 makes "time expended" only one part of one of the items listed, the Standing Committee's Formal Opinion 93 - 379 focused on the basis of hourly rates and hours spent as the determiner of legal fees. Among other things, Formal Opinion 93-379 provides that "absent a contrary understanding, any invoice for professional services should fairly reflect the basis on which the client's charges have been determined." The fact-finder (court or jury) is trying to determine the basis on which a billing for fees "have been determined," and so are embarked on the quest the Standing Committee in its opinion discusses. Because that opinion is so important, every lawyer litigating attorney fees should read the entire opinion.

Quotations from parts of the ABA Formal Opinion 93-379 [80] are appropriate to be considered in almost every discussion of what constitutes a reasonable fee in a particular case. The most apt portions for quotation or use by you, dependant on the situation and the side you are on, follow. We have it here in the handbook so you easily refer to it, and so you can copy and paste it into your brief to the court

ABA Formal Ethics Opinion 93-179 [portions]

> * * * * The legal profession has dedicated a substantial amount of time and energy to developing elaborate sets of ethical guidelines for the benefit of its clients. Similarly, the profession has spent extraordinary resources on interpreting, teaching and enforcing these ethics rules. Yet, ironically, lawyers are not generally regarded by the public as particularly ethical. One major contributing factor to the discouraging public opinion of the legal profession appears to be the billing practices of some of its members.

> * * * * It is a common perceptions that pressure on lawyers to bill a minimum number of hours and on law firms to maintain or improve profits may have led some lawyers to engage in problematic billing practices. These include charges too more than one client for the same work or the same hours, surcharges on services contracted with outside

---

[80] ABA Comm. on Ethics and Professional Responsibility, Formal Op. 93-379

vendors, and charges beyond reasonable costs for in-house services like photocopying and computer searches. Moreover, the bases on which these charges are to be assessed often are not disclosed in advance or are disguised in cryptic invoices so that the client does not fully understand exactly what costs are being charged to him.

* * * * A corollary of the obligation to disclose the basis for future billing is a duty to render statements to the clients that adequately apprise the client as to how that basis for billing has been applied. In an engagement in which the client has agreed to compensate the lawyer on the basis of time expended at regular hourly rates, a bill setting out no more than a total dollar figure for unidentified professional services will often be insufficient to tell the client what he or she needs to know in order to understand how the amount was determined. By the same token, billing other charges without breaking the charges down by type would not provide the client with the information the client needs to understand the basis for the charges.

* * * * An obligation of disclosure is also supported by Model Rule 7.1, which addresses communications concerning a lawyer's services, including the basis on which fees would be charged. The rule provides:

> A lawyer will not make a false or misleading communication about the lawyer or the lawyer's services. A communication is false or misleading if it:
> (a) contains a material misrepresentation of fact or law, or omits a fact necessary to make the statement considered as a whole not materially misleading.

* * * *Implicit in the *Model Rules* and their antecedents is the notion that the attorney-client relationship is not necessarily one of the equals that it is built on trust, and that the client is encouraged to be dependent on the lawyer, who is dealing with matters of great moment to the client. The client should only be charged a reasonable fee for the legal services performed. Rule 1.5 explicitly addresses the reasonableness of legal fees. The rule deals not only with the determination of a reasonable hourly rate, but also with total cost to the client. The Comment to the rule states, for example, that "[a] lawyer should not exploit a fee arrangement based primarily on hourly charges by using wasteful procedures." The goal should be solely to compensate the lawyer fully for time reasonably expended, an approach that if followed will not take advantage of the client.

* * * * It goes without saying that a lawyer who has undertaken to bill on an hourly basis is never justified in charging a client for hours not actually expended. If a lawyer has agreed to charge the client on this basis and it turns out that the lawyer is particularly efficient in accomplishing a given result, it nonetheless will not be permissible to charge the client for more hours than were actually expended on the matter. When that basis for billing the client has been agreed to, the economies associated with the result must inure to the benefit of the client, not give rise to an opportunity to bill a client phantom hours. This is not to say that the lawyer who agreed to hourly compensation is not free, with full disclosure, to suggest additional compensation because of a particularly efficient or outstanding result, or because the lawyer was able to reuse prior work product on the client's behalf. The point here is that fee enhancement cannot be accomplished simply

by presenting the client with a statement reflecting more billable hours than were actually expended.[81]

* * * * in the absence of an agreement to the contrary, it is impermissible for a lawyer to create an additional source of profit for the law firm beyond that which is contained in the provision of professional services themselves. The lawyer's stock in trade is the sale of legal services, not photocopy paper, tuna fish sandwiches, computer time or messenger services.

The third major American Bar Association statement on the subject of the ethics of lawyers' fees is the ABA, Task Force on Lawyer Business Ethics, *Statements of Principles*[82] (1996).   The preamble correctly summarizes the content:

Preamble: This is a statement of general principles in billing for legal services to which, in the view of the Business Law Section of the American Bar Association, lawyers should voluntarily adhere. It states guiding principles intended to be applicable to any type of billing arrangement, followed by commentary, which identifies certain frequently encountered issues in the context of hourly billing arrangements and illustrates the application of the principles to the resolution of such issues.

This Statement of Principles is a practical document for what should be done in charges from attorney to client, not to an adversary. Awards of "reasonable attorneys' fees" in litigation are charges from attorney to adversary. Nonetheless the Statement of Principles illuminates the thinking that underlies many of the comments made by judges as they determine whether what the lawyer charged is really "a proper charge."

§ 04.05   Ethics related publications by investigators and ethics   experts

At the end of this Handbook, among the Appendices, is an appendix listing some of the books and articles on the practice and ethics of fee billing by attorneys. They are only a few of the bountiful supplies of articles and books available for your reading if you want to learn more about the practice and legal ethics of billing. If you are in a fee dispute, both your expert and also the adverse expert probably will have read some of them. They may furnish ideas to you for your direct or cross examinations.

---

[81] This ethics reasoning is one reason why "rounding up" by 15 minute increments is not proper unless it is a matter of contract with the client.

[82] The Statement of Principles is a statement written largely with the input of large law firms, and in some areas reflects their bias toward approval of the practices of their own large law firms, especially in commercial transactional work.

Chapter 05   Timekeeping for the Number of Hours Spent

§ 05.01   Records required

If you are going to ask for an award of a reasonable attorney fee, you should keep time records — from the time you start work on the case — and those time records should contain the elements we discuss in this text. Why? Because the courts demand it.

Almost always, courts start the calculation of a reasonable fee by discussing the time the lawyer spent on the work and *requiring* attorneys requesting an award to present time records for the work done. (I am serious in putting emphasis on the word "*requiring*".) Most courts, federal and state, have adopted the substance of what was said by the United States Supreme Court in *requiring* not only written time documentation, but also *requiring* the documentation to be specific.

> [T]he fee applicant bears the burden of establishing entitlement to an award and documenting the appropriate hours expended and hourly rates. The applicant should exercise "billing judgment" with respect to hours worked . . . . and should maintain billing time records in a manner that will enable a reviewing court to identify distinct claims. *fn12 - We recognize that there is no certain method of determining when claims are "related" or "unrelated." Plaintiff's counsel, of course, is not required to record in great detail how each minute of his time was expended. But at least counsel should identify the general subject matter of his time expenditures . . . As for the future, we would not view with sympathy any claim that a district court abused its discretion in awarding unreasonably low attorney's fees in a suit in which plaintiffs were only partially successful if counsel's records do not provide a proper basis for determining how much time was spent on particular claims.

> *Hensley v. Eckerhart,* 103 S. Ct. 1933, 461 U.S. 424 (1983).

The 1983 *Hensley* case (a civil rights case) cemented the need for attorneys to submit accurate and detailed time records when requesting an award of attorney fees. The Court's requirement of time records in civil rights litigation was expected. Starting about 1980, various courts in employment cases already had begun to mandate that attorneys seeking fees awards present detailed hourly time records and segregate issues and claims in their time slips.[83]   There is, of course, no substantial reason to treat the

---

[83] No compensation is paid for time spent litigating EEOC claims upon which the claimants did not prevail, hence segregation of time slips by issue became necessary. See, e.g., *Copeland v. Secretary of Labor,* 641 F2d 880, 891-892, 23 Fair Empl. Prac. Case (BNA) 967 (CADC, 1980 (En

method of determination of what is a reasonable attorney fee in employment cases and civil rights claims differently than other types of litigation. Hence, the *Hensley* standard has become the de facto federal court standard generally applicable in all federal attorney fee setting. The state courts since the *Hensley* decision likewise have mandated the submission of hourly time records in all state court attorney fee setting.

The ethical lapses of attorneys reporting hours on an hourly billing method are well known and well established: over-billing, double-billing, and flat-out false billing, among others. The courts regard the absence of time records, or vague time records, as probably a cover-up of billing fraud. The courts are well aware of articles such as "*Blue Chip Bilking: Regulation of Billing and Expense Fraud by Lawyers*'"; "*Greed, Ignorance, and Overbilling: Some Lawyers Have Given New Meaning to the Term 'Legal Fiction*"; and *The Honest Hour: The Ethics of Time-Based Billing by Attorneys*[84]. Several such books and articles from scholars detail how lawyers systematically pad time sheets, create entirely fictitious time sheets, or record as highly compensated attorney's legal time the work actually done by paralegals or secretaries. Sloppy time records, or a lack of time records, raise court eyebrows and invite an adverse expert to give interesting testimony to the fact finder.

🔊) WARNING. The pitfalls of hourly billing are not confined to intentional misconduct. You may think your case work is being recorded in 1/10 hour increments by everyone in the office but in fact it is not being so recorded. Firms sometimes profess to bill on six-minute increments, but their bills contain a suspicious number of 1/4 or ½ hour activities. If so, it may be that all the timekeepers are not disciplined to recording time contemporaneously. If time is not recorded contemporaneously (or at least on the date of the event) recording the amount of time spent on tasks in tenths of an hour may prove difficult for even the most well-intentioned young associate. Think about what you've done yesterday: did you spend 1.1 hours drafting a contract or .9 hours? Furthermore, remembering how long it took you to do something yesterday may be complicated by interruptions, which frequently last longer than remembered. Did you subtract time for the brief conversation when you walked over to your secretary's office with a batch of files and discussed how you would like the file folders in another case arranged? Dividing your time up into 1/10 hour blocks — and recording it as you finish each task, or are interrupted, or take on a new task — takes practice and discipline. As you start a case where time records are likely to be submitted to the court, explain the importance of timekeeping anew to each timekeeper on the case, to renew their discipline of recording time contemporaneously.

Banc); *Dillon v. AFBIC Devel.Corp.*, 597 F2d 556, 564 (5th Cir. 1979); *Oldham v. Erhlich*, 617 F2d 163 169, n 9 (8th Cir 1980).

[84] Lisa G. Lerman, "*Blue Chip Bilking: Regulation of Billing and Expense Fraud by Lawyers,*" 12 Geo. J. Legal Ethics 205 (1999); Darelene Ricker, "*Greed, Ignorance, and Overbilling: Some Lawyers Have Given New Meaning to the Term 'Legal Fiction,*'" 80 ABA J. 62 (1994); William G. Ross, *The Honest Hour: The Ethics of Time-Based Billing by Attorneys.* Carolina Academic Press (1996).

Good timekeeping and billing is not only important to the courts. It is important to clients who are looking for court awarded fees. As a matter of reasonable attorney service in recovering the fee award for their clients, attorneys should keep their records so that a reasonable attorney fee can be proven in court. If an award of attorney fees is reduced because of sloppy records, attorneys can be accused of malpractice for failing to keep the records upon which their client's award of attorney's fees needs to be based.

§ 05.02   Over-billing and double-billing

> As a judge stated in one case, a 'day with 10 billable hours, while extraordinary will occasionally occur. But 17 days where billable hours exceeded or equaled 12 hours is not justifiable. A 20-hour day is questionable.'
>
> William G. Ross, *The Honest Hour.*[85]

Courts usually view billing of 10 or more hours in a day to one client ("double-digit days") with skepticism. Well they may. Most published estimates are that an attorney can only bill in the approximate range of three hours for every four hours in the office, some investigators giving only a two to three hour ratio.[86] The nature of the law business involves a lawyer necessarily moving between matters and administrative tasks so that a continuous block of several hours is seldom available for one task only. A handout given by Yale Law School[87] to its graduates assumes spending four hours in the office can only produce three billable hours; thus, to achieve even 10.5 billable hours a day, a lawyer has to be in the office from 8:00 a.m. until 6:30 p.m., without eating or performing any personal function or physical or mental movement other than working.

☞ **TIP.** If you represent the losing party, check the time recorded by the court reporter for the actual time a deposition took and compare that with the time the prevailing attorney claims for the actual deposition attendance without travel time. That is a good way to find convincing evidence, to present to a judge or jury, of fraudulent or negligent time billing, to wit: billed time that does not coordinate well with the time a court reporter records for attendance at depositions. Court reporters routinely record when a deposition starts and when it ends, as well as the beginning and ending time of breaks in the deposition. You can compare the attorney's time charges against the time the court reporter records for the deposition.

---

[85] (Carolina Academic Press 1996) at 27.

[86] William G. Ross, *The Honest Hour* (Carolina Academic Press 1996) at 27, estimates an attorney normally must spend three hours in the office for every two billable hours estimates. See also, Robert W. McMenamin, *Lawyers at Bay*, 31 Law Office Economics and Management, 370 at 373 (1991).

[87] Yale Law School Career Development Office, *The Truth About The Billable Hour* (2005). The publication estimates only 1800 billable hours can be provided by being at the office 10.5 hours a day, with no time off for sick or personal time during the entire year of work,..

A variation of over-billing (i.e., exaggerating) the actual time is double-billing. One type of double-billing is the situation where one attorney bills two clients for the same time period. In most instances, it is not ethical, but it is sometimes done. A common example is billing one client for travel time on an airplane, and billing a second client for drafting a pleading during that same time sitting in the airplane.   It is impossible to discover that form of double-billing unless the billing attorney admits it, or there is access to the firm's billing computer to run a printout of all the time recorded for all clients by that attorney.

A second type of double-billing is always unethical, to wit: billing the same client twice for the same time. This most commonly occurs when travel time is billable, e.g., billing the client for travel time and for work done during the travel time as a second charge, as though the work had been done before leaving for the trip.

A third type of double-billing is two attorneys billing for doing the same task, better described as double staffing. This can be discovered through close examination of the time records submitted in support of the attorney fee award. Although double staffing is common practice in litigation firms today, it frequently is wasteful and frequently not reasonable. E.g., passing the preparation of a motion back and forth among three attorneys over a period of three months is not the time efficient way to accomplish a task that one reasonably skilled attorney could accomplish in two days.

Double-staffing of depositions is an especial evil to a paying client. If there is more than one attorney claiming attendance, preparation and travel time for the same deposition attendance, the double-staffing charges for one task (asking a witness questions) are especially multiplied. Double-staffing of depositions in anything but the most spectacular cases usually is flatly prohibited by insurers and sophisticated clients. Because the universal rule is that only one attorney for a party can ask questions of a witness, double staffing of depositions is done on the theory that a senior attorney's sharp skill was necessary to take the deposition, but he did not know the case sufficiently to take the deposition by himself. The response is that if the senior attorney does not know the case sufficiently to take the deposition by herself, she does not know enough to ask intelligently prepared or phrased questions – and thus should not be taking the deposition or at it.[88] Where there is double-staffing, it is easy for a judge or jury to conclude the prevailing attorneys were padding the time by overstaffing a task the most senior attorney could have accomplished by herself.

§ 05.03   Specifying which claim is involved in the work

It is rare that a plaintiff prevails on all the claims initially made. Pleadings are made broad so that nothing is lost by time bar or a court's decision that the wrong cause of

---

[88] A second person is sometimes legitimately needed to handle the exhibits and be able to extract a needed exhibit while the interrogating attorney is asking questions. But that second person usually only needs to be a paralegal, charging at a much lower rate than an attorney.

action was alleged. Where a plaintiff is deemed prevailing although he succeeded on only some claims for relief, the court must address two questions: (1) did plaintiff fail to prevail on claims that were unrelated to claims on which he succeeded; and (2) did plaintiff achieve a level of success that makes the hours expended a satisfactory basis for a fee award?[89]

If the claims can be split apart on the basis of proper time records, the time spent on unrelated claims usually are disregarded in computed the time "needed" to prevail. For example, fees attributable to the defense of a counterclaim are not recoverable unless the facts necessary for the plaintiff to recover also serve to defeat the counterclaim.[90]

When much of counsel's time is spent litigating the case as a whole, and all claims involve a common core of facts and/or related legal theories, it may be difficult to divide hours spent on a claim-by-claim basis. Instead, the court might focus on the significance of overall relief obtained by the plaintiff in relation to hours reasonably spent on the entire litigation.[91] A party may recover attorney fees rendered in connection with all claims if they arise out of the same transaction and are "so interrelated that their prosecution or defense entails proof or denial of essentially the same facts."[92]

In summary: not only must a law firm seeking an award of attorney's fees for its client as a prevailing party keep contemporaneous 1/10 hour time records, and write details of what was done — where more than one cause of action is alleged and some might not be "prevailing," then the time records must have enough detail so that a court can determine to which cause of action a time item refers.

☞ **TIP.** If you represent a party defending against a complaint that includes a claim for attorney fees, and the bills of the adverse attorney are in the hundreds of thousands of dollars, within your own firm you are not going to find either the time or the expertise to examine the hundreds of time entries the adverse side is putting forth.There are accounting firms and expert witnesses that specialize in doing the detail work of examining attorney fee bills item by item for vague descriptions, work done on claims on which the party did not prevail, over-billing, double-staffing, excessive work, and all the other billing data details that cumulate to lead the fact finder to cut the fee submission

---

[89] See *Hensley v. Eckerhart*, 461 U.S. 424, 434, 103 S.Ct. 1933, 76 L.Ed.2d 40 (1983)

[90] *Republic Bank Dallas, N.A. v. Shook*, 653 S.W.2d 278, 278 (Tex. 1983); *Crow v. Central Soya Co., Inc.*, 651 S.W.2d 392, 396 (Tex.App.--Fort Worth 1983, writ ref'd n.r.e.),

[91] See *Gorini v. AMP,* Inc., No. 03-2052, 2004 WL 2809997, at * 3 (3rd Cir., 2004); see also Hensley, 461 U.S. at 435; for a state case sample, see also *Cordova v. Southwestern Bell Yellow Pages, Inc.*, No. 08-03-00362-CV (Tex.App. Dist.8, 2004) citing *Wilkins v. Bain*, 615 S.W.2d 314 (Tex.Civ.App.--Dallas 1981, no writ).

[92] *Flint & Assocs. v. Intercontinental Pipe & Steel, Inc.*, 739 S.W.2d 622, 624-25 (Tex.App.--Dallas 1987, writ denied).

by large percentages. Most of these firms and experts can be found through an internet search. One of the firms with respected principals is The Devil's Advocate (www.devilsadvocate.com) which does legal fee management for major large corporations or insurers. Another good bill examiner on the reasonableness of the asserted fee is Accountability Services, Inc. (www.legalbills.com) which has clients throughout the country. Judith Bronsther, the principal of the firm, is intelligent, hard-working, develops an excellent report, and is an excellent negotiator you can bring to the settlement table on your side. She, or someone like her, is who you want on your defense side during a settlement conference when huge attorney fees are a part of the settlement package.

Chapter 06   The Top Four Elements of Good Time Records

§ 06.01   The top four elements

Billing methodology is important. Good timekeeping practices are necessary to justify an award of a "reasonable attorney fee." Whichever side you are on in a billing dispute, take note — *the following "Top Four" are the four most important components of the good timekeeping practices on which attorney fee awards are based.*

> If you represent the prevailing party, these four items are what you need to have in your time records.

> If you represent the defending party, these four items are the timekeeping elements on which to focus in your investigation and attack.

If you are seeking an award of attorney fees — or if you are the unsuccessful side seeking to cut down the prevailing party's attorney fee award — concentrate on the time records. Whether you are on the offensive or the defensive, the battle on the amount of time spent on the case usually will be won or lost on the following Top Four Elements of Good Time Records.

> # 1. A reasonable time increment.

> # 2. Detailed task descriptions.

> # 3. Itemized time entries.

> # 4. Accurate and contemporaneous time records.

§ 06.02   # 1. A reasonable time increment

Don't start keeping time records for a future attorney fee award without it — a reasonable time increment. A reasonable time increment for bills to support an attorney fee award request never is an hour increment or a half hour increment — even if that is the billing charge increment upon which you and your client contractually have agreed. Most courts are now requiring requests for time awards to be submitted using not more than a 1/10 hour (6 minute) increment, on the rationale that 1/10 of an hour is the highest reasonable increment to use in recording time to be compensated by the adverse party. The way the court enforces that requirement is to penalize attorneys who submit fee requests using larger increments. Yet many attorneys still bill their clients, whenever they can, on the 1/4 hour increment, and march into court requesting an attorney fee award based on the 1/4 hour (or more) increment![93]

> [A]ll of the time entries contained in the fee application for services rendered are charged in minimum *one-quarter hour increments*. At the hourly rates charged, this type of billing practice *inherently inflates and distorts the time actually expended, and hence is unacceptable*. [citing cases] Consequently, the Court will discount the compensation requested to take into account the likely overcharge from such inflationary distortion resulting from minimum billing increments.
>
> *In re Price*, 143 B.R. 190 (Bankr. N.D. Ill 1992) "[Emphasis supplied.]

Why is it that some law firms choose to keep their time in 1/4 hour (15 minute) increments and not 1/10 hour (6 minute) increments? The answer unfortunately is simple: the use of 15 minute increments has a great inflationary (thus profitable) effect on legal bills. It is a form of bill padding.

The use of recording time charges with a minimum increment is commonly understood in the business of law to mean that if any part of the next time period is consumed, then all of that time charge is billed. In other words if a timekeeper is recording in 1/10 hour (six minute) billing increments, a 1 minute up to a 6 minute telephone call is billed as 0.10 hour; a 7 minute up to a 14 minute telephone call is billed as 0.20 hour. A phone call lasting only 5 minutes and a second phone call of 7 minutes result in a bill for attorney time of 0.30 hours (20 minutes) Hence, the 0.10 hour increment inflates the time charged from an actual 12 to a billed 20, an 85% inflation. But watch the zoom that occurs (below) when a 1/4 hour increment is used in billing.

The 1/4 quarter hour increment means that if a timekeeper spent 5 minutes on a telephone call or casual assignment, the client is billed for 15 minutes of work. Likewise if a timekeeper spent 7 minutes on a telephone call the client is billed for 15 minutes of time. The total charged the client for a 5 minute and a 7 minute telephone call is 0.50 hours (30 minutes). Time charged is inflated from an actual 12 minutes to a billed 30 minutes – a 250% inflation!

The following is a battle-tested quick way to explain the 1/4 hour billing increment to a jury without using percentages in the explanation.

> "An attorney who spends five minutes on four different tasks, and writes each of them down on a separate time record, and then bills a minimum increment of 1/4 hour (15 minutes) for each task, gets paid for one full hour of work for what was really only took him 20 minutes. Do you think getting paid an hour for doing 20 minutes work is fair? They say they

---

[93] Cf., in a Kansas case, the lawyer admitted he regularly rounded three-fourths of an hour of work up to a full hour for billing purposes, but did not record time for work that took less than a quarter-hour. That practice crossed the line for the Kansas Supreme Court. "Billing in one-hour increments when one hour is not spent working on a matter is an improper billing practice.... In this case, it is impossible to know exactly how much time the Respondent spent working in behalf of Mr. and Mrs. Brown and Mr. Brown's estate, given the Respondent's billing practices....The Respondent violated his duty to his client to charge a reasonable fee." *In re Myers*, 127 P.3d 325, 280 Kan. 956 (2006).

charge by the time spent, but they show you a bill that only shows you how much time they want to charge, not the time they actually spent."

Today, judges, insurers, and sophisticated purchasers of legal services take the position that time billed on 1/4 hour increments is over-billed time. Today, courts refuse billings that are based on a 1/4 hour increment, or "rounding up" more than about 4 minutes.

Modern day accounting systems for law firms are capable of recording time in 1/10 hour (0.10 hour) (6 minute) billing increments. There is no reason not to use 1/10 of an hour as the increment. Most modern day systems, such as the popular TimeSlips® billing accounting software, and even the elementary QuickBooks® Pro, supply a computer screen stopwatch that can be started and stopped by the press of a key. It records time increments even as small as 1/100 of an hour.[94] An attorney or legal assistant at his/her desk simply has to click the stopwatch button on the computer screen when he/she starts and finishes, and the time is recorded. Even if the work is done away from the office, and the time is entered in the billing system at a later date, the popular attorney timekeeping systems allow the entry of time in any chosen increment.

The inflationary effect of the use of the 15-minute billing increment may, in part, be the explanation for what appears in many legal bills to be extraordinary total hours of time recorded every month by an attorney choosing to make short telephone calls or do other short routine work that a legal secretary or legal assistant could handle.

In most cases, it is not reasonable for an attorney to bill an adverse party in increments in excess of .10 of an hour (6 minutes). While "rounding up" is permissible in six minute increments (and perhaps occasionally to 15 minutes), repeatedly rounding to fifteen minutes is questionable at best and raises substantial issues as to whether the total of the asserted time was in fact expended.[95] The litigated cases have held that clients (and courts) are due more than mere estimates or remembrances of time spent on their matters. When a bill lists "0.5" of an hour, the courts and persons asked to pay an attorney's fee billing should have every expectation that the attorney creating the bill actually spent close to 30 minutes on the client's matter. If, in truth, the attorney did not spent 20 minutes, but recorded it as 30 minutes (two 1/4 hour increments), the attorney may have violated the state equivalent of *Model Rule* 7.2 and *Model Rule* 8.4 because the billing statement is misleading.

> 7.02 Communications Concerning a Lawyers Services. (a) A lawyer shall not make a false or misleading communication about the qualifications or the services of any lawyer or firm. A communication is false or misleading if it:(1) contains a material misrepresentation of fact or law, or omits a fact necessary to make the statement considered as a whole not materially misleading.

---

[94] When bills are to be computed from the time entries in the computer, the firm's billing clerk has the option to have the Timeslips® program "round upward" to 1/10 hour or 1/4 hour (15 minutes) increments for the bills to be produced. Other programs have similar options.

[95] See ABA Formal Opinion 93-379 (December 6, 1993).

8.04   Misconduct. (A) A lawyers will not: . . . (3) engage in conduct involving . . . misrepresentation.

Because of the inherently inflationary effect of "rounding up" from "actual time" when using a 1/4 hour increments, it is appropriate to reduce the fee hours submitted on a 1/4 hour increment base by *at least* a factor of 10%. A 10% reduction is minimal; courts have reduced 1/4 hour fee increment billing by 50% or even rejected them entirely.[96] A factor of 50% mathematically may be low in cases where 80% of the work is shown in quarter hour blocks of time.

Expert witnesses working for the defense commonly start their testimony to the jury by showing how the firm submitting the fee award request inflated their time by using more than a 1/10 hour minimum billing increment. If you are defending against the fee award request, attacking a time increment of more than 1/10 an hour is an excellent place to start the defense. Why? Because:

✓   Showing over-billing fits right in with the juror or judge's inherent suspicion of any lawyer's bill as probably "too high."

✓   A defense expert's example of how four separate 5 minute tasks, billed on a quarter-hour increment, can grow into a fee for a full hour, is easily understood. It also is a great illustration for the defense attorney to use on a chalkboard or posterboard when cross-examining the billing attorney!

✓   A fee-requesting attorney's common rebuttal explanation that the "extra 40 minutes" in the above example is to pay him for unbilled time spent in putting down his pen on one matter and getting his mind ready to make a phone call on another matter is a weak explanation. The explanation sounds as though he does not want to admit his wrongdoing but only is making excuses for morally bad overcharging.

✓   The defense expert's explanation cannot be attacked successfully as bad math, contrary to reason, inaccurate, defense biased, or unfair.

✓   There is no accounting or computer software reason why the submitting attorney could not have used 1/10 hour increments had he/she chose to keep accurate records. It appears to the jury that the submitting attorney chose to use a larger billing increment solely to make money without doing anything for the extra money.

✓   Without the defense attorney making the statement, the jury makes its own conclusion that the fee-requesting lawyers are shady characters not to be trusted.

---

[96] E.g., "Further, the Court will no longer accept itemizations of service that use a minimum increment of time for billing unless the applicant can show that the increment is reasonable." *In re Temple Retirement Community, Inc.*, 97 B.R. 333, 339 (Bankr. W.D. Texas 1989); *Kronfeld v. Transworld Airlines, Inc.* 129 F.R.D. 598 (S.D.N.Y. 1990) (ruling excessive the billing of 15 minutes each for telephone calls that might last only five minutes).

✓   Both the defense expert, and also the defense attorney, can use the inflated time records as an easy way to suggest that the first thing the fact finder should do is take 50% off the time claimed. ("Folks, this attorney bill more than doubles up the time they charged. They more than doubled up a somewhat accurate 1/10 increment all the way up to a 1/4 increment. That's like taking 10 dimes and making them into 10 quarters; changing $1 into $2.50. The best way to adjust for what they did is to take 50% off what they billed.")

If you are on the defending side, you will want to bear down hard on the requesting attorney's use of anything more than a 1/10 hour increment. If you are the requesting attorney, you want to avoid being subject to such an attack.

§ 06.03   # 2. Detailed task descriptions

Task descriptions should be sufficiently detailed to enable the reader to identify the specific activity performed, the time spent on the activity, and its purpose and relationship to the matter.[97] Task descriptions should identify (a) the date the work was performed, (b) the attorney or staff person performing the work, (c) the specific task performed, and (d) the time spent on the activity. Vague descriptions such as "review file," "research," "strategy meeting," "draft brief," and "witness conference" are non-descriptive. Here is a quick instruction to use, and to give your attorneys and staff.

Entries for "review" should identify the specific item(s) reviewed and the purpose of the review (e.g., "Review plaintiff's medical records from Memorial Hospital (10 pages) in preparation for deposition of Dr. Smith").

Entries for "research" should identify the particular issue(s) researched and the purpose of the research (e.g., "Research regarding statute of limitations on cause of action for breach of warranty in connection with preparation of motion for summary judgment").

Entries for "conference" and entries for "telephone call" should identify the participants and the purpose or subject matter (e.g., "Conference with Tommy Goodman to find out what he knows about the hole in the ceiling of the house." "Telephone call with plaintiff's attorney Smith regarding his settlement demand").

Entries for the drafting or review of "correspondence" should identify the recipient or sender and the purpose or subject matter of the correspondence. (E.g., "Draft letter to Blatherskite asking for information in preparation for further investigation regarding Smithfield's knowledge of

---

[97] For examples of good and bad time records, see *Chrapliwy v. Uniroyal Inc.*, 583 F. Supp. 40, 47 (N.D. Ind. 1983).

defect." or "Receipt and review of letter from Blatersmith regarding Smithfield's knowledge of defect.")

Entries for "trial preparation" should identify the specific activities performed (e.g., "Prepare outline for cross-examination of Sally Smith.").

Here is an even shorter quick instruction to use, and to give your attorneys and staff.

Use a What-Why-Who task description. If you write What-Why-Who, you automatically get correctly detailed time records. A What-Why-Who time record states WHAT specifically was done, WHY was it done, and WHO was involved other than the timekeeper.

Most attorneys fail in recording the WHY. If you consciously think "What-Why-Who" you will automatically include the important "WHY."

Instruct everyone in the office making time records to get into the habit of writing a detailed task description that will induce the highest attorney fee award. Tell them to remember to include in every time record the "What - Why - Who."

Courts disallow hours that are described in vague terms that do not allow the court to determine if the time was excessive or not for the task described. Courts are today treating as "vague" the sort of records that attorneys in your firm tomorrow may be creating because they do not know better. You need to set an example, and you need to instruct other attorneys billing on the matter for which you want a fee award. For examples of records the courts call "vague" and what they do about it, see the following.

> Additionally, USA objects to many of the time entries pertaining to telephone conversations. Pursuant to the standards set forth in this district, a time entry of "telephone call" or "telephone call with IRS" is insufficient. See Wildman, 72 B.R. at 708. The purpose and length of the conversation and the person called or calling must be clearly set forth in the application. Id. The entries pertaining to telephone calls in the instant application are insufficient in that they fail to provide the Court with the requisite information in order to determine if the services were reasonable and necessary. . . . . .Moreover, there are several other entries which inadequately describe the tasks performed. For instance, many of the entries reflect time expended reviewing the file, conferencing, and writing letters to the client without the requisite detailed specificity. A proper billing entry must adequately explain what services the professional was rendering at the time..... With respect to conferences, the entry should note the nature and purpose of the conference as well as the parties involved.

> *In re Price,* 143 B.R. 190 (Bankr. N.D. Ill 1992)

> With regard to Schnapper's records, the requirement for specificity has not been met with respect to 73.6 hours ....where the entry reads simply "research for brief," "research and draft brief," and "draft and edit brief." Orshan v. Macchiarola, 629 F.Supp. 1014, 1019 (E.D.N.Y.1986) (fees disallowed for time supported only by such vagaries as "prepare correspondence" and "review correspondence."). Additional examples of vague entries include: "telephone call to S. Berger," "Review Macklowe files," "conference with T. Holman," "Telephone conference," "letter to Suzanne Berger," "research," "Telephone conference with Holman and Berger," "working travel to NY," "phone calls to NY," "continue to work on reply brief," "Research for reply brief.."....In light of the numerous entries which contain insufficient descriptions of the work done, a lack of

contemporaneous records for a significant number of hours, duplicative billing and other errors found throughout the record, there will be a reduction of the lodestar of 30%.

> *Ragin v. Harry Macklowe Real Estate Co.*, 870 F.Supp. 510 (S.D.N.Y. 1994).

For Attorney Dague, the court eliminated 205.7 hours for inadequate description. For Attorney Dusman, the court eliminated 145.6 hours for inadequate description or duplication or excessiveness. For paralegal Karl, the court eliminated 101.7 hours for inadequate description or duplication.

> *Rode v. Dellarciprete*, 892 F.2d 1177 (3d Cir. 01/04/1990).

As the courts have pointed out, there are substantial penalties, some up to 50%, for a client whose lawyer writes vauge descriptions of what was done for the time period, and yet seeks attorney fees.[98]

Role Models America, Inc. v. Brownlee reiterated the established law on the subject of time billing that is not sufficiently descriptive. Because the decision describes so well the type of time records needed, and the consequences of a law firm's failure to do so, we quote liberally here. (It also gives you an easy way to cut and paste into your brief some helpful language if you are defending against a request for a fee award.) If you only read one case on preparation of billing records to submit in evidence for a fee award, read the Role Models case.

> To begin with, many time records lump together multiple tasks, making it impossible to evaluate their reasonableness. . . .Many time records also lack adequate detail. . . . do not adequately describe the legal work for which the client is being billed. This makes it impossible for the court to verify the reasonableness of the billings, either as to the necessity of the particular service or the amount of time expended on a given legal task.. . . The law clerk's time records, for instance, give an identical one-line entry, "[r]esearch and writing for appellate brief." . . . See *In re Meese*, 907 F.2d 1192, 1204 (D.C. Cir. 1990) (per curiam) (reducing an award because "[t]he time records maintained by the attorneys, paralegals and law clerks are replete with instances where no mention is made of the subject matter of a meeting, telephone conference or the work performed during hours billed"); *Olson*, 884 F.2d at 1428 ("[T]here are multitudinous billing entries, included among other entries for a particular day, that wholly fail to state, or to make any reference to the subject discussed at a conference, meeting or telephone conference.").
>
> Attorneys also billed for time spent dealing with individuals whose roles in the case are never explained.. . . ("[W]e are also compelled to deduct - charges incurred when attorneys held conferences and teleconferences with persons referenced as 'Geiser' and 'Wells.' The application fails to document who these individuals are or the nature of their relationship to the investigation; consequently, we cannot evaluate whether such fees were reasonably incurred."). . . . .But because the time records contain so little information, we have no basis for concluding that hours that appear to be excessive and redundant are in fact anything other than excessive and redundant. . . .

---

[98] See., e.g., *Role Models America, Inc. v. Brownlee,* 353 F.3d 962 (D.C.Cir., 2004) which reduced the attorneys fee 50% because of sloppy billing time records. See also, *Bonnie & Co Fashion Inc. v Bankers Trust Co.*,970 F. Supp 333 (S.D.N.Y. 1977) (Even a 30% reduction in the claimed time may be too generous to the attorney in light of the vagueness of the law firm's records).

Second, several time records include tasks that do not warrant reimbursement. . . . In this circuit, the government cannot be charged for time spent in discussions with the press. . . . Nor should it have to reimburse Role Models for two hours that a partner spent "[c]ompleting application for admission to D.C. Circuit Bar" and fifteen minutes that the associate spent "[r]esearch[ing] admission to D.C. Circuit Bar [and] prepar[ing] application materials" for the partner.. . . . We agree that [the relevant fee-shifting statute] should not be used to require the government to fund the enhancement of an attorney's versatility or capability.").. . . .

In view of all this -- inadequate documentation, failure to justify the number of hours sought, inconsistencies, and improper billing entries -- we will allow reimbursement for only fifty percent of the attorney hours that Role Models requests. See *Hensley*, 461 U.S. at 433 ("Where the documentation of hours is inadequate, the district court may reduce the award accordingly."). A fixed reduction is appropriate given the large number of entries that suffer from one or more of the deficiencies we have described. . . .; see also *Okla. Aerotronics,* 943 F.2d at 1347 (affirming the district court's flat forty percent reduction in allowable hours).

Role Models America, Inc. v. Brownlee,353 F.3d 962 (D.C.Cir., 2004).

🔊 **WARNING.** You cannot use the attorney-client or work-product privilege as a sword. If you are claiming an award for work done, to the extent necessary to let a fact-finder determine if the amount of time and skill you brought to the task was needed, you cannot prevent disclosing the facts of what work was done. Distinguish between disclosing the event from the content of the work or communication. The difference in writing a non-privileged disclosable time record is the difference between recording a conference with a client as "conference with client to secure answers to interrogatories" [adequate description, yet discloses no content of the attorney-client discussion] versus "conference with client re how many dates she went to the doctor" [bad description because it discloses content of an attorney client conference].

☞ **TIP.** The What-Why-Who method is not only good for requesting attorney fee awards. The What-Why-Who method also produces bills that clients want to pay and that induce client appreciation for what you did. So you have a double bonus: both courts and clients see bills that induce appreciation for what you did. *Carpe Libra* – Seize a book! Bills that clients want to pay are also bills that judges and juries think should be paid. The book "*How to Draft Bills Clients Rush to Pay*" contains the sound advice that J. Harris Morgan has been giving for decades. If you want both good client relations and also bills that clients rush to pay, read Morgan's advice for bills that motivate clients to pay. He gives you a longer version of what I gave you above as my What-Why-Who task description, along with a clear explanation of why a method like this works best. The reason I mention "bills clients rush to pay" is that bills that motivate clients to pay also are bills that motivate courts and juries to award fees. If you don't buy Morgan's book, at least follow my What-Why-Who method of writing time slips.

In summary, you need to submit to the court time entries that enable the reader (client, juror, or judge) to identify the specific activity performed, the time spent on the activity, and its purpose and relationship to the matter. Using the What-Why-Who task description will automatically give you the needed time entry – and will show the client, juror, and judge your thought and care in handling the client's matter

§ 06.04 # 3. Itemized time entries

"Block billing" (also sometimes called "lumped" billing) refers to the practice of grouping multiple task descriptions together under a single total block of time, rather than describing each task and the actual time associated with it individually. Block billing is billing that states a total block of time spent on more than one discrete legal activity, e.g., a record that a full morning of three hours was spent in "telephone calls and legal research."

Courts will almost always question block billing and assess some sort of penalty for using it, maybe even disregarding the time entirely. Block billing, showing a total for a number of discrete tasks does not show the information on which either a client or the court can make an informed judgment on the reasonableness of the time spent on the items shown in the block. There is a suspicion that block billing is a fraudulent inflation of the actual time spent.

Do not do block billing. Each task performed on a case and the time associated with it should be described separately (e.g., "Draft statement of undisputed facts for summary judgment motion: 4.2 hours; Conference with plaintiff's attorney re settlement: .5 hour; Review interrogatory responses from plaintiff: 1.8 hours; Draft letter to client re plaintiff's deposition: .2 hour"). A requirement of accurate time records is that the records describe tasks separately and do not use time block billing descriptions.

Block billing is a practice that is generally prohibited by sophisticated consumers of legal services, has frequently been criticized by the courts in fee cases, and has resulted in lowered fee awards. Courts are supposed to determine if the amount of time spent on services is excessive. Clients are supposed to be able to determine from bills if the services are excessive. Block billing that lumps several items together into one time charge frustrates courts and clients in their time-reasonableness investigations. "Prepare for depositions, letter to Jones, telephone call to Smith, and interview of Adams, time spent: 6.3 hours" gives no clue whether it was a half hour or 5 hours that was spent for any one of the four mentioned items. While painstaking work may segregate it out (e.g., physically looking at the notes and papers and the computer metadata on the work done in the block of time), no court wants to do that sort of work to determine if the hours being spent by the attorney are excessive.

> [When] more than a single service was provided, the services are combined, and there is no information concerning what part of the total charge is allocated to each service. Hercules' challenge of cleansing the Augean Stables pales by comparison with the task presented.
>
> *Mokover v. Neco Enterprises, Inc.*[99]

---

[99] 785 F. Supp. 1083 (D.R.I. 1992)

§ 06.05   # 4. Accurate and contemporaneous time records

Time should be recorded contemporaneously with the task performed. The courts demand accurate time records. The first hallmark of accurate time records is that the records are contemporaneous with the legal work done, that is, the records are made at or near the time of the event.

> The burden is on counsel to keep and present records from which the court may determine the nature of the work done, the need for it, and the amount of time reasonably required; where adequate contemporaneous records have not been kept, the courts should not award the full amount requested.
>
> *F.H.Krear & Co. v. Nineteen Named Trustees*, 810 F2 1250,1265 (2nd Cir. 1987)

If time records are not kept contemporaneously the reliability of the time records is called into question. An individual who reconstructs his or her day schedule and work done the next day or even weeks after the work was actually performed cannot hope to achieve the accuracy that the client or court deserves. Several courts, acting as fact finders to determine a reasonable fee, have held that the absence of detailed contemporaneous time records, except in extraordinary circumstances, will call for a substantial reduction (up to 50%) in any award of a reasonable attorney fee or, in egregious cases, complete disallowance.[100]

Sophisticated expert witnesses on "reasonableness of attorney fees" will sometimes place all of the time billed by a firm onto a chart tracking the billing increments. If the reported times for tasks by the law firm are not randomly distributed, or do not follow a normal curve, this is an indication of time not having been recorded at the time the work was performed, but rather the time was "guessed and recorded" at a later date. The "guess and record" method tends to record time in even amounts of similar lengths of time.

A non-random distribution of time spent on tasks, or an excessive number of times that a timekeeper shows full exact hour increments suggests non-contemporaneous time keeping, leading to an inexact estimate of the "hours for what I did." It is rare that a litigation attorney works an even number of exact full hours on one item, most of the time. Suppose one were to have a billing for time that has the distribution of more than 400 entries in even hour units, about 150 entries in even half hour units, and no time entries for a tenth or quarter hour, three quarters of an hour (taken from an actual audit I did of one attorney's time slips submitted to support a request for an attorney fee award). It is not a familiar distribution of work time intervals. What this distribution strongly suggests is that this timekeeper was entering his time a day (or days or weeks or months) later than he did the work, and then estimating the time he spent, not recording the time actually spent. A judge or jury gets that point easily.

---

[100] E.g, *Grendel's Den, Inc. v. Larkin*, 749 F. 2d 945 (1st Cir, 1984); *Ragin v. Harry Macklowe,Real Estate Co.*, 870 F.Supp. 510 at 521 (listing cases)(30% flat reduction in fee for failure to keep contemporaneous time records).

There are other markers of non-contemporaneous time entry. Most computer timekeeper programs for attorneys, e.g., the Timeslips™ program, generate a serial number for the time entry. These time entry serial numbers sometimes are out of order from the order the timekeeper said the work was done, indicating non-contemporaneous time records.

☞ **TIP.** Note that to be admissible as a business record, a time record must be "A memorandum, report, record, or data compilation, in any form, of acts, events, conditions, opinions, or diagnoses, *made at or near the time* by, or from information transmitted by, a person with knowledge." Fed. R. Evid. , Rule 803 [Emphasis added.] While an opinion by the person testifying as to reasonableness of the fee need not be based entirely on admissible evidence, it certainly does nothing to help an award if the underlying data is excluded from evidence as unreliable hearsay, because not "made at or near the time!"

Chapter 07   Finding the Hours Reasonably Expended

There are a number of factors which can be considered to determine the number of attorney hours of time reasonably expended on the matter to be the subject of compensation.

§ 07.01   Time actually spent: the starting point

The attorney's own time records show the number of hours actually spent on the matter. Hours actually spent and hours reasonably spent are not necessarily the same. Proving the reasonableness of the time expenditure involves more than saying the total time lawyer A spent was X hours. Determining the amount of time actually spent is only the start of a judicial investigation on which an expert opinion of time reasonably spent can be based, and that investigation requires time records that have sufficient detail Woe to an attorney whose records are so lacking in detail that the reviewing court decides that are worthless in its investigation of whether the time spent was reasonable. See, e.g., *Pontarelli v. Stone.*[101] Plaintiff requested a half-million dollars in attorney's fees, but filed vague supporting documentation which was characterized by the district court as "questionable." Because of the inadequate documentation of actual time spent, the court ruled the plaintiff was entitled to no attorney's fees. The need for adequate time records is one of the reasons why we spent so much time describing "Detailed task descriptions" in our chapter on The Top Four Elements of Good Time Records.

§ 07.02   The measure of time "reasonably expended"

Excessive, redundant, or unnecessary hours are to be eliminated from the billed hours to find the total hours "reasonably expended." That is what experts on attorney fees awards do, and that is the law's requirement in determining a reasonable attorney fee. The difficulty in the elimination of excessive, redundant, or unnecessary hours from the time actually spent is the task of reviewing what was done and bringing experience and knowledge to bear on the question of what was reasonable and what was excessive. It takes time to do the review. It takes informed judgment to do the review.

To move from the number of hours actually spent to the number of hours reasonably spent needs the bridge of an expert opinion. A non-lawyer does not know whether it takes one or a hundred hours to bring a summary judgment motion in a case. Neither does a lawyer, unless he/she knows what the case is about, a summary of the facts, a

---

[101]   978 F.2d 773 (1st Cir. 1992).

summary of the law, what has been done in the case prior to the hearing on the attorney fees, and the nature of the arguments advanced by both sides.

The first harsh truth to be understood on looking at an attorney's time records is that some attorneys spend time doing things that do not reasonably need to be done. "Everything that reasonably should be done" does not necessarily equate to "Everything that can be done." There are two main reasons why some attorneys act as though the two terms equate.

> # 1. Hourly billing creates an attorney's need to earn money by billing time. The attorney has an inherent conflict of interest that causes him to be biased, whether or not he knows it, to think an attorney doing work for the client is always a good "reasonable" objective for the client.

> # 2. The profession's present problem is that many litigators today have never tried a case. They cannot discriminate between reasonably relevant tasks and excessive tasks because they have never tried a case. These attorneys derive their professional livelihood from the process of litigation rather than from a trial. These attorneys are doing a perfect job of doing excessive work that really doesn't count. Attorneys who have imagination and the ambition to contribute to a better result in trial can list all sorts of peripheral research, discovery, objections, and motions that might possibly bring a better trial result. Unless restrained by the hand of an experienced attorney who has tried cases, they will do all the projects they list even though some on the list are not reasonably going to make any difference to the final result in the litigation. A young associate's enormous energy and desire to succeed drives the law firm into doing everything possible.

If the court is the fact-finder in an award for attorney fees, the court will use their own expertise to comment on the total billed amount of work as excessive (or not) for what was reasonably needed to get the job done. The court then makes (or does not make) a reduction from hours billed to obtain a reasonable number of hours expended. This approach by the court is not necessarily addressed to a perceived venality of the lawyer involved (point # 1 above) but rather addresses the point # 2 above. The court's work does give the court much more experience on what is reasonably needed to be done by the trial attorney. As a result, the court's determination, of what was reasonably done to handle the litigation before it and what was excessively done, or what was left undone, may be sharply worded.

The second harsh truth about excessive time billed is that attorneys all too often undertake lucrative work even though they are not knowledgeable in the subject matter or field of law.   "Everything I personally know on the subject involved" does not necessarily equate to "what a reasonable attorney, competent in the subject involved, knows."

It is true that, as the comment to Rule 1.1 of the ABA's *Model Code* of Professional Responsibility states:

> A newly admitted lawyer can be as competent as a practitioner with long experience....
> A lawyer can provide adequate representation in a wholly novel field through necessary
> study. Competent representation can also be provided through the association of a lawyer
> of established competence in the field in question.

In setting a fee award amount, "reasonable hours expended on the case" do not include the education of a lawyer on basic tenets, procedure, and problems in the subject field needed to make him/her self competent to handle the matter. When the lawyer must get legal education to become competent in regard to the case, the client should not be charged for the legal education of the lawyer.

In like manner, hours spent by the less competent lawyer doing a task that could have been handled more cheaply by the competent lawyer (who does have the needed basic knowledge in the field) are not necessarily hours reasonably expended on the matter. If an average lawyer could do a particular job of legal research in a half-hour, then two hours is not "reasonably expended" to do the job (unless, in that example, the sub-average lawyer's hourly rate was only 25% of the average attorney's rate).

Also, hours attributable to litigation of other claims on which plaintiffs did not succeed have to be considered in calculations of the time "reasonably expended" to recover on the successful claim. Thus a court or an expert determining a reasonable fee has to look not only at the course of the litigation or transaction involved, but also at each item in the fee billing submitted by the attorney seeking payment. This line-by-line examination of fee bills is not a favorite occupation of judges, so expert testimony, directing attention only where it needs to go, normally is welcomed by the judge (or jury if it is the fact finder).

Time records frequently disallowed by courts, as *not* showing time reasonably spent, include the following:

> 1.   time that should be allocated to other matters than the particular claim on which the winning party prevailed.

> 2.   time that does not appear to have been recorded accurately.

> 3.   time vaguely described, rendering the record useless to a client or court in determining whether the time was reasonably expended.

> 4.   time of attorneys reviewing each others work, instead of one attorney simply doing the work.

> 5.   time of multiple attorneys attendance at hearings and depositions.

§ 07.03   Expert testimony as a source

The general rule is that the billing attorney can give an opinion that he/she spent all that time because it was reasonably necessary to accomplish the job. The billing attorney is accepted as an expert on his/her own work. Hence, his/her opinion accomplishes an initial establishment of the number of hours reasonably spent.

But no judge or jury has to accept the opinion of any expert. The judge or jury suspects, as biased by self-interest, the opinion of the one who wants the money. Faced with opposing self-interested opinions of the parties, the trier of fact seeks a nonparty expert opinion. Even a court seeks an expert opinion that has additional credibility over that of the parties' opinions. An expert opinion by a credible expert — other than by the billing attorney or by the opposing attorney — on the amount of time "reasonably" spent will considerably advance the cause of the witness-proffering party.

Can a judge be its own expert on what is reasonable for an attorney to do in the matter before the court? Generally, yes. In the federal courts, and many jurisdictions, a trial judges are considered to be an expert on the amount of time reasonably spent by an attorney on a matter reviewed by the court. However, in those states giving the jury the task of deciding what is a reasonable fee, some take the position that when the court substitutes for the jury as a fact finder, the judge also needs expert testimony and cannot simply use her own experience as "judicial notice" of what is a reasonable fee.

§ 07.04   Case law and statutes as a source

There are many published cases in which state and federal courts throughout the country have addressed the reasonableness of attorney's fees and billing practices. Sometimes in the process of the reasoning the court indicates a minimum or maximum time that seemed reasonable or excessive for the sort of matter involved. For example, you might find a quote from a court which has said something like "in the average case involving...., it should not reasonably take more than X hours to do the discovery necessary to bring the case to trial." If you find such a quote, citing that language might be helpful to you. Therefore, take the time to do a quick research survey on the last 10 years or so of fee award cases in your jurisdiction. This is true whether you are in federal court (where a factor that must be considered is "awards in similar cases") or you are in a state court (where "awards in similar cases" is not a factor for consideration). Judges are human, and predisposed to travel a road previously traveled by fellow judges.

§ 07.05   Sophisticated consumers of legal services as sources

Sophisticated consumers of legal services such as major corporations and insurance companies provide standards of what they will accept as reasonable. Often they have detailed billing guidelines which set forth the billing and timekeeping standards that they expect will be followed by their attorneys.

A plaintiff's defending against a fee award requested by a defendant may want to use discovery to find the Defense Research Institute (DRI) *Recommended case handling guidelines for law firms*. Those guidelines include standards for billing and timekeeping.

The DRI materials are only available to members of DRI, but can be discovered as material "under the control" of the defendant to obtain. If the defense attorney is a member of DRI, you often can characterize the defense attorney's fee submission as a departure from "defense attorney industry standards."

In like manner, use discovery to ask if the client for whom a fee award is sought has billing guidelines. Such guidelines often will become sources for your cross examination of the fee award proponent attorney.

§ 07.06   Internal information captured by the computer as a source

Large law firms must depend for work flow volume on satisfying corporations and insurance companies. Thus, they follow the standards of billing those sophisticated consumers demand. This in turn has influenced the design of the computer software programs to prepare the legal firm's bills that are needed in today's business of law, whether defendant or plaintiff. For example, insurers now generally demand itemized bills that separate different types of services (e.g., a telephone call must be recorded separately from the legal research done immediately following the telephone call) and demand the time records show not only the individual item done, but also the date of service, the person doing the service, the number of hours worked expressed in no larger increments than tenths of an hour, plus a description of the service sufficient so that a claim manager familiar with the case can tell if the time spent appears excessive.

As a consequence of the need to satisfy corporations and insurance companies, all major computer programs for lawyers to use in generating bills capture that level of information. The information is available; so if the proponent does not show it, demand it. Ask for a printout of all the raw information stored. More than that, if the proponent attorney has sent bills to the client, demand the actual bills sent to the client. You may be surprised at the differences between the description or amount of detail given to the client and the listing given in support of the demand for an attorney fee award.

Remember, attorney-client privilege cannot be used as a sword. If a party is asking for an award of an attorney fee, they waive the attorney client privilege as to the information you are probably seeking to defend against it. If the judge to whom you are arguing the matter favors the privilege to bar your discovery, use the quick analogy of the waiver of medical privilege that occurs when a plaintiff sues for personal injuries.

§ 07.07   Custom and practice of attorneys as a source

The amount customarily billed by lawyers in the firm involved, or in the specialty or jurisdiction involved, may be instructive in finding "reasonable hours expended." For example, if a firm has an insurance company for a major client, the firm's billing practices may include a guideline statement of the amount of time to spend on a particular type of proceeding, e.g., drafting a pleading. Even without a major client's demand, the custom and practice of a law firm becomes the firm's internal standard of "custom and practice" for not only for dollars charged per hour, but also for hours charged per proceeding. Where firms too often fall down is in the failure of the firm's internal standard (custom and practice) to conform up to the external standards expected by clients and courts. Such a mismatch of the firm's internal practice to the client's expectations may not be intentional, but rather simply a matter of momentary forgetfulness. Unfortunately, sometimes a firm's internal practice of what hours or resources it devotes to the client's matters can be intentionally so overcharging or so without relationship to what was accomplished that the failure to measure up to the expectations of clients may be negligence or "not a reasonable number of hours expended." Inquiry of a proposing attorney of what he and his firm view as "customary" or "normal" hours spent on a proceeding (e.g., drafting a standard demand for production of documents) may suggest a divergence from what courts or outside experts may regard as normal.

§ 07.08   Charges of the opposing attorneys as a source

Frequently overlooked is the option of using discovery to find the total fees and costs billed by the adversary attorney in the same case. It is relevant to the issue of determining a reasonable attorney fee.

> The court further considered that Arrowhealth's counsel billed the company in excess of $200,000 in defending the action. A comparison of hours and rates charged by opposing counsel is probative of the reasonableness of a request for attorney fees by prevailing counsel.
>
> *Heng v. Rotech Medical Corp.*, 2006 ND 176 [following *Duchscherer v. W.W. Wallwork, Inc.*, 534 N.W.2d 13, 16 (N.D. 1995)].

Chapter 08   Other Factors Than Hours of Time

§ 08.01   The lodestar calculation

In Chapter 03, we told you that in both the state and federal courts, the determination of what a reasonable fee is starts with fact finding:

> (1) the number of hours of time reasonably spent on the matter, and

> (2) the customary hourly fee for similar work, done in the geographical area of the work performed, by attorneys of the skill reasonably needed to do the job.

When these two amounts are determined, mechanically multiplying those factors together will produce the "lodestar amount." The dictionary definition of a "lodestar" is "a star that is used to guide the course of a ship." A lodestar is a point of reference to aid in finding a destination; it is not the destination itself. Finding the lodestar amount is part of the course of discovering a reasonable fee amount; the lodestar amount is not the end of the end of the fact finder's job.

After the lodestar amount is determined, than other factors are examined to adjust the lodestar amount upward or downward (if and as appropriate) to yield the endpoint: the reasonable attorney fee for the job. No matter how it is sliced or stated, all courts look at all of the listed factors. A wise trial court routinely mentions all of them to assure an appellate court that all were considered. Hence, you as an attorney should give the trial court the benefit of your thinking and available facts in regard to each of the factors listed by the law in your jurisdiction.

Is there a limit to the number of adjusting factors the court may define and examine in determining a reasonable fee? The federal courts say that all of the basic listed factors must be considered but that additional other factors may be considered. A startling example of this consideration of additional factors occurred in *D.F. v. Mt. Sinai-NYU Medical Center Health Systems,* [102] in which the judge applied two additional factors: ethics of the lawyer, and legal workmanship of the lawyer. In that case the judge ordered that an attorney who settled a $2.4 million medical malpractice suit should receive no fee whatsoever because of unethical inflation of the fee. The judge added that even if an appeals court determined there was no ethical misconduct in inflating the fee, the attorney should receive no more than $100,000 for his work because of the "grossly incompetent and inexplicable manner in which [he] conducted himself" *after* the proper settlement was reached. Among the acts cited by the court were failing to properly assess the needs of his infant client, failing to understand the importance of a Special

---

[102] 04-CV-1507, E.D. New York, 2nd Federal Circuit.

Needs Trust, failing to understand the need of proper asset accounts to ensure that the child's needs are met in the future. Korman, the chief judge of the Eastern District, wrote "I am not going to allow him to be compensated in the same way as attorneys who do their job."

Most states are in accord with the federal courts in allowing additional factors to be considered. Considering other factors than the listed factors does conform with the official comment to ABA Model Rule 1.5 [103] from which the list of factors is derived. The comment clearly states:

> [1] Paragraph (a) requires that lawyers charge fees that are reasonable under the circumstances. The factors specified in (1) through (8) are not exclusive. Nor will each factor be relevant in each instance.

Not only is such an approach in accordance with the comment concerning the intent of the rule listing the factors, but also it is rational to consider all the circumstances of the handling of a matter in determining reasonableness of the fee in handling the matter. However, there is a minority of states that make the list of factors exclusive. E.g.:

> This Court has uniformly held that when determining the reasonableness of attorney fees, all factors must be considered and no single factor controls. In determining fees on remand, the district court shall first decide the number of hours reasonably expended, and then determine a reasonable hourly rate ....[In examining the various factors] evidence and specific findings are necessary... After this analysis, the fees shall not be reduced based on any other factor.

> *T.F. James Co. v. Vakoch, 2001 ND 112, 628 N.W.2d 298.*

§ 08.02   The skill level needed during hours reasonably expended

Although hours claimed by the prevailing attorneys as the time they spent on a case should be a factor in determining a fee, their claimed hours are not the only ingredient to be considered.[104] Notice that the factor is the hours of time *"reasonably needed,"* not the hours of time *actually spent or claimed.* Hand in glove with the time needed is the skill reasonably needed to do the job in a reasonable time. An attorney can spend time which is not reasonably expended on the matter. For example, if an inexperienced or incompetent lawyer must spend time to get legal education to acquire the basic

---

[103] American Bar Assoc., *Model Rules of Professional Conduct*, Rule 1.5 Fees, Comment (2006)

[104] In discussing the nature of the additional factors considered, you generally will not go wrong citing and quoting the wording of statements made in *Johnson v. Georgia Highway Exp., Inc.*, 488 F.2d 714 (5th Cir. 1974). The opinion is succinct and is classic in statement, and equally applicable to federal and most state law.

knowledge needed to handle the case[105], the adverse party against whom the fee award is assessed is not charged for basic legal education of the lawyer. Likewise if an average lawyer could do a particular job of legal research in a half-hour, it is wasteful to take two hours to do the job. Thus, if an attorney merely claims time for "research" without specifying the subject of the research, a real question arises whether the time was reasonably expended on the matter which was actually litigated. (That is why the courts require detailed and itemized hourly time records.)

The skill level "needed" involves determining the novelty and legal difficulty of the task. The skill level "needed" does not always match the skill level that the law firm applied during the hours billed. Work can be either overpriced or underpriced. Work done at a contract price that is lower than justified by the legal or practical difficulties by the case may call for an increase in the lodestar amount; overpriced work may call for a decrease in the lodestar amount. The most common example of unneeded skill level that the defense may look for to attack a proposed award is a billing by a senior lawyer at $500 an hour in "drafting notice of deposition of Mr. Smith," a task usually delegated to a paralegal. The skill level needed is not enhanced just because a lawyer does it. Skillful counsel for a prevailing party probably should avoid attack by exercising "billing judgment" to reduce the total billed amount for which could have been done by Mr. Smith's paralegal, even if it was done by Mr. Smith.

§ 08.03   Acceptance of the job precludes other employment

A reasonable fee includes adjustment if acceptance of the job by the lawyer is likely to decrease the attorney's future expected income because he took on an undesirable client, and will lose future clients because of that.

Likewise, it is also possible to argue that a fee award should include an upward adjustment because the attorney was prevented by the instant case from doing work during the same time period for a client that normally paid higher hourly fees.

On the other side of the coin, consider lowering the lodestar amount when the purpose of undertaking the work was to generate publicity for the lawyer; hence the likelihood is that the acceptance of the job would increase, not preclude, other employment.

§ 08.04   The fee customarily charged in the locality

Courts say the base for determining a reasonable fee is found by multiplying the number of hours reasonably expended by each attorney by the hourly rate normally charged:

    (1) for similar work

---

[105] See e.g., *Model Rules of Professional Conduct,* Rule 1.01, Comment.

(2) by attorneys of like skill
(3) in the geographic area.

Notice that even if the court uses the shorthand and undifferentiated phrase "customary rate" (instead of using a cumbersome phrase such as "hourly rate normally charged for similar work by attorneys of like skill in the geographic area"), the "customary"rate they discuss almost always is the modal[106] or median[107] hourly rate for similar work by attorneys of like skill.[108]   The "fee customarily charged" for the particular work, by attorneys of like skill to the one that did the billed work, does not mean the average[109] hourly rate for all attorneys in the geographic locality.

What fee rate is used when the prevailing party's counsel practices outside the forum jurisdiction? Generally the courts pick the forum's rates as applicable. The relevant community for a fee determination is a judicial district or the state in which the trial court sits.[110] Nonetheless, the high-priced out of town counsel may be awarded his/her rate instead of a lower rate paid in the forum community if local counsel was unavailable, either because they are unwilling or because they lack the degree of experience or expertise required to handle properly the case.[111]

In litigation lasting many years, the losing party may argue that an attorney fee award must be limited to the market rates prevailing for each of the years the suit was litigated. However, in *Missouri v. Jenkins*,[112] the U.S. Supreme held that for the federal courts, instead of a prejudgment interest award for past work done "an appropriate adjustment for delay in payment—whether by the application of current rather than historic hourly rates or otherwise—" is appropriate. Thus, in multi-year litigation a court could either award current rates for the entire case—the easiest solution—or award historical rates

---

[106] Statistics. The mode is the value occurring most frequently in a distribution of data.

[107] Statistics. The median is the middle value in a distribution.

[108] Cf., *Di Filippo v. Morizio*, 759 F.2d 231, 235 (2d Cir.1985) ("the hourly rates governing fee awards to non-profit legal services organizations are calculated according to prevailing private market rates").

[109] Statistics. The average is the value obtained by dividing the sum of the values in a data distribution by the number of quantities in the distribution.

[110] See, e.g.,In re *"Agent Orange"* Prod. Liab. Litig., 818 F.2d 226, 232 (2d Cir.1987); *Shlomchik v. Richmond 103 Equities Co.*, 763 F.Supp. 732, 743-44 (S.D.N.Y.1991) (awarding suburban Philadelphia attorney a higher New York City rate as action was litigated in New York).

[111] *See, e.g., Barjon v. Dalton*, 132 F.3d 496, 500 (9th Cir. 1997) and *Gates v. Deukmejian*, 987 F.2d 1392, 1405 (9th Cir. 1992)).

[112] 491 U.S. 274, 284 (1989).

augmented by an interest factor or other a multiplier to compensate for delay in payment.[113]

A defense contention often is made, in connection with determination of rates to be paid, that too much of the work was done by experienced attorneys at the high end of the hourly rate scale. Sometimes the facts are such that the argument has force. Most of the time courts and juries seem to reject that contention, on the general theory that: "Presumably, the skill and experience of the partners places them further along the learning curve and enhances their ability to operate efficiently so that the higher partner rate is likely to be offset, at least in part, by a reduction in the number of hours multiplying that rate."[114]

The proponent has the burden of proving relevant "customary" market rates through evidence. Typically most proponents only put forward a friendly attorney to say the proponent's hourly rate is customary or reasonable. However, specific hourly rate information is more persuasive than a declaration of one attorney that she thinks a certain rate is like hers and therefore "reasonable."The latter type of declaration "might properly be characterized by a reviewing court as one given out of courtesy, but it provides little or no evidentiary support for an award." [115] Better than one attorney's opinion of "customary" rates, would be multiple declarations from attorneys in a range of private law firms in the relevant community reporting hourly rates charged by those firms for attorneys with the same number of years of practice. However, such evidence by individuals of their own rates is merely a collection of data points, hardly rising to the level of a scientifically conducted study of fee rates.

There are a number of surveys that may be available to draw upon when determining what is the "customary" hourly charge. For example, The National Law Journal's survey of billing rates of the largest U.S. law firms[116] provides the high and low rates for partners and associates, the principal billing rates, and associate and partner billing averages and medians. It could be used if you wanted to show that a large law firm in Cincinnati was billing $140 an hour for 1st year associates and $210 an hour for 7th year associates (or if you wanted to show a firm in Hartford billing 1st year associates at $190 an hour and

---

[113] See the later section in this handbook regarding the awarding of interest for past years attorney work.

[114] *American Petroleum Institute v. Environmental Protection Agency*, 72 F.3d 907, 916 (D.C. Cir. 1996). See also, *Daggett v. Kimmelman*, 811 F.2d 793 (3d Cir. 1987); *Muehler v. Land O'Lakes* Inc., 617 F. Supp. 1370, 1379 (D.Minn. 1985); *Laffey v. Northwest Airlines* Inc., 572 F. Supp. 354, 366 (D.D.C. 1983), reversed on other grounds, 746 F.2d 4 (D.C. Cir. 1985). See also the discussion by Gary Greenfield, *Efficient Litigation: An Ethical Imperative?*, 20 American Lawyer 38 (Apr. 1994) ("it usually would be cheaper to have the senior lawyer simply sit down and draft it").

[115] *Quote is from Norman v. Housing Authority of Montgomery*, 836 F.2d 1292, 1304 (11th Cir. 1988).

[116] The survey, done annually, costs about $250 per copy.

7[117] year associates at $390 an hour)[117]. Altman and Weil does an annual national survey of firms that want to participate in the survey. The survey has a great amount of statistical data, and it costs a substantial amount per copy. If available to you it does have the advantage of being more broadly representative of the law firms in an area. On the internet, one can find attorney salary comparisons, such as available at Salary.com and FindLaw. Knowing the salary paid to an associate is of some help in determining a reasonable fee to produce that salary plus overhead and partner profit. More importantly, successive years' salary data tends to show whether a reasonable fee would be lower or higher in successive years of a long term transaction or litigation.

The most helpful surveys of actual fees charged by lawyers in a state are those done by bar associations. Bar associations do them primarily as an aid to their members in setting fees in the range the customer-clients are paying to other lawyers. As one attorney advising lawyers how to set their fees said: "The more common method is to set the hourly rate at the rate customarily charged in the geographic area. . . . A lawyer should obtain the rate that the market will support."[118] Lawyers want to know what the competition is generally charging, and bar associations like to be responsive to their members' needs. Hence, a state bar association that does a survey to find the customary fee rates in the state [119] generally will try to accomplish a statistically valid survey of their membership.

◀)) **WARNING.** Before stating to a court what is the "customary" hourly rate, check if the state bar involved had done a survey of attorney rates, and if so, what that state bar survey establishes. Then build your argument with recognition of that survey. All too often a failure to recognize an existing bar survey leads to enduring a withering cross-examination or argument.

☞ **TIP.** A fruitful cross-examination of local attorney witnesses put on the stand to testify regarding the reasonable fee amount is a cross-examination regarding the foundation for their opinion on customary rates. Often the foundation is only what that lawyer charges and what some of his friends have said they charge. Indeed it is

---

[117] See, e.g., *Salazar v. District of Columbia*, 123 F. Supp. 2d 8, 14 (D.D.C. 2000) (relying upon National Survey Center and National Law Journal surveys to determine reasonable hourly rates in the District of Columbia).

[118] *2001: An Attorney's Fee Odyssey: Setting and Collecting Fees in the New Millennium*, by Mike McCurley and Stacy Glenn, McCurley, Kinser, McCurley & Nelson , Dallas, TX, paper delivered at the March 3-10, 2001, Seminar of the American Academy of Matrimonial Lawyers.

[119] Note the state may have different legal markets and hence different customary rates for the area of the court. E.g., see *Davis v. City and County of San Francisco*, 976 F.2d 1536, 1542 (9th Cir. 1992), vacated in part on other grounds, 984 F.2d 345 (9th Cir. 1993) at 1547 (rejecting reliance on survey that reported only statewide average rates rather than rates specific to San Francisco, where case was litigated).

surprising, in this Daubert[120] era, that more attorneys do not seek to disqualify adverse experts from testifying on "customary fees" on the ground that they do not have sufficient data to form a reliable opinion.

§ 08.05   The amount involved and the results obtained

The amount involved and the results obtained must be considered. A million-dollar matter usually does not warrant ten million dollars of attorney time to recover, whether the client is paying the bill or the adversary. Court opinions require bills submitted to the courts or to adversaries to show the same "billing judgment" that would be shown in bills to clients. Time and effort spent must be proportionate in some measure to the importance of the matter.

Sometimes, in matters of great public principal, it is not the dollar amount that is important; it is the establishment of a public principal. Therefore, in civil rights or discrimination cases, the relative success of the results to the attorney time expended is measured in the vindication of rights, not in the dollars recovered. Even outside of civil rights cases, an attorney's fee considerably larger than the ultimate dollars of the verdict amount may be an appropriate reasonable fee for the effort that reasonably had to be expended.[121]

The factor of "results obtained" becomes greatly important in litigation where an attorney fee is to be awarded to the "prevailing party," but the party did not prevail on all the claims that were made. If a case involves more than one claim, then only those fees attributable to the claim falling within the scope of the statute, contract, or law providing for recovery by a prevailing party are recoverable.[122] An example from the state courts is found in a marathon case in Texas where the prevailing attorneys had not kept time records: "We reversed and remanded the award of nearly $21 million in attorneys' fees because only the claim for declaratory judgment would support the award and the fees

---

[120] In the federal trial cou*rts, Daubert v. Merrell Dow Pharmaceuticals,* Inc., 509 US 579 (1993), and the line of cases subsequent to Daubert, provides that the admissibility of an expert's opinion testimony is dependent on the expert's method and procedures. Many state courts now have similar requirements. Thus, defect in foundational data can be a bar to admissibility of the opinion into evidence, rather than just a factor to judge the value of the opinion after it is admitted.

[121] E.g., see *Stuckey v. White*, 647 S.W.2d 35, 37 (Tex.App.--Houston [1st Dist.] 1982, no writ). (Even fees which amount to three times the amount of actual damages may be reasonable, depending on the facts of the case); *Murrco Agency, Inc. v. Ryan*, 800 S.W.2d 600, 602 (Tex.App.--Dallas 1990, no pet.)(fee award of $92,000 upheld where damages were only $28,000).

[122] *International Sec. Life Ins. Co. v. Finck*, 496 S.W.2d 544, 546-547 (Tex. 1973); *4M Linen Supply Co., Inc. v. W.P. Ballard & Co., Inc.*, 793 S.W.2d 320, 327 (Tex.App.--Houston [1st Dist.] 1990, writ denied); *Hill v. Heritage Resources, Inc.*, No. 08-93-00266-CV (Tex.App. Dist.8 12/31/1997).

attributable to the declaratory judgment action had not been properly segregated."[123] An example from the federal courts is a Seventh Circuit case in which the plaintiff sued the police alleging an unconstitutional use of excessive force, an equal protection violation, and a malicious prosecution. The plaintiff prevailed only on the equal protection claim and was awarded $267,000 in damages and all his attorney fees for the total case ($377,000). The Circuit Court found that the equal protection claim and the malicious prosecution claim were not related. Because the fee award in the trial court was based on the total number of hours the attorney expended on the litigation, not solely on the time spent on the equal protection claim, the Seventh Circuit remanded the case for a lowering of the attorney's fees.[124] So, whether it is a state or federal court involved, segregation of work time charges according to whether it was work on the prevailing claim, not on a rejected claim in the pleadings, probably will be needed.

However, awarding payment for all the hours spent in the entire case where only partial victory was achieved may be appropriate — if all the claims involve the same common cores of facts and legal theories.[125] Segregation is not required if services are rendered in connection with claims arising out of the same transaction and are so interrelated that their prosecution or defense entails proof or denial of essentially the same facts.[126] The key phrase to awarding total hours expended is "all the claims involve a common core of facts or legal theories to the extent that division of hours spent on claim basis is inappropriate for the items of work done."[127] Notice that the impossibility of division of the hours by claim has to exist because of the "common core of facts or legal theories" — not because the time records kept by counsel were inadequate to show on which claim each item of work was done.

---

[123] *Heritage Resources, Inc. v. Hill,* 104 S.W.3d 612 (Tex.App. Dist.8 02/13/2003)

[124] *Lenard v. Argento,* 808 F.2d 1242 (7th Cir. 1987).

[125] See *Gorini v. AMP, Inc.,* No. 03-2052, 2004 WL 2809997, at * 3 (3d Cir., 2004)

[126] *Stewart Title Guar. Co. v. Sterling,* 822 S.W.2d 1, 10 (Tex. 1991)

[127] E.g., *see Gorini v. AMP,* Inc., No. 03-2052, 2004 WL 2809997, at * 3 (3d Cir. Dec.8, 2004) (when much of counsel's time is spent litigating case as a whole, and claims involve a common core of facts and/or related legal theories, it may be difficult to divide hours spent on a claim-by-claim basis; instead, district court should focus on the significance of overall relief obtained by the plaintiff in relation to hours reasonably spent on litigation); see also *Henley,* 461 U.S. at 435; *Hooven v. Exxon Mobil Corp.,* 2005 L 417416 (E.D.Pa.) at fn.16 ("Here, the four counts in the Complaint were pled as alternative theories of the case, and they were all related claims.. . . Since the remedy was fully favorable to Plaintiffs, and Plaintiffs prevailed in a "material respect," the Court will not limit attorneys' fees to the actual time spent litigating Count III. . . .Furthermore, it is quite apparent that such parsing of claims would be impossible given the nature of the litigation in this matter."); and *Cordova v. Southwestern Bell Yellow Pages,* Inc., No. 08-03-00362-CV (Tex.App. Dist.8, 2004).

§ 08.06   Time limitations

It is rare that time limitations imposed by the client or by the circumstances are a factor in a reasonable fee. When they do occur, it usually means demanding physical and mental work and often overtime payments to employees, so an increase in the amount to come to the ultimate "reasonable fee" for such emergency work is justified.

§ 08.07   Nature and length of professional relationship with client

Lawyers in the legal community involved customarily may reduce their fees to attract a client who will produce a reliable volume of work during the future. Even if not customary, a law firm may do it in a specific case. If a lawyer has a longstanding relationship with a client, as for example, a corporation supplies a steady flow of work to the lawyer, and has lowered their fee because of that relationship, that does not mean the client receives less than a "reasonable attorney fee" if it is the prevailing party in an appropriate case. The measure of the award is a "reasonable" fee, not the "actual" fee.

☞ **TIP.** "The nature and length of the professional relationship with the client" is a factor which frequently affects the "customary fee" charged by insurance defense lawyers. An insurance company that can supply a half million dollars of work a year to a lawfirm can well demand to be charged $50 an hour less than the firm would do the work for an individual prospective client who only has one case to offer the firm. Consequently, if you represent an insurance company as the prevailing party entitled to an attorney fee award, you may have to spend time and effort proving to the court, or jury as fact finder, that the factor of "The skill level needed during those hours reasonably expended" calls for an increase above that actually charged by your firm up to a "reasonable" fee.

§ 08.08   Experience, reputation, and ability of the lawyer

The fee is to be approved as a reasonable fee is a reasonable fee, (1) for this specific matter, (2) for this specific attorney the client has chosen, provided that the fee is reasonable considering the nature of the case. It is not to be a fee based solely on the lowest price and lowest quality attorney that could have done the job. Generally, lawyers just out of law school are paid less per hour than lawyers with 25 years of experience. It is the increase in skill and ability to do things faster and better, plus the increase in the capacity to assess situations or circumstances and draw sound conclusions, that usually accompanies experience that is recognized by the higher hourly fee. Reputation is a major reason why one lawyer can charge more per hour than another. Reputation generally — although not always — correlates with experience and ability.

§ 08.09   Fixed or contingent fee; certain or uncertain payment of fee

A stated factor in both the federal and state courts list of factors to be considered is "whether the fee is fixed or contingent." Nonetheless, in the federal courts, (unlike the state courts) in statutory fee award cases, there is a United States Supreme Court pronouncement that stands as a bar to directly considering the fee contract as evidence calling for a specific enhancement (or lowering) of the lodestar amount. *City of Burlington v. Dague*[128] prohibits – in fee shifting statute cases – contingency contract enhancements to the lodestar amount. After *Dauge*, even federal circuits that previously held it necessary to provide fee enhancement for a contingent fee contract fell in to line and have reversed awards for a contingency fee enhancement. E.g., *Murphy v. Reliance Standard Life Insurance Co.*, 247 F.3d 1313 (11th Cir. 2001).

An able court sometimes gets around the *Dauge* case bar by discussing the factor of "whether the fee is fixed or contingent" not in terms of considering the *fee contract per se*, but rather discussing either whether the fee was contingent because case success was contingent (i.e., subject to chance) or the lawyer getting adequately paid for time expended was contingent. Under this approach the "contingent nature of success" is viewed at the time of filing the suit in terms of the probability of the defendant's liability, and of whether the attorney is asserting under well settled law or is advancing a novel theory, and of risks assumed by counsel in hours of labor and costs paid out by the firm without a guarantee of remuneration. An excellent example of this "way around *Dauge*" is *Hooven v. Exxon Mobil Corp.*[129], where the trial court used the "contingent nature of success" to add six hundred thousand dollars to the lodestar figure so that the attorney fee award just happened to be the same amount as the contingency fee contract provided.

Other federal courts have added a percentage to the lodestar amount for attorneys working on a contingency fee contract by adjusting the fee to account for the necessity of attracting competent counsel. This type of contingency multiplier adjustment has been approved by the U.S. Supreme Court, with the caveat that it is to be granted only in rare cases.[130] To obtain this specific type of contingency multiplier in federal court, to avoid the *Dauge* bar on directly referring to the attorney's own contingent fee contract to establish the award amount, the applicant attorney must establish:

> (1) the legal services market treats contingency fee cases as a class differently from hourly fee cases,

---

[128] See *City of Burlington v. Dague*, 505 U.S. 557, 565, 112 S.Ct. 2638, 120 L.Ed.2d 449 (1992)(holding that federal fee-shifting statutes do not permit enhancement of fee award beyond lodestar amount to reflect fact that a party agreed to pay on a contingency-fee basis). However, unlike statutory fee-shifting, contractual fee-shifting is not subject to the prohibition on contingency enhancements to the lodestar calculation of fees.

[129] *Hooven v. Exxon Mobil Corp.*, Slip Copy, 2005 WL 417416, E.D.Pa.,2005., Feb 14, 2005. As this text goes to the publisher only the Westlaw citation is currently available.

[130] *Delaware Valley, II,* 483 U.S. 711, 97 L. Ed. 2d 585, 107 S. Ct. 3078 (1987).

(2) the degree to which the relevant market compensates attorneys upward or downward for a contingency,
(3) the amount determined by the market to compensate for a contingency contract is not more than would be necessary to attract competent counsel,
(4) that without an adjustment for risk the prevailing party would have faced substantial difficulties in finding counsel in the local or other relevant legal market.[131]

Still other federal courts have creatively bypassed the *Dauge* bar by granting an overall hourly rate enhancement because use of a contingent fee contract attracted expert counsel who were able to create a common benefit to a whole class of persons not party to the litigation, e.g., establishing a legal benefit to employees.[132] This is in line with the majority opinion in *Dauge*,[133] which ruled against direct consideration of a contingency contract, but stated that one might have to award the "higher hourly rate of a superior attorney skilled and experienced enough" needed to win a chancy case. As Justice Blackman, dissenting, stated: "it is a fact of the market that an attorney who is paid only when his client prevails will tend to charge a higher fee than one who is paid regardless of outcome." Using this tactic, first, assert that an attorney of the skill involved in the case would reasonably charge a much higher hourly fee per hour if the actual collection of the fee was uncertain, and then, second, use the higher hourly fee in calculating the lodestar amount.[134]

In the federal courts, in fee-shifting statute cases, since they do not consider the attorney's contract as relevant to changes in the lodestar amount, cases such as *Duncan v. Poythress,*[135] are a natural conclusion: a pro se litigant, who incurs no attorney fees, can be awarded an attorney's fee.

State courts are another matter; they do not have without the stricture of the U.S. Supreme Court that is effective in federal courts, directly commanding the federal courts not to take a contingent contract directly into consideration. In the state courts, the risk-

---

[131] *Delaware Valley II,* 483 U.S. at 731 (O'Connor, J., concurring); id. at 733; id. at 731 n. 12 (White, J., plurality opinion), 733 (O'Connor, J., concurring); and Id. at 733 (quoting plurality, ante at 730 See also, *Blum v. Witco,* 888 F.2d 975, slip op. at 9-17 (3d Cir. 1989); *McKenzie v. Kennickell,* 277 U.S. App. D.C. 297, 875 F.2d 330, 336-37 (D.C.Cir. 1989); *Lattimore v. Oman Construction,* 868 F.2d 437, 439 (11th Cir. 1989); *Fadhl v. City and County of San Francisco,* 859 F.2d 649 (9th Cir. 1988).

[132] E.g., Cook v. Niedert, 142 F.3d 1004, 1015 (7th Cir.1998) (risk multipliers are appropriate in cases that are initiated under ERISA).

[133] *City of Burlington v. Dague,* 505 U.S. 557, 565, 112 S.Ct. 2638, 120 L.Ed.2d 449 (1992)

[134] This is the method used in *Hooven v. Exxon Mobil Corp.,* 2005 WL 417416 (E.D.Pa.). See fn.39 ("enhancement of attorneys' fees for contingency is unnecessary as higher hourly rates for more experienced counsel and higher number of hours worked to overcome the uncertainty of outcome already compensate attorneys adequately").

[135] 750 F2d 1540 (11th Cir. 1985)

taking involved by a lawyer taking the matter on a contingent fee contract is often recognized directly as a reason to enhance the lodestar amount. An example of a state court's approach to the contingency fee contract being direct evidence involved in setting the attorney fee award can be found in New Jersey.

> 4. As a matter of economic reality and simple fairness, a counsel fee award under a fee-shifting statute cannot be "reasonable" unless the lodestar, calculated as if the attorney's compensation were guaranteed regardless of result, is adjusted to reflect the actual risk that the attorney will not receive payment if the suit does not succeed. The Court adopts standards to guide the award of contingency enhancements that will address concerns about overpayment and double counting. Those standards will serve as a limit on the amount of contingency enhancements and will require a relationship between the amount of the enhancement awarded and the extent of the risk of nonpayment assumed by counsel for the prevailing party.
>
> 5. The trial court must determine whether a case was taken on a contingent basis, whether the attorney was able to mitigate the risk of nonpayment in any way, and whether other economic risks were aggravated by the contingency of payment. . . . Moreover, there need not be evidence in the record that without risk enhancement plaintiff would have faced substantial difficulties in finding counsel in the local market . . .
>
> 6. . . .Contingency enhancements in fee-shifting cases ordinarily should range between five and fifty-percent of the lodestar fee, with the enhancement in typical contingency cases ranging between twenty and thirty-five percent of the lodestar. Here, the Court exercises original jurisdiction and modifies the counsel-fee award. . . . a contingency enhancement equal to one-third of the lodestar fee is appropriate.
>
> *Rendine v. Pantzer*, 141 N.J. 292, 661 A.2d 1202 (N.J. 1995).

Now, let's turn back to looking at the federal courts' consideration of the contingent fee contract of counsel, but this time looking at the category of cases regarding attorney fee awards which do *not* arise under fee-shifting statutes. In that category of cases, e.g., contract award cases or common fund cases, the federal courts can decide to award based on a contingency fee contract enhancement. See, e.g., the approach taken by the district court in *Hooven v. Exxon Mobil Corp.* in the following quotation.

> FN19. The Third Circuit favors the use of contingency fees in cases involving a common fund, and the lodestar method in cases involving fee shifting statutes. In re Prudential Ins. Co. of Am. Sales Practices Litig., 148 F.3d 283, 333 (3d Cir.1998). This case involves neither a common fund nor a fee shifting statute, but rather a contract term providing that Defendants will pay all reasonable attorneys' fees and expenses incurred by prevailing employees. As the fees will be paid by Defendants and not by Plaintiffs from a common fund, the situation is more akin to a statutory fee shifting case. However, unlike statutory fee-shifting, contractual fee-shifting is not subject to the prohibition on contingency enhancements to the lodestar calculation of fees.
>
> *Hooven v. Exxon Mobil Corp.*, 2005 WL 417416 (E.D.Pa.)

The *Hooven* opinion is such a poster child opinion for prevailing attorneys who did all the right things in making their application for fees, and illustrations of several of the points made in this handbook, that I have included the opinion in the Appendices to this Attorney Fee Award Handbook. The opinion is worth reading to see what good applications for fee awards can produce.

Chapter 09   Awards for Paralegal Time

§ 09.01   Paralegal time "Yes"; clerical time "No"

In *Jenkins v. Missouri*[136] the United States Supreme Court effectively laid to rest any dispute whether payment for paralegal work should be included in an award of "attorney's fees."[137] However, a few state decisions have not yet announced they have joined the trend.[138]

Often the key to getting the legal assistant's fees approved (or disapproved) as legal fees is the testimony of an expert or a court finding that the work done in the case by the legal assistant indeed was work normally otherwise done by a lawyer and was not mere clerical or typing work.[139] To provide the evidentiary basis for approval of legal assistant work as attorney fees, show the following, To attack, show the negative of the following.

1.   The legal assistant was to have been qualified through education, training, or work experience to perform substantive legal work.

2.   The legal assistant work that was done is identified and described.

3.   The legal assistant work was legal work that traditionally has been done by lawyers.

4.   The legal work was performed under the direction and supervision of an attorney.

---

[136] 110 S. Ct. 1651, 495 U.S. 33 (1990). Read this case if you are involved with a dispute regarding billing for paralegal time as part of a reasonable attorney fee.

[137] E.g., *Gill Savings Association v. International Supply*, 759 S.W.2d 697 (Tex. App.-Dallas 1988, writ denied).

[138] E.g., *Hines v. Hines*, 1997 WL 112346 (Idaho 1997) (54(e)(3).(The rationale used in *Missouri v. Jenkins* was not applicable to Idaho.); *Joerger v. Gordon Food Service*, 224 Mich. App. 167, 568 N.W.2d 365 (Mich. Ct. App. 1997) (The court acknowledged federal and sister state precedent which recognizes legal assistant fees as a separate element of attorney fees damages but found there was a lack of precedent in Michigan. The court urged the Michigan Supreme Court to address the issue.) See also, *Annotation, Attorneys Fees: Cost of Services Provided by Paralegals or the Like as Compensable Element of Award in State Court*, 73 A.L.R. 938.

[139] See *In the Interest of JLB*, 1999 Tex. App. LEXIS 4901; *Stamp-Ad, Inc.*,915 S.W.2d 932; *Arthur Anderson & Co.*, 898 S.W.2d 914.

5.   The number of hours expended by the legal assistant

6.   The hourly rate being charged for the legal assistant.

7.   The customary range for legal assistant work of like skill in the relevant legal community.

The legal assistant work for which courts will award an amount for "attorney fee" is only the substantive work which traditionally has been done by lawyers. Clerical tasks cannot be charged as attorney fees. Clerical tasks should be deducted from any billing for paralegal fees.

Clerical tasks are not considered as a part of the computation of hours of a reasonable attorney fee, whether submitted as attorney or paralegal work. Clerical and secretarial tasks are considered office overhead and part of the normal expenses of operating a business, not as an additional profit center for a law office.

Because the award of paralegal time is sometimes a matter of convincing a judge that other judges make such an award, we include a list of several cases that are often cited for the proposition that legal work done by a paralegal is compensable as part of an attorney fee award. The list is at Appendix B to this handbook.

Chapter 10   Awards for Prejudgment Interest

§ 10.01   More than one way to enhance for the passage of time

Prejudgment interest may be recovered and awarded on the attorney fees and costs. Statutes may authorize the award of prejudgment interest. If the statute is silent, the fact finder may add it as part of a reasonable fee. Powerful arguments and case law support it being added.

The rationale for awarding prejudgment on attorney fees has been expressed by the courts either:

> as a determination of a total reasonable fee to be paid at the end of the case, or

> as interest on an attorney fee incurred and normally due to be paid by a client earlier as the case proceeded.

If you represent a prevailing party, hammer on the mandatory language in the following quotations. Paste these quotations into your brief.

> "If the rate used in calculating the fee does not already include some factor for risk or the time-value of money, it *ought to be enhanced* by some percentage figure." *Henley v. Eckerhart,* 103 S. Ct. 1933, 461 U.S. 424 (1983). [Emphasis supplied.]

> "[It must be understood that the awarding of interest is in no sense a windfall. Because a dollar today is worth more than a dollar in the future, *the only way [the party] can be made whole is to award him interest.*" *Gates v. Collier,* 616 F2d 1268, at 1273-1297 (5th Cir 1980). [Emphasis supplied.]

Instead of making a percentage adjustment or addition to the lodestar amount, some courts achieve the rough justice equivalent of prejudgment interest on the attorney fee award by calculating the lodestar amount using counsel's current hourly rates rather than a lower market hourly rate in effect at the time the work actually was done and billable to the client.[140]

---

[140] E.g., see *Missouri v. Jenkins,* 491 U.S. 274, 283-284 (1989) (finding that application of current rather than historic hourly rates is an appropriate adjustment for delay in payment of attorneys' fees); *Rode v. Dellarciprete,* 892 F.2d 1177 at 1188-89 (3d Cir. 1990) (describing petition based on current rates as premised on a theory of "delay compensation"); *Rendine v. Pantzer,* 661 A.2d 1202, 1127 (N.J. 1995)(To take into account delay in payment, the hourly rate at which compensation is to be awarded should be based on current rates rather than those in effect when the services were performed.").

☞ **TIP.** To generate the most enthusiasm of the fact finder (court or jury) for the award of prejudgement interest on your fee charges as part of a reasonable fee, have your computer generate your exhibits of the time spent on the matter as a series of monthly invoices.   Then have the computer generate an end of case summary statement including interest due on each unpaid invoice, computed at the maximum legal rate from 30 days after the date of each monthly invoice until the date of trial. (Separately submit a sheet adding up the monthly totals without interest charges.) Because most litigation takes more than a year to complete, the pile of monthly invoices surmounted by the summary statement looks impressive as to the time you have gone without payment, and have been financing the payment of your office staff. Everyone who sees a pile of monthly bills (and who pays their bills monthly or who looks forward to a monthly payment check) can understand visually that an interest payment is fair.

Chapter 11   Awards for Attorney Expenses

§ 11.01   Traditionally billed expenses

The statutes providing for the prevailing party to receive a reasonable "attorney fee" do not usually mention the expenses the attorney pays out to conduct the litigation. Expert fees, court reporter fees, travel expenses, conversion fees to change paper documents into PDF format to file as required by court rules, computer research time, photocopies, FedEx messenger charges, and such items can easily run the expenses of the case into thousands or tens of thousands of dollars. Can those expense items be included in the term "attorney fee?"

In the *ABA Formal Ethics Opinion 93-179* [141] it is said:

> In the absence of an agreement to the contrary, it is impermissible for a lawyer to create an additional source of profit for the law firm beyond that which is contained in the provision of professional services themselves. The lawyer's stock in trade is the sale of legal services, not photocopy paper, tuna fish sandwiches, computer time or messenger services.

That dour prohibition catches your eye, doesn't it? Are attorney expenses properly part of an "attorney fee" award?

The answer is: legal industry's traditional charges to client — yes; legal industry's non-traditional charges to client --- no, mostly. Courts routinely state that all expenses normally billed to fee paying clients, reasonably incurred in the litigation, can and should be awarded as part of the reasonable attorney fee. The key is in the phrase "expenses normally billed to fee paying clients." The judge uses his own judgement of what is "normally billed," and that judgment is formed by what she has done before she went on the bench and the few attorney bills she has seen since donning the judicial robe. Times change, and therefore what is "normal" or "traditional" changes. Although you may have the 1993 *ABA Formal Ethics Opinion 93-179* in front of you, forbidding photocopy charges and FedEx messenger charges, clients in your city and state probably long since have become accustomed to bills asking for reimbursement for photocopies and FedEx bills. What is customary in to charge clients first occurs in the legal community, and only when the judge knows of the new customs does she think of the charges as "normally billed to fee paying clients."

If you are requesting a fee award, you might want a laundry list of expenses "normally" billed to clients. Here is such a suggested list, from a respected ABA source which

---

[141] ABA Comm. on Ethics and Professional Responsibility, Formal Op. 93-379.

included what corporate counsel on the committee thought was normally billed to them as fee-paying clients.[142]

> Arbitrators' and mediators' fees and expenses;
> Copying of documents (but not the firm's own file copies of documents produced by the billing attorney);
> Court reporter and deposition transcripts or recordings;
> Court fees and service of process fees;
> Delivery services or special messengers;
> Experts;
> Litigation support vendors;
> Local counsel;
> Meals (of the sort that the IRS would recognize as business expenses);
> Online computer research;
> Outside printing;
> Private investigators;
> Subpoena and witness fees;
> Telephone charges;
> Travel in town;
> Travel out of town;
> Trial transcripts;
> Trial exhibits;
> Word processing beyond that of normal secretarial production of the firm's work product.

☞ **TIP.** If you are proposing a fee award, include in your fee submission evidence some evidence that the costs you are asking for as a part of "attorney fees" are normally charged to clients by lawyers outside of your own law firm. The above list from the ABA may be sufficient for your purposes. If there is some other item of substance, you might, for example, have the office manager of a large law firm in your area sign an affidavit that clients are normally charged the items in question as a separate charge from attorney time, that the costs are not included in the firm's calculation of a reasonable time charge, and that his/her experience is that other law firms also normally charge such items. Even if the ABA report list or the affidavit is not directly admissible, the opinion of your billing attorney (remember he/she is automatically an expert on attorney fees) can specifically mention that ABA list and the affidavit as part of his/her expert opinion on what are "expenses normally billed to fee paying clients in the legal community." Under federal evidence Rule 703, the judge always knows about the proposed evidence, and in most cases will allow it to be disclosed to a jury sitting as a fact finder as part of the foundation of the expert's testimony.

---

[142] This list is based on the ABA Section of Litigation's Uniform Task-Based Management System (1995) coding for expenses. The coding list was developed by a tripartite initiative of the American Bar Association Section of Litigation, the American Corporate Counsel Association, and a sponsoring group of major corporate law departments and law firms coordinated and supported by Price Waterhouse LLP (In other words, the list of common expenses for which billing codes are needed was developed by a group that has seen a lot of law firm bills.).

☞ **TIP.** If you are opposing a fee award, use discovery to look at the proponent attorney's fee contract, and see what the limits are that can be charged the client under that contract. That might set some boundaries on costs to be awarded as part of a "reasonable fee." After all, if the attorney did not seek to obtain the costs as apart of the legal services contract, the cost cannot be part of a fee award intended only to reimburse the client for the cost of hiring the attorney.

◀)) **WARNING.** If you are undertaking a claim on a contingent basis, and a fee award is a possibility, you may be tempted to have some broad language in the fee contract on what the costs will be that the client will pay if the case is successful. Careful attention to your state's ethics rules is necessary, to ensure that you are not engaging in an improper financing of litigation.

§ 11.02   Handy quotes

ABA statements will be of some help in making your arguments on what is an appropriate expense charge. For example, if you represent a losing party, you pull out of the *ABA Statements of Principles* the statement that:

> The Task Force concurs with the position of the Standing Committee that, absent agreement to the contrary, ethical obligations of lawyers limit rather significantly the latitude available for creative charging of clients for costs.[143]

On the other side, if you represent a winning party, you pull out of the *ABA Model Rules Comments* and the *ABA Statement of Principles* the following statements and quote them in your brief on the attorney fee award.

> Paragraph (a) requires that lawyers charge fees that are reasonable under the circumstances. . . . A lawyer may seek reimbursement for the cost of services performed in-house, such as copying, or for other expenses incurred in-house, such as telephone charges, either by charging a reasonable amount to which the client has agreed in advance or by charging an amount that reasonably reflects the cost incurred by the lawyer.[144]

> With regard to disbursements, firms generally should charge their clients only their actual out-of-pocket amounts incurred on behalf of the client. With regard to other charges incurred on behalf of a client, such as photocopying and computer research, firms should charge its costs, unless an understanding with the client specifies otherwise. "Costs" as

---

[143] Task Force on Lawyer Business Ethics, *Statements of Principles*, 51(4) ABA Journal 1303–30 (Aug. 1996)[Revised and republished from *Statements of Principles*, 51 Bus. Law. (1996)].

[144] American Bar Assoc., *Model Rules* of Professional Conduct, Rule 1.5 Fees, Comment (2006)

used in connection with other charges incurred on behalf of a client may include indirect costs reasonably allocable to the service provided as well as direct costs.[145]

As with attorney time records, expense records or charges need to be specific, (e.g., "Federal Express charges for September 2003" may be disallowed as not shown to be applicable to the action or shown as needed because ordinary mail could not have been used. Just as with a phone call time record, the costs record needs to show item by item the Who ("to"), What (was sent), and Why (ordinary postal mail was not sufficient to be used.)"

Do not submit an expense billing that just says "$20,000 for Photocopies." Break the amount into the amount charged for internal duplicating charges and charges of outside vendors, and state how many copies were made by you and included in your in-house photocopy charges. If outside vendors charge between $.05 and $.10 per page, the maximum reasonable per page charge for you is probably a $.10 per page charge. For the best treatment by the court of your photocopy expenses, you need to indicate that you are not charging photocopy expense for your own in-house file copies of the documents you have generated yourself and sent to the client and other counsel.

In general, a request for a travel expense to be considered, as an addition to an attorney's hourly fee, needs the same level of detail required by the IRS records requirements (each individual date, place, expense type, expense amount, and the business purpose for the expense).

§ 11.03   Witness and experts' fees

One of the expenses that an attorney has and that is clearly normally and traditionally charged to, and paid by, by the client is the amount paid as proper fees to lay and expert witnesses. Nevertheless, courts ordinarily reject witness fees, lay or expert, as part of an award of an attorney fee. E.g., the U.S. Supreme Court rejected expert fees in the context of an award of attorney fees in civil rights actions under 42 U.S.C. §1988.[146] The almost universal rejection of witness fees, whether expert or lay, as part of an attorney fee award, is based on the historic role of legislatures to provide by specific statutes for the payment of the fees and expenses of expert and lay witnesses.

Where experts' fees are allowed, either by part of an attorney fee award or under some other rubric, the courts require such experts or consultants, rendering professional services, to furnish time documentation similar to that required by court for the time documentation by the attorneys hiring the expert.

---

[145] Task Force on Lawyer Business Ethics, Statements of Principles, 51(4) ABA Journal 1303–30 (Aug. 1996)[Revised and republished from Statements of Principles, 51 Bus. Law. (1996].

[146] Congress later amended the civil rights law to allow expert fees as part of the attorney fee award to the prevailing party.

Chapter 12   Special Considerations in Settlements

§ 12.01   Attorney fee award disposition in settlement

Most cases are settled; not tried. If a statute or case law regarding your lawsuit provides for an award of attorney fees to the prevailing party, take special notice of that law during your negotiations for settlement. If you are not explicit during settlement, questions arise whether the settlement was intended to include attorney's fees, and whether attorney fees were waived.

In the settlement agreement make it clear whether:

    ✓   there is a waiver of attorney fees as a part of the settlement, or

    ✓   the amount of attorney fees has been agreed upon, or

    ✓   the issue of attorney fees is outstanding — and the court retains jurisdiction of the case to decide that issue.

Most commonly, when cases are resolved by a settlement agreement, the parties end the case by a stipulation of dismissal. In *Kokkonen v. Guardian Life Insurance Co.,*[147] the dismissal order entered by the parties' agreement neither incorporated the terms of the settlement in the body of the order nor reserved enforcement power in the court. The *Kokkonen* case held that enforcement of the settlement agreement was not a matter of a renewal or continuation of the original case but rather an entirely new contract beach cause of action. As such, the alleged breach of the settlement agreement had to be brought as a new action, one that the federal *Kokkonen* court observed would have to be brought in state court, because no federal cause of action was involved in a simple breach of contract case. So unless jurisdiction of the case is reserved to the trial court to enforce the settlement agreement, there will be problems of enforcement.

There is a further problem for the party that believes they prevailed in obtaining the settlement, perhaps even a settlement providing 100% of everything sought in the pleading filed in the case. If you are not a "prevailing party," then you are not entitled to an amount for attorney fees. You do not qualify as a "prevailing party" because of a settlement agreement — unless the settlement agreement is incorporated into an order of a court. In the federal courts, *Buckhannon v. West Virginia Department of Health and*

---

[147] 511 U.S. 375 (1994).

Human Resources,[148] mandated that unless a court has issued an order which creates a "material alteration of the legal relationship between the parties" or "a judicially sanctioned change in the legal relationship of the parties," then there is no "prevailing party" for an award of attorney fees. State decision law is tending to follow this pattern for the future. In short, if you represent the plaintiff, do not settle and dismiss the case, expecting an attorney fee to be awarded by the court because your settlement agreement paid the plaintiff money and everything else the plaintiff wanted.

On the other hand, if the settlement agreement is incorporated into the dismissal order, and the court retains jurisdiction to enforce the terms of the agreement in the order of dismissal, then the court's order of dismissal based on the settlement agreement becomes the legal equivalent of a consent decree on the merits. Note the two separate requirements: incorporation into the decree, and the court's retention of enforcement powers.

In a consent decree on the merits, a winning party can be a "prevailing party."[149] A consent decree, in an appropriate case, may serve as the basis for an award of attorney's fees. If the consent decree does not include an admission of liability by the defendant, there needs to be some court-ordered change in the legal relationship between the parties.[150] To define a plaintiff as a "prevailing party," defendants could agree to a declaration ordered by the court's consent decree that plaintiffs have certain rights or that defendant's procedures will be improved, or both. If there is neither a declaration of rights, nor an ordered change in what defendant will do in the future, nor an admission of liability, a court in an enforcement proceeding may decline to find the plaintiff was a "prevailing party" or award attorney fees.

◀)) **WARNING.** If the defendants insist on a nonadmission-of-liability clause in a settlement agreement, plaintiffs' counsel should insist three items: (1) additional or more specific language defining and implementing relief, (2) a specific agreement that plaintiffs are the prevailing party, and (3) a specific agreement that plaintiffs are entitled to attorney fees.   Each of these three items must be included; otherwise a

---

[148] 532 U.S. 598, 604 (2001)

[149] Cf., *American Disability Association v. Chmielarz*, 289 F.3d 1315, 1319–21 (11th Cir. 2002) (either by adopting the terms of the settlement in the court order or by expressly retaining jurisdiction, parties obtain the functional equivalents of consent decrees); *Board of Trustees of Hotel and Restaurant Employees Local 25 v.Madison Hotel*, 97 F.3d 1479, 1483 (D.C. Cir. 1996) (whether a mere reference to the existence of a settlement in the dismissal order is sufficient to retain jurisdiction is unclear, and the parties also should expressly provide that the court retains jurisdiction); and *Kokkonen v. Guardian Life Insurance Co.* 511 U.S. 375 (1994)(noting that if the explicit terms of the settlement agreement had been incorporated into the order of dismissal or if the order had provided for continued jurisdiction over the settlement, then the lower court would have had the authority to enforce the agreement, but not noting that such authority would make the plaintiff a prevailing party.)

[150] *See Maher v. Gagne*, 448 U. S. 122 (1980); *Texas State Teachers Assn. v. Garland Independent School Dist.*, 489 U. S. 782, 792 (1989); and *Rhodes v. Stewart*, 488 U. S. 1, 3-4 (1988) (per curiam).

nonadmission-of-liability clause can be interpreted to mean that as a matter of law the plaintiff was not a prevailing party. The court (prodded by counsel) can declare that the parties joint agreement that plaintiff is a "prevailing party" does not legally make it true, and the court's decision on the law is otherwise.

§ 12.02   Settlement tactic for defendants; trap for plaintiff's counsel

Some attorneys have gotten caught up in disputes with their clients and grievance committees because of the lawyer's faulty understanding of "who owns the attorney fee award."

Do attorney fees awarded to a prevailing party belong to the attorneys who labored to earn them or to their clients? The answer to that question is important in settlements. For example, if the attorney fee award is likely to be more than the attorney's fee contract with the client provides, if the client "owns" the fee award, the client may benefit by waiving the attorney fee award as a condition of a comfortable settlement, or may want to keep the awarded attorney fee for herself. As another example of why that question is important, consider that the answer to that question of "ownership" of the fee award determines who must sign the settlement agreement as a party to the settlement contract.

In some few states, and in some few instances, — if the fee contract between attorney and client specifies that the attorney fee award will be the attorney's fee due from the client, then it is held that the attorney fees awarded to a prevailing party belong to the attorneys, not to their clients, absent an agreement to the contrary.[151] The theory of such fee ownership is that to increase public vindication of fundamental public policies attorneys need assurance that, if they obtain a favorable result for their client, they will actually receive reasonable attorney fees, instead of the sum a middle class or poor client is willing to pay to prosecute the matter.

However, in most states and under most federal statutes, and almost always in federal court, the reasoning is that where fees can be awarded to the "prevailing party," the right to receive the attorney fee award belongs exclusively to that party and not to the party's lawyer, thus allowing clients – not the lawyer – to bargain with the adversary about the attorney fees, including waiving statutory attorney fee awards. [152]

Generally, the legal theory is that the right to seek and to receive an attorney fee is a cause of action (or part of it) that the client owns. Attorneys are ethically forbidden from

---

[151] E.g., see *Flannery v. Prentice*, 26 Cal.4th 572, 28 P.3d 860, 110 Cal.Rptr.2d 809 (Cal. 08/13/2001).

[152] E.g., see *Evans v. Jeff D*. 475 U.S. 717 (1986). Cf., *U.S. ex rel. Virani v. Jerry M. Lewis Truck Parts & Equipment* (9th Cir. 1996) 89 F.3d 574, 577, cert. den. (1997) 519 U.S. 1109. [Under the federal False Claims Act, a client's "right" to reasonable attorney fees "is really a power to obtain fees for his attorney; the attorneys' right does not come into being until the client exercises that power; the defendant's liability will only arise if that power is exercised"].)

taking an assignment of the cause of action they are prosecuting for the client. That means, among other things, just as the client cannot assign his/her entire liability cause of action to the attorney, so too the attorney ethically cannot request the client to assign the right to recover the attorney fee to the attorney.

This fact of non-assignabilty of causes of action to the attorney for the client forms the base for a settlement tactic for defendants in cases involving fee-shifting states authorizing an attorney fee award to the prevailing party. Here's why. The norm in most civil rights, employment, and like cases is for the attorney to undertake the case on the basis of a contingent fee. Defendants in such cases can use the tactic of offering a lump-sum settlement that could benefit a plaintiff but not provide enough for their lawyer's time investment in the case. It's a tactic that works in small damages cases.

For example, suppose a case of racial discrimination in employment, that the claimant's attorney has the case on a 33% contingency fee contract, and has put in $50,000 of time bringing the case up to the courthouse door. Suppose further that the main economic damage of the plaintiff is the payment of $20,000 in lost wages until she found alternative better-paying employment. The defendant offers a total of $60,000 for a total settlement "including any claim for attorney fees." To the plaintiff such a settlement sounds good: she gets $60,000, deducts and pays her attorney $20,000 in accord with the fee contract, and she winds up with $40,000 for her $20,000 in economic loss. But to the attorney, he winds up with $20,000 in fees to pay for $50,000 of time invested.

Alert defense counsel will always issue a demand for production of the plaintiff attorney's fee contract. If the fee award is a part of the issues, then the attorney-fee contract is a legitimate target of discovery. Once a contingent fee contract is found, the defense always should think in terms of a lump sum settlement "including any claim for attorney fees."

There are many civil rights and other cases that present legitimate claims by an individual where the plaintiff secures an attorney even though the case is a low-value case with little damages to be recovered for the injury. Attorneys seek various ways of protecting themselves, often by fee contract clauses that are not ethically proper or are otherwise unenforceable. For example, the lawyer in *Pony v. County of Los Angeles*[153] was working on such a case, and reasonably expected that the defendant would offer to settle for a small amount including the attorney fee award. To protect himself he devised a retainer agreement that transferred a plaintiff's right to seek fees to the attorney himself -- letting him sue for his fees even after his client settled. As happens in these cases with regularity, the U.S. Circuit Court of Appeals held the fee contract clause invalid.

> The Supreme Court has held that Section 1988 vests the right to seek attorney's fees in the prevailing party, not her attorney, and that attorneys therefore lack standing to pursue them. *[citing numerous cases]* . . . Once the prevailing party exercises her right to receive fees, [assuming the fee contract gives the attorney the fee award] the attorney's right to collect the vests, and he may then pursue them on his own. Virani, 89 F.3d at 578. Unless and until the party exercises this

---

[153] 433 F.3d 1138 (9th Cir. 2006).

power, however, the attorney has no right to collect fees from the non-prevailing party, and the non-prevailing party has no duty to pay them. Id. A prevailing party may waive her statutory eligibility for attorney's fees as a condition of settlement. Evans, 475 U.S. at 737-38 (concluding that 42 U.S.C. § 1988 does not create a general rule prohibiting settlements conditioned on the waiver of fees).

In this case, Pony, the prevailing party, did not exercise her rights to pursue attorney's fees. To the contrary, she waived them as a condition of settlement with the County. Accordingly, under the Court's ruling in Evans and our ruling in Virani, Mitchell has no standing to pursue attorney's fees merely as a result of his position as Pony's former attorney.

Mitchell argues that he need not rely on his status as Pony's former attorney. He contends that he has standing under his retainer agreement with Pony, whereby she assigned her rights to apply for attorney's fees to him. If the assignment is valid, Mitchell argues, he stands in her shoes and may assert her rights to statutory attorney's fees as if she had asserted them herself. However, Pony's putative assignment to Mitchell is invalid because the right to seek attorney's fees under 42 U.S.C. § 1988 is a substantive cause of action which cannot be transferred contractually.

Pony v. County of Los Angeles, 433 F.3d 1138 (9th Cir. 2006).

§ 12.03   Tax problem in settlements

It is common for parties to settle a case after a verdict. Clients of the prevailing party normally will assume the award of attorney's fees goes to the attorney and hence the attorney fee is not income to be reported to, or taxed by, the IRS. Clients may make the same assumption if the settlement agreement provides for payment of an attorney fee directly to the attorneys. The clients' assumption is wrong. To prevent later claims of legal malpractice in the attorney's advice regarding settlement, the attorneys for the prevailing party should keep in mind that the client's normal expectation may be wrong.

The Internal Revenue Department takes the position that the award of the attorney fee is owned by the party, not her attorney, and taxes the full award received by the party, including the attorney fee, even if the fee is paid directly to the attorney. In cases where attorney fees exceed the damage awards -- such as in public interest litigation where relief is injunctive or awards are minimal -- a client could be forced to pay more in taxes than he or she won in the award.

> In the case of a litigation recovery the income-generating asset is the cause of action derived from the plaintiff's legal injury. The plaintiff retains dominion over this asset throughout the litigation. . . . When a litigant's recovery constitutes income, the litigant's income includes the portion of the recovery paid to the attorney as a contingent fee.
>
> *Commissioner of Internal Revenue v. Banks*, 125 S.Ct. 826, 543 U.S. 426, 160 L.Ed.2d 859 (U.S. 01/24/2005).[154]

(After the client has paid the IRS, then the IRS gets a second bite of the apple by taxing the income received by the attorney!)

---

[154] The fees in the *Banks* case were calculated on the basis of the attorney fee contract. There is still a small ray of hope for taxpayers who received statutory attorney fee awards prior to the effective date of the new legislation. The court specifically left open the issue of how statutory attorney fees should be treated. But it is a dim small ray of hope.

Plaintiffs in lawsuits alleging employment discrimination and other civil rights claims fare better on their taxes—if they recovered their awards after the American Jobs Creation Act became law in October 2004. A provision in the Jobs Creation Act[155] relieves plaintiffs who settle or win court awards under a broad array of federal and state civil rights statutes from having to pay taxes on the attorney fee portions of their awards. Before the American Jobs Creation Act, a prevailing plaintiff would have had to pay taxes on the entire award amount. For some taxpayers a deduction is available for the expense of recovering the income. For others the operation of the Alternative Minimum Tax[156] comes into play and does not allow any miscellaneous itemized deductions.

Notice the Jobs Creation Act relief statute applies only to prevailing plaintiffs, not to prevailing defendants. Furthermore, it does not address awards of attorney fees outside the specified federal and state civil right statutes.

What all this boils down to is that trial counsel should probably disclaim professional ability to advise the client on tax consequences, tell the client the attorney fee may be taxable to the client, and tell the client to see tax counsel for advice before a settlement, if taxes are a concern to the client.

---

[155] 118 Stat. 1418. Section 703 of the Act amended the Internal Revenue Code by adding §62(a)(19). Id., at 1546. The amendment allows a taxpayer, in computing adjusted gross income, to deduct "attorney fees and court costs paid by, or on behalf of, the taxpayer in connection with" a number of federal and state civil right statutes.

[156] 26 U. S. C. §§56(b)(1)(A)(I)

Chapter 13   Traps in the Procedure for an Award

§ 13.01   Attorney fee awards procedure

This chapter points out problems you may encounter in federal and state law procedure. Be aware of the possibilities, and do your homework in your own jurisdiction on when, to whom, and you submit the evidence on a requested attorney fee award.

We start with a warning. It is especially applicable to plaintiffs' counsel. Before you start a lawsuit, you need to be aware of all the attorney fee statutes that might apply. Do not assume that the procedural requirements to get an award for a fee award are like all other procedures for recovering damages. You know the normal requirements for recovering damages: give notice of the fact of damages in the pleading, request the damages in the ad daman of the complaint and then prove the facts and opinions as a part of the evidence in the main case, following which the fact finder will make a decision on the amount of the attorney fee at the same time other damages are awarded. Alternatively, do not assume that an award for a fee award is like the usual trial or post trial motion procedure is used to obtain an attorney fee award. Both of these alternative assumptions can be dangerous assumptions in the peculiar field of attorney awards law – in your jurisdiction. For example, there may be a statutory requirement of a specific demand for payment before the complaint is filed to recover reasonable attorney's fees against an insurer.[157] The failure to establish compliance with a pre-suit demand requirement will deny recovery of attorney's fees under such a statute. In other jurisdictions, failure to place evidence into the trial record prevents a motion for fees after the trial.

Most states have multiple statutes and case law doctrines allowing recovery of attorney fees. Those statutes and doctrines often specify a particular procedure to be followed. Sometimes those various statutory procedures are not uniform within a state. You cannot assume that if you comply with the procedure jurisdictional hoops of one statute you can use that same statutory procedure for recovering an attorney's fee under a different statute or court-made doctrine. You may lose under some legal theories in the case but may win under the one legal theory embodied in the state or doctrine which had a procedure with which you did not comply. So before you sue, check all the attorney fee statutes that might apply. When you prevail, you must have followed the specific procedure for the attorney fee award for the specific theory on which you prevailed.

---

[157] See e.g., *International Sec. Life Ins. Co. v. Redwine*, 481 S.W.2d 792 (Tex. 1972); *McFarland v. Franklin Life Ins. Co.*, 416 S.W.2d 378 (Tex. 1967).

§ 13.02   The required fact finder — and when to present your evidence

Whether you are on the prevailing side, or on the responding side, you should determine, first, whether (1) the law of your jurisdiction for (2) the involved specific theory of recovery — requires (A) the jury or (B) the judge to find the facts of what is a reasonable fee and award the attorney fee. In the states, the law varies, and may vary according to the legal basis for recovery of the attorney fee. On the prevailing party's side, your failure to submit evidence to the correct fact finder will make your attempt for fees a nullity. On the responding side, your failure to object to an incorrect fact finder until after final judgement is entered is one way to lose a sophisticated client for the future.

Second, you need to determine when during the course of the litigation the factual evidence on the attorney fee award is to be submitted, and when the issues will be heard. Those times vary among the states, although commonly the state law takes one of two different routes. The first route makes the jury the fact finder on the attorney fee award. You present the attorney fee evidence to the jury (or judge if the jury is waived) along with the presentation of all the other damages evidence in the case. The second route makes the judge the fact finder on the attorney fee award. You present the evidence on the issues of attorney's fees but only after the liability and other damage issues have been decided by a jury (or judge if the jury is waived). You have to look at the statutory and case law of the state, as well as procedural rules, to find the answers as to whom and when you present the attorney fee evidence. Make the presentation to the wrong entity, or at the wrong time, and you are out of luck.

In the various states it is not always the judge; sometimes it is the jury, who sets the amount. Statutes, case law, and court rules, vary not only as to whether it is a matter of substantive damages or a procedural matter of costs, but also whether it is judge or jury that determines substantive damage attorney fees. Further, who sets the amount depends on which jurisdiction's law is being litigated in the state court. Read the following quotation[158] as an example to understand that the matter of who decides the attorney fee (judge or jury) depends both on whether substantive of procedural law is involved, on whether the substantive law is state or federal law, and also on whether you are in federal or state court. It's a Texas state case where the attorney finished the jury trial on a claim of violation of federal statute and thought he would then submit his evidence on his attorney fee to the judge in accordance with the federal procedure.

> In Smith v. Davis, 453 S.W.2d 340 (Tex.Civ.App.--Fort Worth 1970, writ ref'd n.r.e.), the court stated:
>
> > "It is established law in Texas now that in a case where there is a question as to what would constitute a reasonable attorney's fee, such question is one of fact to be determined by the fact finder in the case,

---

[158] This quotation is from *Martin v. Body*, 1976.TX.40139, 533 S.W.2d 461 (Tx. App. Corpus Christi, 1976). See also two case cited in *Martin v. Body*, to wit: *Great American Reserve Insurance Company v. Britton*, 406 S.W.2d 901 (Texas 1966); and *Johns v. Jaeb*, 518 S.W.2d 857 (Tex.Civ.App.--Dallas 1974, no writ)

and in order to have a determination of such fact is [sic] must be supported by evidence...."

In Bagby Land and Cattle Company v. California Livestock Commission Company, 439 F.2d 315 (5th Cir. 1971), the Court said:

."... although the procedure in Texas courts would apparently require proof of reasonable attorney's fees, Federal courts are not bound by this procedure in diversity actions. It was entirely permissible for the district court to fix attorney's fees on the basis of its own experience and without the aid of testimony of witnesses."

In this case, *even though we are dealing with a Federal statute, we are bound by the law as determined by the Texas Supreme Court.* The record shows that defendants are entitled to attorney's fees under 15 U.S.C.A. § 1640(a)(2). But, there is no evidence [submitted to the Texas jury in this case, so therefore there is no attorney fee that can be awarded]. [Emphasis supplied.]

Martin v. Body, 1976.TX.40139, 533 S.W.2d 461 (TX. App. Corpus Christi, 1976).

Look beyond your general state law regarding who is to decide the amount of attorney fees. If you are dealing with a specific statute or specific case law doctrine, look there also. Specific statutes and legal doctrines may differ from the state general law, e.g., giving the court the power to determine the amount of a fee award even though the other substantive damages are set by a jury. For example, suppose you are trying a trade secret case in state court. Section 4 of the *Uniform Trade Secrets Act,* enacted by the states, provides "the court may award reasonable attorney's fees to the prevailing party." The commissioners' comments to this section state "patent law is followed in allowing the judge to determine whether attorney's fees should be awarded even if there is a jury."

You may even find there is a statutory procedure and a conflicting, overruling, court rule procedure (or vice versa). An example is Oregon, where ORCP 68 C(1) overrules everything you may read elsewhere[159] in the state statutes, case law, and court rules, by stating:

Notwithstanding Rule 1 A and the procedure provided in any rule or statute permitting recovery of attorney fees in a particular case, this section governs the pleading, proof, and award of attorney fees in all cases, regardless of the source of the right to recovery of such fees.

In the federal courts, if the theory of liability is one of federal law, or if the fees are *not a substantive element* of damage under a state theory of liability involved, the matter is determined by a federal judge. Let's break that long sentence in parts, and expand the thoughts in that last sentence. In federal courts, the answer to "who" and "when" is a two-step answer:

In the federal courts, the judge determines attorney fee awards, even if the case is a jury case, and even if the cause of action arises from a state

---

[159] *Pointe West Apts v. Anderson*, 145 Or App 596, 931 P2d 100 (1997) is a case reversed for the trial court's failure to follow the ORCP 68(C)(1) statute that makes every other procedure a nullity..

stature that specifies the jury is to determine an attorney fee award — unless, and this is a big unless — the state law of the case provides the fees are an element of *substantive* damage involved in the cause of action.

If the *substantive* law of a state is the theory of liability, and the state law provides the fees are a *substantive* element of damages, then you follow the *state* law as to *who* is the decision maker and as to *when* you submit the issues to the decision maker. For example, state laws granting a cause of action to recover insurance policy proceeds often provide that the damages involved in the cause of action include the attorney fees to recover the policy proceeds. If the *substantive* law of the state so provides for an attorney fee as part of the *substantive* damages, then if you are in federal court, the state law still controls the who and when; you submit the matter of attorney fees to the decision finder on the damages in the cause of action and you submit attorney fee facts when you are proving the other damage facts on the main case.

If federal law controls the award of attorney fees, then the decision maker is the trial judge. The when and how the issue of fees is to be presented to the federal judge is found in *Fed. Rules Civ. Proc.*, Rule 54 (d).

> (2) Attorneys' Fees.
>
>> (A) Claims for attorneys' fees and related nontaxable expenses shall be made by motion *unless the substantive law governing the action provides for the recovery of such fees as an element of damages to be proved at trial.* [Emphasis supplied.]
>>
>> (B) *Unless otherwise provided by statute or order of the court*, the motion must be filed and served no later than 14 days after entry of judgment; must specify the judgment and the statute, rule, or other grounds entitling the moving party to the award; and must state the amount or provide a fair estimate of the amount sought. If directed by the court, the motion shall also disclose the terms of any agreement with respect to fees to be paid for the services for which claim is made. [Emphasis supplied.]
>>
>> (C) On request of a party or class member, the court shall afford an opportunity for adversary submissions with respect to the motion in accordance with Rule 43(e) or Rule 78. The court may determine issues of liability for fees before receiving submissions bearing on issues of evaluation of services for which liability is imposed by the court. The court shall find the facts and state its conclusions of law as provided in Rule 52(a).
>>
>> (D) By local rule the court may establish special procedures by which issues relating to such fees may be resolved without extensive evidentiary hearings.

Many federal districts do use the subsection (D) to set in place a special rule for the timing and submission and procedure for determination of attorney fees. Some of those local rules impose extremely short deadlines for fee motions after a judgment has been entered. The best way to avoid a 14 day after judgment deadline or a local rule's even shorter deadline, and get the time that may be needed to prepare your supporting documents and testimony, is simple: obtain an order postponing the deadline. There is a second, less preferable way, if you are the applicant. Rule 54 (B) requires only that the fee applicant state the basis for an award and either the actual amount or "fair estimate" of the amount. Thus, Rule 54 (B) appears to permit a time stop motion with details to be filled in later.

Whether or not there is a subsection (D) special rule in place, the safest thing[160] to do, is to follow Rule 54(d)(2) (C) and ask the court to proceed to use 54(d)(2) B to set a specified time and procedure for your submission of attorney fee documents. This avoids all the problems of guessing the time and procedure for the specific federal judge involved. There is no reason such a motion has to wait until after the verdict or entry of judgement. You can make this motion before the trial.

◁)) **WARNING.** Each federal judge runs her own ship. In some multi-judge federal districts, the district will have a subsection (D) rule in place, setting forth the procedure to follow ----but hidden in another set of rules applicable only to the judge trying your case may be a different time or procedure.

☞ **TIP.** If you are a claimant's attorney on a case getting close to settlement, making a pre-trial motion to set a procedure for attorney's fees may enhance settlement. In the moving papers assert the expected large size of the attorney fee award, the extensive evidence that will be presented (e.g., expert testimony), and that events during trial will increase the evidence on attorney fees and will have to be considered. The motion then serves as a wake-up call to the other side that it may be less expensive to settle the case now than during the course of the case, after more attorney time has been invested. The motion tells the other side in the negotiations that you are serious and prepared on the issue of attorney's fees. Many lawyers wrongly assume that the issue of attorney fees is something that you are willing to throw away during negotiations as worthless in the bargaining. Awaken defense counsel to seriously include the issue of attorney fees in their settlement conference with their client.

§ 13.03   Bundle all your motions for fees together

In general, it is both safest and also best that you must bundle all your requests for fee awards to be heard at the same time. First, a court might take the position that determining a reasonable fee should be decided at one time. Second, determining penalties against opposing counsel needs to take into consideration the compensatory fee award; doing one motion before the other may void attempts for the other.[161]

---

[160] Assuming that the federal judge is the determiner of the attorney fee in your case.

[161] See, e.g., *Smallwood v. Perez*, 717 So. 2d 154 (Fla. Dist. Ct. App. 1998) (Spouse's motion for attorney's fees from opposing counsel for bad-faith litigation must be heard together with the request for attorney's fees from the lawyer's client in the action; making one later than the other does not allow proper consideration.)

§ 13.04   The five pathways to an attorney fee award

There are five possible pathways to a judgment setting the amount of a reasonable attorney fee award.

Settled Amount

You and your adversaries agree on the amount of the attorney fee award and submit it to be included in the ultimate judgment in the case by motion to the judge.

Agreement for separate submission to the judge

You and your adversaries agree to the time and place and manner you will submit the matter of attorneys fees to the court for its decision. Usually the content of a stipulation following this pathway is to agree that after the main trial, the evidence will be submitted to the court solely on briefs and written affidavits.

Judge trial, and judge as determiner

If the amount of the attorney's fee is to be set by the judge, and the trial of the substantive issues is before the judge, before the trial of the substantive issues, ask the judge when she wants to hear the evidence to determine the amount of attorney's fee. If you do not make a request before trial of the substantive issues ends, some judges will rule that you did not submit any evidence on the issue of fees and no longer have an opportunity to submit evidence regarding the attorney fee. That is because some judges want evidence of attorney fee amounts as a part of the main trial. Other judges want to wait until after they write their memo decision on the case, and regard earlier submission of attorney fee evidence with irritation.

Jury trial and jury as determiner

If the amount of the attorney fee is required to be set by a jury as the finder of fact in the case, you will need to give the evidence to the jury and ask the jury to set the amount — unless you have agreed to have the judge be the fact finder of the amount of attorney's fees after the trial of the substantive issues.

Jury trial, but judge as determiner

If the amount of the attorney's fee is required by your state law to be set by the judge, but there is a trial of the substantive issues before a jury, generally the best procedure is a motion made before trial asking for the court to determine the attorney fee by a hearing immediately after the jury verdict jury but before the entry of any order for judgment on the jury verdict. The problem of delay until after a court action is taken on the jury verdict is that authorizing statute for an award of attorney's fee may be interpreted or require that the court award at attorney fees be made be "made at the trial," or "summarily taxed at the trial." In such a situation, what your state believes is "after trial" may be too late for action to be taken to award fees.[162]

§ 13.05   Contingency fees

Now let us turn our attention to what evidence you should submit to the fact finders. Let us get rid of a common misconception immediately. Many personal injury attorneys wrongly assume that a contingency fee contract is almost uniform in the industry, so surely the contingent fee contract is **all** that is necessary to establish a "reasonable" fee. A contingency fee agreement — by itself – is not sufficient evidence to establish the amount of a reasonable attorney fee.[163] A plaintiff cannot ask the judge or jury to award a contracted percentage of the recovery as a fee, only because he/she had a contract specifying X percent. The award is against the adverse party, and the "reasonable fee" is to be a reasonable fee, not a fee contracted with someone other than the party having to pay the attorney fee award. Without evidence of the time spent, customary hourly fee and the other factors involved, there is no meaningful evidence to determine if the fee was in fact reasonable and necessary.

But read what we said in Chapter 08 regarding contingency fees and the uncertainly of payment as a factor in setting the reasonable fee. There are ways to obtain the contingency fee or something equivalent to it.

§ 13.06   Time at the trial and on a future appeal

Proof at the hearing or trial on the amount of the fee needs to include evidence of the hours spent in the days of trial — even the time after the presentation of the evidence on which the award is to be based. The best way to handle this is to have evidence that a reasonable fee for every day the fact finder sees the prevailing attorney in the courtroom day at trial there normally is involved not only X hours in the courtroom, but also an additional Y hours of preparation before and after the hours in the courtroom for the main attorney, the second chair attorney, and the paralegal working in the office doing legal support work daily. Have evidence of the trial hourly rates of the attorneys

---

[162] See, e.g., what happened in **Estate of Nelson**, 281 N.W.2d 245 (N.D. 1979) and *People ex rel. Henderson v. Redfern*, 104 Ill.App.2d 132, 243 N.E.2d 252, 254 (1968).

[163] Regarding the federal courts, see *City of Burlington v. Dague*, 505 U.S. 557, 565, 112 S.Ct. 2638, 120 L.Ed.2d 449 (1992)(holding that federal fee-shifting statutes do not permit enhancement of fee award beyond lodestar amount to reflect fact that a party agreed to pay on a contingency-fee basis). However, unlike statutory fee-shifting, contractual fee-shifting is not subject to the prohibition on contingency enhancements to the lodestar calculation of fees. Re state courts, see e.g.,*Arthur Anderson & Co., v. Perry Equipment Corp.*,1997.TX.672 (Tex., 1997)(evidence of a contingency fee contract by itself cannot support an award of attorney's fees.)("A party's contingent fee agreement should be considered by the fact finder and is therefore admissible in evidence."). See also, Brister, *Proof of Attorney's Fees in Texas*, 24 St. Mary's L.J. 313 (1993)

and paralegals involved. Together the hours per day and the hourly rate give the fact finder a basis for an award for trial time that accrues after the evidence is in the record.

Evidence on the hours spent for trial of the issues even includes time spent in proving and litigating the fee request. This time is compensable as part of the reasonable fee. If the judgment debtor challenges the submission for attorney fees then additional amounts should be awarded. Even separate outside counsel's fee spent solely in litigating the fee request is compensable as a "reasonable attorney fee" for the prevailing party.[164] This is understandable if you keep in mind that it is the prevailing party who recovers the attorney fee. The attorney fee is paid to the party, not to the attorney.[165]

If the fact finder to determine the reasonable attorney fee is the jury, there is a potential procedural problem. In some states attorney's fees for handling a case in the event of an appeal may be decided (and probably can only be decided) by the appeals court. In other states attorney's fees for handling a case in the event of an appeal may be decided (and probably can only be decided) by the jury. If the fact finder is the jury, it means the jury must be given evidence on which to base a reasonable fee on a piecework basis for handling a successful appeal. *International Security Life Insurance v. Spray*,[166] suggests two ways of handling the problem.

> (1) include in the judgement in the trial court an attorney fee large enough to protect the prevailing party in the event of an appeal, and provide for piecework deductions "if an appeal is not made"

> (2) include in the judgement in the trial court a piecework addition "in the event of an appeal."

The award of attorney's fees is to include an award for the time spent litigating the amount of the attorney's fees. Although some judges instinctively recoil against it, especially where the amount being litigated is excessive, the general rule of the decided cases is that the expense of reasonable attorney's fees in claiming and proving attorney's fees can be awarded in litigation in which attorneys fees are allowed. E.g., see *Thompson v. Pharmacy Corporation of America, Inc.*, 334 F.3d 1242 (11th Cir. 2003)(reversing district court). Lawyers will not be compensated for excessive disputes or time on the matter of fees, for there can be a penalty for turning the litigation about attorneys' fees into a "second major litigation." *Henley v. Eckerhart*, 103 S.Ct. 1933, 1941 (1983). The effect of completely denying compensation for the time spent on the

---

[164] See, e.g., *Environmental Defense Fund v. Environmental Protection Agency*, 672 F2d 42, at 61 et seq (DC Clr 1982); *Thompson v. Pharmacy Corp. of America Inc.*, 334 F.3d 1242 (11th Cir./2003)

[165] The attorney fee for recovery of the items due the prevailing party, including the fee for recovering the attorney fee, is the property of the client, not of the attorney. *Tax lawyers love this concept. This concept is why the client, not the lawyer, suffered income taxation in Commissioner of Internal Revenue v. Banks*, No. 03-892 (U.S. 01/24/2005)(The plaintiff retains dominion over the recoverable amount throughout the litigation.)

[166] 468 S.W.2d 347 (Tex. 1971).

fee issue is to diminish the proper net award of attorney's fees for the successful civil claim: a diminishment that frustrates the theory of awarding attorney fees. If there is no payment for the litigation about the fees, the attorney's effective rate for all the hours expended on the case is decreased.[167]

---

[167] See, Prandini v. National Tea Co., 585 F.2d 47, 53 (3d Cir. 1978).

§ 13.07   Form: order for severance

<u>ORDER FOR SEVERANCE AND TRIAL ADMINISTRATION</u>

Upon the agreement and application of all the parties, and good cause appearing, pursuant to Rule 42 of the Federal Rules of Civil Procedure, in furtherance of convenience, and for expedition and economy in the trial of the case, the court makes the following ORDER.

<u>SEVERANCE</u>

1.   The amount and value of the attorney's services of the plaintiff's attorney are severed to be tried by the Court after the determination of the other issues by the jury.

<u>HEARING ON WRITTEN MATERIALS ONLY</u>

2.   The matter of the attorney's services and the values thereof will be submitted to the Court by the parties in written materials. Experts' reports and witness testimony to be submitted will be submitted in affidavit form. There will be no oral testimony unless upon request of a party the Court in its discretion orders oral testimony. There will be no oral argument unless upon request of a party the Court in its discretion orders oral argument.

<u>DATES AND HEARING ADMINISTRATION</u>

3.   After a determination of the issues in the main case, and it is appropriate to determine the amount and reasonable value of the services of the attorney for a party, then the Court will set a hearing date for the determination of attorney fees. For convenience and economy, until after the trial of the main case neither party needs submit evidence or materials to the court regarding attorney fees. Both parties shall have until 30 days after issuance of the Court's order setting the hearing date to supplement their responses to discovery directed to the issues of the attorney's services and fees, and an additional 15 days to furnish any supplemental reports from their experts regarding attorney fees. The hearing date order will include both a date certain for the parties to submit affidavits, written evidence, or other supporting written materials to the Court and also a date certain thereafter for the parties to submit to the court written materials to respond to materials submitted by the adverse side.

4.   On the date certain to submit written materials to respond to materials submitted by the adverse side, each party shall a brief and a proposed order setting forth the requested findings and conclusions by the Court on the issues of attorney's fees and services.

SO ORDERED:

[Judge's usual date and signature block]

Chapter 14   Documents Supporting an Attorney Fee Award

§ 14.01   The five basic documents

Most lay persons think lawyers overcharge.[168]   So if a jury is setting the amount of a fee award, a proponent has his/her work to show why there is no overcharge. Likewise, courts seem almost automatically to assume that if the opponent objects, the proper amount of time or rate per hour is less than requested.

To maximize the chances of success of a motion to obtain attorney's fees in the requested amount, the prevailing attorney always should present the following six basic supporting documents. The local jurisdiction may require others. However, even if not required, to maximize your chances of receiving the attorney fee award you want, always submit the following six basic supporting documents:

✓   time records,

✓   fee agreement,

✓   biographies of the attorneys and legal assistants,

✓   evidence of the prevailing, customary or market, hourly rate,

✓   factual background and opinion given by a primary billing attorney, and

✓   opinion of an expert witness.

---

[168] Peter D. Hart Assoc., *A Survey of Attitudes Nationwide Toward Lawyers and the Legal System* 18-19 (1993), cited in Roy Simon, *Gross Profits? An Introduction to a Program on Legal Fees,* 22 Hofstra L. Rev. 625, 625 n.1 (1994). Although this survey is old, there is little reason to think the public attitude on fees has changed. Indeed the many surveys taken in the last few years show a steady decline in the approval rating of lawyers as a class.

§ 14.02   Time records

Submit the type of document used in an invoice or bill sent to a client. The theory of this evidence is that you are submitting a summary[169] of what is shown by the raw time slips or computer time records. Normally, this type of document will (and should) show a detailed itemization of the time and cost records and will establish what was done, on what dates, by which attorney or legal assistant, how much time was spent, and the hourly rate charged.

This itemization summary should be verified by affidavit or testimony, stating that the summary is a true and correct summary of the work done in the matter.

[170]Because this document is the sort of document used in a bill sent to a client, it will show the "lodestar dollar figure" you will be arguing to the court, that is the sum generated by multiplying the hours spent times the hourly rates. Further, if you are following our advice regarding the request of prejudgement interest, the documents will be submitted as monthly bills, showing accrued interest on the past months' billings.

Do not submit to the adverse counsel or the court the original time slips or raw computer data, unless it is requested by adverse counsel or the court.

§ 14.03   Fee agreement

You want the court to award at least as much as the client agreed to pay. Thus, you want to give the court the fee agreement under which you did the work. Submit a written affidavit summarizing the fee agreement with the client, with a copy of the fee agreement attached to the affidavit.

§ 14.04   Biographies of the attorneys and legal assistants

One of the classes of documents that prevailing attorneys should submit is biographies of the attorneys and legal assistants who did the work, showing their education, experience and qualifications for doing the work. How else can the finder of fact determine the prevailing market rate for an attorney of the skill and experience of the attorney doing the work? Both the federal and also the state criteria to be used in determining a reasonable fee contain the item "the experience, reputation, and

---

[169] Fed. R. Evidence, Rule 1006. Summaries. The contents of voluminous writings, recordings, or photographs which cannot conveniently be examined in court may be presented in the form of a chart, summary, or calculation. The originals, or duplicates, shall be made available for examination or copying, or both, by other parties at reasonable time and place. The court may order that they be produced in court.

[170] *Fed. R. Evid.*, Rule 803. All states have a similar rule.

ability of the lawyer or lawyers performing the services." Hence, a biography is needed.

☞ **TIP.** One of the exceptions to the hearsay rule is for "(17) Market reports, commercial publications. Market quotations, tabulations, lists, directories, or other published compilations, generally used and relied upon by the public or by persons in particular occupations." This allows you to put in a Martindale-Hubble directory page and explain it to the fact finder. If you are the prevailing party, you may want to show your biography and an AV rating. On the other side of the table, defense may want to show that other attorneys consider the prevailing attorney only "C" grade, and the matter in litigation did not need high hourly rates to get the work done.

☞ **TIP.** The requirement that the finder of fact consider the "the experience, reputation, and ability of the lawyer or lawyers performing the services" creates a splendid opportunity for prevailing counsel to have other attorneys extol the virtues and ethics of the prevailing attorney. It eliminates the need for the prevailing attorney to "brag." It allows the use of attorney witnesses who can state they cannot express an opinion on the number of hours needed, because they are not familiar with the case, but they are there solely to express an opinion regarding the experience (tell them how many other public service related cases have been worked on) and reputation of the prevailing lawyer.

§ 14.05   Evidence of the prevailing hourly rate

Specific evidence of the prevailing, customary or market, hourly rate in the community for the type of work done by attorneys and legal assistants of like skill in the state or area. Other than affidavits or testimony of the billing attorney and an expert witness, consider additional testimony or affidavits, if available, by knowledgeable sophisticated consumers or knowledgeable attorneys as to the prevailing customary hourly rates or the market value of the services rendered.

§ 14.06   Opinions of experts

We have said this elsewhere in this Handbook, but we'll say it again. Lay persons are not able to adjudicate the matter of a reasonable attorney fee without the testimonial opinion of an expert. Even where a judge is the finder of fact of a reasonable fee, don't rely on the judge's expertise. The prevailing party, and the defending party, should make expert opinion available to the fact-finder.

An expert opinion needs to show the facts upon which the opinion is based. This factual description should start with a narrative of the nature of the case and the progression of events, including the number of hours spent, why and how various attorneys or legal assistants were used, and the hourly rates of attorneys and legal assistants. Then this opinion should summarize the factual considerations in *all* the factors that might be involved in upward or downward adjustments to the fee from a lodestar amount. If the determination of the amount is to be by the court, and it is ordered or stipulated to be on documentary evidence only, this factual description and the opinion can be by written affidavit. Otherwise, if the presentation is to a jury or with live testimony to a judge, oral testimony should be used.

§ 14.07   Who the experts are

We will discuses the need for expert testimony in Chapter 16 of this Handbook. But right now, keep in mind that there are three kinds of experts on a reasonable attorney fee: (1) the attorneys in the case, (2) the attorney friends of the attorneys in the case, and (3) "real" experts with experience in determining and testifying regarding attorney fees. The attorneys in the litigation are considered "experts" on the work they did and the reasonable value of it, much as the owner of an automobile is allowed to testify on the market value of his own car. However, just as the car-owner's testimony is considered suspect for lack of breath of market knowledge and for his/her dose of self-interest, the opinions of the attorneys in the case are suspect.

This is not to say that the billing attorney should not testify. The billing attorney always *should* submit his/her own opinion on the amount of a reasonable attorney fee. It's a necessary base for the determination of the fee. Furthermore, there is a phenomenon known as "anchoring" that occurs when two sides are discussing a matter of numerical measurement. The studies of negotiation show that the figure first stated "anchors" the discussion that follows, so that the final decision on the amount tends to be closer to that figure than to the figure put forth by the adversary.

If the case involved is only a $1000 contract dispute, the opinions of the billing attorney and the contrasting opinion of the adverse attorney will probably be all that are economically justifiable as expenses. The next step up in expense of expert witnesses is having other attorneys review the materials in the case, and give opinions. Invariably, these attorneys are friends of the attorney asking them to testify, have no time to do the job, and lack the experience know what is needed for an adequate foundation for their opinion. *Daubert* style challenges may well succeed to keep the opinions of "an attorney down the street from my office" out of evidence.

The final step upward in experts is the "real" expert, a professional who charges for his/her opinion. You should get such an expert, as a rule of thumb, whenever the dollar difference between the amounts of fee the two sides suggest as reasonable is more than double the cost of the expert witness.

There are piecemeal experts that can be obtained. By "piecemeal" I mean experts who can supply only one part of the total opinions needed, thus accomplishing the total expert opinion. For example, many state bar associations have had statistically solid surveys done to show the prevailing market rate of attorneys in various size firms and with various experience levels, and in various counties in the state. The bar executive in charge may be happy to testify on his/her work and what is shown for market rates. As another example, there are a number of auditor services for insurers, who are skilled in picking apart bills and showing the excess hours (or lack of them) in a list of time expended.

☞ **TIP.** The biggest problem arising for the claimant when the claimant's attorney herself/himself is declared to be a testifying "expert" is that an expert is subject to a deposition. The defense attorney has the right to demand to see every document which a testifying expert has considered in determining the value of services. In most states and the federal courts "every document" means "every document" including privileged and work product documents. An expert has no privilege to withhold documents if they were seen during the course of the expert's work. So two points emerge. # 1. If you are the defending attorney take the deposition of the adverse attorney and look at all their office notes. # 2. The law firm for the prevailing party may want to designate some attorney other than the lead attorney in the case as the testifying expert for your law firm. Alternatively, have firm members testify only as to the facts of what was done, and leave all opinion-giving to a paid expert witness.

§ 14.08   Content of the billing attorney's affidavit or testimony

There simply is no way to make a reliable "form" for what should be contained in the affidavit of a prevailing attorney seeking fees. Each case is so individualized that a form cannot do as much "fits all" as most forms are expected to do. That is the reason why in later you will see "Exemplar Format: Billing Attorney's Affidavit" does not label that section as a "form" but rather as "Exemplar Format." The Exemplar Format will give you enough of an idea of the general format and content that you will be able to dictate your own affidavit efficiently.

Although all we can give you is an Exemplar and not an all-purpose form, the Exemplar plus the following checklist on what you should have in an affidavit of a prevailing attorney will provide a roadmap of the general content. If testimony is used in addition to, or instead of, an affidavit, the testimony can follow the same basic roadmap.

§ 14.09   Checklist: the billing attorney's affidavit or testimony

Checklist: Billing Attorney's Affidavit or Testimony

❑   Personal knowledge of the affiant. It is a basic law in most jurisdictions that evidence upon which a judicial act is to be taken needs to be based on testimony by a witness who has personal knowledge of the facts stated. Therefore, in addition to identifying the affiant as being an attorney senior in the process of the presentation of the matter of the case in court for the client, it is necessary always to make the formalistic statements about having personal knowledge of the facts stated in the affidavit.

❑   Verification of work and costs and business record foundation. You want your fee billings into evidence. These are the basic documents. But you do not ordinarily put into evidence a huge pile of paper time slips or a computer printout of raw data. You put into evidence your fee bills showing the necessary itemization.   These bills are admissible as either being business records[171] or as being a summary of computer records.[172]   Therefore a business record foundation and a summary document foundation should be stated in whatever format is usual in your jurisdiction.

❑   Fee agreement with client, and uncertainty of fee. The item of whether the fee was certain or uncertain is used in fact by the courts because from the court's standpoint they want to be sure that there is a supply of attorneys handling unpopular cases. More, the fact finder really wants to know what the fee agreement with the client is. It is relevant to determining what is a reasonable fee. On the prevailing party's side in a civil rights or other case of an individual versus big business, you may as well secure the emotional help to your side in pointing the need for a contingent fee was because of the financial need of the client and the need to fight injustice and that the client is going to be paying that full contingent amount even if the attorney fee awarded is smaller.

❑   Initial need for legal services. If the court is deciding the amount of fee, the court is probably going to use the affidavit as a basis for writing a decision. The court will

---

[171] See Fed. R. Evid., Rule 803. "(6) Records of regularly conducted activity. A memorandum, report, record, or data compilation, in any form, of acts, events, conditions, opinions, or diagnoses, made at or near the time by, or from information transmitted by, a person with knowledge, if kept in the course of a regularly conducted business activity, and if it was the regular practice of that business activity to make the memorandum, report, record or data compilation, all as shown by the testimony of the custodian or other qualified witness, or by certification. . . " If the adversary does not stipulate to admission of the bills, your testimony needs to establish, inter alia, that you do in fact use time records and it is a regular practice of your business to have the computer print out bills.

[172] See Fed. R. Evid., Rule 1006. "Rule 1006. Summaries The contents of voluminous writings, recordings, or photographs which cannot conveniently be examined in court may be presented in the form of a chart, summary, or calculation."

appreciate having a refreshment of the basic situation and why it was that the client needed to have legal services and could not have simply relied upon the adverse party to resolve the matter in some sort of informal or out of court manner. You are trying to show the court how difficult the matter was for you to accomplish.

❑   Billing judgment.   In the case law approving or disapproving legal fee submissions there is almost invariably a statement about the need for the submitting attorney to have used "billing judgment" to eliminate those items that would have been excessive or that really did not produce much for the client. The billing attorney's affidavit or testimony specifically should use the ritual language that "billing judgment has been used to eliminate any excessive or unproductive time from the time for which fees are sought." The phrase is not magical, but it is almost mandatory. Further, if the prevailing party did not prevail on all issues, the billing attorney affirmatively should state that fees are not being sought on issues where the claimant did not prevail or which were unrelated to the prevailing issues. Be sure to exclude from the time records included in the fee request any marginal items, or reduce the time in an item where excess time incurred, so that you can point out items, upon request by the court or adverse counsel, to show that "billing judgment" was in fact used.

❑   Market value of services. In some jurisdictions the applicable authority calls for a "market" valuation of services; in some jurisdictions, for the "customary" value of services; in some for the "normal" value of services. However it is phrased this is a phrase that you want to track and repeat as you offer evidence that the rates used in your calculation are the market, customary or normal value of the services.

❑   Lodestar amount — and that it is only a minimum fee. At this point in the recitation of the affidavit you have achieved showing the court the factors to be used to set the "lodestar" amount. That is the amount of fee based solely on hours expended multiplied by the customary hourly fee. Your job at this point on the prevailing side is to prevent the court or jury from using various factors to lower the fee from that you have set out in your billing. You want to court or jury to award something more than the lodestar amount. But first — remember that the jury or court starts by thinking about the amount of fee as the number of hours spent times the hourly rate of pay. Do the math for them. Give them that lodestar amount.

❑   Lodestar amount is only a minimum fee. Go on to affirmatively state an opinion that a "reasonable" attorney fee is more than the lodestar base amount for the reasons set forth in the following paragraphs of the affidavit. [Remember that this is an affidavit of an expert (attorney) on the facts and opinions to be the evidentiary support for an award].

If this is a state case, here is the point to state the applicable law from your jurisdiction to point out the additional factors to be considered. If it is a state case, ordinarily these are factors which you will find in your jurisdiction's rule 1.5 of the Professional Rules. The point is that you should list the "additional factors to be considered" that you want the state fact finder to look at.

The federal judges are experienced in setting attorney fees awards, and normally know the law and factors involved well. Ordinarily, you would not want to insult their intelligence by anything other than a one sentence reference to *Johnson v. Georgia Highway Express, Inc*[173] (or whatever local district or circuit opinion has been used often by the court involved) as the case stating the factors that "must be considered" in setting a reasonable attorney fee.

❑   Novelty and difficulty of question. Try to find something that you can point to as "different" or "more difficult" than the average case or transaction of the type. It might have been a factual question; it might have been a legal question. Some place along the line of handling this case or transaction there probably was a question of law to be debated, at least internally in your office. Point these things out and buttress the idea that indeed this case or transaction was not just a routine matter.

❑   Preclusion of other work. Any attorney worth her salt has a limited amount of time and more work that this case to do. Ordinarily you as a prevailing party's counsel can construct an argument that doing this particular work prevented you from doing other work. The loss of opportunity time idea used in validating charges for travel time (otherwise you would be back in the office earning more money) can be used in any case where the hourly fee is lower than normal.

❑   Amount involved and results obtained. It is on the amount involved and the results obtained that many attorneys and experts fall down on their presentation and testimony on behalf of the prevailing party. If for example, there were ten causes of action, but five of them were dropped out or dismissed along the way to judgment, you may find the defense arguing that 50 percent of your total fee is all that should be awarded for the issues on which you "prevailed." On the prevailing side, you need to argue that all of the items were necessarily intertwined; hence, the fee award should be for all the hours of all the work that was done.

❑   Opinion as to total a reasonable attorney fee ("Based upon all of the factors I have described, and upon my education, training and experience, it is my opinion to a reasonable degree of professional certainty that a reasonable attorney's fee, including expenses, in this case is $___.")

---

[173] , 8 F.2d 714 (5th Cir. 1974)(criteria specifically approved in *Henley v. Eckerhart,* 103 S. Ct. 1933, 461 U.S. 424 (1983).

§ 14.10   Exemplar format: billing attorney's affidavit

Above we gave you a checklist for testimony or affidavit of a prevailing attorney seeking fees.   Now, let's see what it looks like when put into practice as an affidavit.

[Usual court heading]

AFFIDAVIT OF [Billing Attorney]
REGARDING AWARD OF ATTORNEY FEES

STATE OF [State]
COUNTY OF [County]

___[   ]___   being first duly sworn states:

1. Identification of Affiant. I am an attorney at, law duly licensed to practice in the State of North Dakota. I am a senior partner in the firm of ___[   ]___. I am the attorney in the firm who is in charge of prosecution of the plaintiff's claims for relief in the above-entitled action. I have personal knowledge of the facts stated in this affidavit.

2. Verification of Work and Costs, and Business Record Foundation. Our firm was initially retained on ___[   ]___, when Mr. Client saw me. Exhibit #1 presented on this motion is an itemization of the work performed by this firm, from that date to today's date of ___[   ]___, together with costs charged to the client for the work. Exhibit # 1 is a business record created by our firm's computer business records from entries made in the normal course of business, at or near the time of the events recorded, by persons authorized to make the entries. The records have been kept safely and securely from unauthorized changes. It is the normal practice of our law firm to prepare billings such as exhibit # 1 from the computer business records.   Exhibit # 1 is a true and correct record of time and costs for the period of time shown thereon, for the events shown thereon.

3. To date Mr. Client has paid $120 on fees and costs. We believe this is all that he can pay us to date, because of the limited nature of his resources. We have spent a great deal of our attorney firm's money, to pay personnel and expenses to do this work for Mr. Client.

4. Fee Agreement with Client. Our agreement with Mr. Client was that we would render services to him on an hourly fee basis. The hourly fee basis and the charge per hour for each of the attorneys that worked on the file are set out in the attached Exhibit #1 A copy of the fee agreement with Mr. Client is attached as Exhibit # 2.

5. Under the fee agreement with Mr. Client, Mr. Client will be paying our fee after the judgment is entered on this case. If the fee award is less than Mr. Client has agreed to pay, he still will have to pay the full contracted amount to us.   Mr. Client's recovery of

a full reasonable attorney fee award will encourage us and others to bring deserving claims to uphold the rights of injured persons.

6. Initial Need for Legal Services. When Mr. Client came to see us he had already been denied admission to the Soldiers' Home. The work that was obviously involved was legal work and not investigative work. It was necessary to appeal the decision of the initial admission board to the governing body that the statutes of North Dakota specify, to wit: the Administrative Subcommittee on Veterans Affairs. This appeal was in the nature of a trial de novo before that body. The Administrative Subcommittee on Veterans Affairs denied admission and therefore a lawsuit was started in Morton County, North Dakota.

7. Short History of Legal Work Required. Before the trial of the Morton County lawsuit was scheduled, a new statute of the State of North Dakota took effect, namely the statute prohibiting discrimination in the furnishing of public services because of a history of past mental impairment. This statute created a new set of administrative remedies and a new cause of action for persons denied admission into the Soldiers' Home after the date of that statute. This statute also raised the possibility that relief in the pending lawsuit for Mr. Client might be denied for failure to exhaust the now new administrative remedies. However, the statute provided a different venue for the new causes of action than the Morton County venue in which Mr. Client's then action was pending. Therefore, it became necessary for our law firm to prepare a new application to the Home, go to the initial board of admissions, then appeal to the Administrative Subcommittee on Veterans Affairs. Again the board of admissions and the Administrative Subcommittee on Veterans Affairs denied the second application, in spite of the new North Dakota statute. The present North Dakota statute on discrimination requires that a lawsuit on the allowable causes of action be started only in the judicial district where the services were to be performed. Therefore it became necessary for us to start a second lawsuit, based on the second application and denial, in a different judicial district than the district in which Morton County lies. Then, to conserve judicial and client's time and expense, and for the furtherance of the administration of justice, it was necessary for our firm to do the necessary legal work to consolidate the two cases in Morton County and proceed to a full trial in Morton County. Our work for Mr. Client was opposed by the State of North Dakota, which utilized multiple attorneys and engaged in a full and vigorous defense in its attempt to defeat the rights of Mr. Client.

8. Billing Judgment; Only Related Items; Only Legal Work. In the Exhibit #1 "(itemization of time and work done). billing judgment has been used to eliminate any excessive or unproductive time. Further, billing judgment has been used to eliminate time spent on issues which were unrelated to the prevailing issues. The time and labor rendered by attorneys in this case was time and labor on legal work, as distinguished from clerical and investigative work. Except as otherwise specifically shown in the billing, no charge has been made in the itemized billing (Exhibit #1) for clerical work or for work which is primarily investigative in nature or otherwise did not need the insight and training usually possessed by an attorney.

9. Market Rate Knowledge. As the senior attorney in the firm I have had to set attorney fees for the sale of our services. For the past 15 years I have kept current on the market

rate for attorney's services for the type of services used in this case and in the geographic areas of the state that are involved in Mr. Client's matters in this case.

10. , Customary, Market, Value of Services; Lodestar Amount. The amount set out in the attached Exhibit #1 (fee billings) is the market value of the services rendered. The hourly fees set out in Exhibit # 1 are at the hourly rate normally charged for similar work by attorneys of like skill in the area. Exhibit # 1 show an amount which is a "lodestar" amount in a minimum sum.

11. Lodestar Sum is Minimum Fee to be Awarded. Because of the additional factors to be considered, it is my opinion that the Lodestar Amount (the amount shown) set out in the bills for services (Exhibit #1 presented on this motion) is only a the minimum base attorney fee and not a full reasonable attorney fee for this specific matter for Mr. Client. The amount of a reasonable attorney fee is more than the base lodestar amount, for the reasons set forth in the following paragraphs of this affidavit.

12. Additional Factors to be Considered. In the case of [insert your jurisdiction's case law, e.g, *City of Bismarck v. Thom,* (N.D. 1977)] it was held that the base for determining a reasonable fee is found by multiplying the number of hours expended by each attorney by the hourly rate normally charged for similar work by attorneys of like skill in the area. When this base rate is established other less objective factors are introduced to determine a reasonable fee The court noted the various factors to be considered, and the remainder of this affidavit will comment upon those factors noted by the Court, such as:

> (1) the time and labor required, the novelty and difficulty of the questions involved, and the skill requisite to perform the legal service properly;

> (2) the likelihood, if apparent to the client, that the acceptance of the particular employment will preclude other employment by the lawyer;

> (3) the fee customarily charged in the locality for similar legal services;

> (4) the amount involved and the results obtained;

> (5) the time limitations imposed by the client or by the circumstances;

> (6) the nature and length of the professional relationship with the client;

> (7) the experience, reputation, and ability of the lawyer or lawyers performing the services; and

> (8) whether the fee is fixed or contingent.

13. Novelty and Difficulty of Questions. At the time that this lawsuit was undertaken on behalf of Client the questions involved were novel legal questions. In the last two years in North Dakota there have been some federal court cases on similar type of actions,

but as noted by This Court in its memorandum decision of ____[___], there were new questions of law for which we as attorneys had to expend above routine consideration.

14. Skill Requisite to Perform the Legal Service Properly. As will be noted from Exhibit #1, the plaintiff engaged in limited discovery. On the other hand the defendant State took depositions and engaged in relatively extensive discovery, which resulted in the plaintiff's attorneys having to spend considerable time and costs to respond thereto. The defendant State was represented by skilled and experienced attorneys, with ample resources for whatever they wished to do. The skill needed by Mr. Client's attorneys had to be of above the average level of attorneys engaged in the practice of law in this state, to combat the defense tactics and resources. Indeed, the skill needed to present the new questions of, law and the witnesses and facts in an effective manner, required an above average attorney who can command above average rates in the market.

15. Prevention of Other Work; Acceptance of the Employment Precluded Other Employment. The undersigned attorney is requested to do more work by clients than I can physically do. This was discussed with Mr. Client at the time the possibility of representation was discussed. Mr. Client responded that it was difficult for him to obtain other attorneys to represent him and that he needed our services. By reason of the finite number of hours in a day, week, month, and year, to work on this matter for Mr. Client, I had to give up working on other matters for other prospective or actual clients. Accordingly, doing the work for Client precluded other employment, not only at my regular hourly fee rate of $_____an hour, but also it precluded contingent fee work which regularly produces an income to the undersigned attorney well in excess of my hourly fee rate of $____ an hour.

16. Skill and Experience of Attorney. The biographical information set out in Exhibit #6 presented on this motion is correct information. It summarizes the experience, reputation, and ability of the lawyers performing services for our law firm.

17. Uncertainty of Fee for Work Done and Costs Advanced. Courts frequently introduce a "multiplier" over and above the usual fee if the attorney undertook the case knowing that if he did not recover for the client, the attorney also would lose his own investment of time and costs. (Because if the case was unsuccessful the client would have no funds to pay legal fees.) A reasonable fee, when the uncertainty of fee is involved, is a greater fee amount that a fee that is certain, whatever the result of the litigation. Also, from the public's standpoint, the reason for the multiplier is to induce other attorneys to take clients who are otherwise unable to secure experienced and able counsel. If this case had been lost we would not have recovered any substantial fee. Because of the modest financial circumstances of our client, he would not have been able to pay our fee. If our firm's attorneys, and other attorneys, are to be encouraged to undertake litigation for persons in limited financial circumstances, a multiplier or factor for the uncertainties should be utilized. An upward addition should be made to take consideration of the uncertainty of the outcome of the case, and the uncertainty of any payment, to find a reasonable fee for undertaking and completing this matter for Mr. Client.

18. Amount involved and the Results Obtained; Success and Importance. The attorneys for Mr. Client were successful on all the causes of action asserted in this case. The success was not limited, but rather was total. Further, the results obtained were important for Mr. Client. Before this lawsuit and during its entire three year course of litigation, he has been living on a pension of less than $400 a month (as testified by him in court). The basic necessities of life were beyond his financial ability, causing him to be a homeless person living on the streets. The room and board and other various and sundry services available in the Soldiers Home as described to the court during the trial of the case (and shown in the brochures which were exhibits in the case) are extremely important for the physical and mental well-being of Mr. Client. The results obtained were exceptionally important to Mr. Client. Further, the results obtained advanced an important public policy and created law available for other like situated veterans to obtain to decent housing.

19. Based upon all of the factors I have described, and upon my education, training and experience, it is my opinion to a reasonable degree of professional certainty that a reasonable attorneys fee in this case would be a total amount of $_____, including the following items.

  A. For work from the time work started until the start of the trial. $_____.

  B. For work at trial. ($_____ per day for ___ days). $_____.

  C. For Attorney Expenses. $_____.

  D. If an appeal is made to the state Supreme Court:

    1. For attorney time involved in presenting the matter to the state Supreme Court and then providing the entry of final judgement after the opinion of the Supreme Court. $_____.

    2. For Attorney Expenses, excluding adjudicated and allowed costs. $_____.

[date line]

[attorney's signature block]

Subscribed and sworn to before me this _____
[Notary]

Chapter 15   Forms: Requesting An Attorney Fee Award

§ 15.01   Form: motion to seek attorney fee award

[Usual Court Heading]

PLAINTIFF'S MOTION FOR ATTORNEY FEES

Pursuant to statute, providing for the payment of a reasonable attorney fee to be awarded to a prevailing party, Plaintiff moves the Court to determine and adjudge the attorney fees to be awarded to plaintiff.

Pursuant to [statutory citation] Plaintiff is entitled to attorney fees and costs.

This motion is made upon all of the files and proceedings herein, including the briefs, affidavits, testimony, and itemization of time and expenses submitted. The following are filed with this motion.

1.   Brief of plaintiff on motion for attorney fees, with citation of applicable authority.

2.   Affidavit of custodian of records with itemized fee bill showing dates, work done, time spent, and costs incurred to [closing date shown in affidavit of time expended] , which is the date of this motion to be submitted to the court.

3.   Affidavit by plaintiff's attorney regarding the factors to be considered in determining the reasonableness of a fee including those factors specified in our state Rules of Professional Responsibility at Rule 1.5.

4.   Affidavit by attorney expert on reasonable fees.

5.   Affidavit by client on fee agreement.

6.   Affidavit of biographical information on plaintiff's attorneys.

7.   Affidavit of plaintiff's attorney showing the expected future time and costs for work after the date of preparation of this motion. (Attorney fees in presenting this matter to the Court are recoverable. The court may set a reasonable fee for work to be performed following presentation of this motion to the court.)

Plaintiff requests the Court to determine the amount of plaintiff's reasonable attorney fees and costs to be as follows.

    1. $_____ is the reasonable, proper and just amount to be awarded to plaintiff for attorney fees, and

    2. $_____ is the reasonable, proper and just amount to be awarded to plaintiff for costs to [closing date shown in affidavit of time expended] , for the performance of legal services in time period from [opening date shown in affidavit of time expended] to [closing date shown in affidavit of time expended].

    plus,

    3. An amount to be determined by the court for the performance of legal services after [closing date shown in affidavit of time expended] , for the further legal services in proceedings necessary to present this matter to the Court, to respond to any attempt by defendant to dispute or litigate this motion, and other proceedings exclusive of appeals leading to the entry of final judgment herein by the trial court.

Further plaintiff notes that it would be expedient for the Court and all concerned for the Court to order that after the entry of judgment herein, the court will retains jurisdiction to set additional amounts for any additional future attorneys fees and costs in appeals, hearings, motions, or presentations of matters in this case and will not require the filing of a new case to determine the same.

WHEREFORE, plaintiff prays for an order of the Court, as set out above, finding and adjudging a reasonable attorney fee. Further plaintiff prays that the Court order that it retains jurisdiction to set additional amounts for any additional future attorneys fees and costs in appeals, hearings, motions, or presentations of matters in this case.

[date line]

[attorneys usual signature block]

§ 15.02   Form: jury submission of attorney fee

One proposed form of special issue submission to the jury, which, of course, should be supported by expert testimony as to the projected services to be rendered on any appeal and the reasonable fees for appeal may be as follows:

Special Jury Question on Attorney Fees

What sum of money, if any, would reasonably compensate Andrew Anderson's attorneys for their services and costs in asserting his rights in this case under Article 3.62 of the Insurance Code of Texas, for each of the following:

A. From the time the attorneys started work until the start of the trial. (Answer in Dollars and ¢):

_____

B. Trial (Answer in Dollars and ¢):

_____

C. In the Court of Civil Appeals, if an appeal occurs. (Answer in Dollars and ¢):

_____

D. In the Texas Supreme Court if writ of error is not granted.(Answer in Dollars and ¢):

_____

E. In the Texas Supreme Court if writ of error is granted. (Answer in Dollars and ¢):

_____

§ 15.03   Form: order finding and awarding attorney fee amount

Order For Attorney Fee Award

[Usual court heading and recital of your jurisdiction].

This matter can duly on for hearing for a determination of an award of attorney's fees in this matter.   This court has considered all of the papers and proceedings in this litigation, as well as all the evidence, testimony and arguments of counsel. The court's memorandum decision, dated _____, is incorporated and made a part of this Order.

The Court determines, finds, and Orders that _____is the prevailing party in this litigation, and that an award should be made, and is now made, for an attorney fee to _____as a prevailing party in this litigation.

This Court determines, finds, and adjudicates that a reasonable attorney fee includes:

> A. For services and expenses from the time the attorneys started work until the start of the trial, the sum of $_____

> B. Prejudgment interest or a factor for the time in which this case has been in litigation, based upon the amount set out in item A above, which prejudgement interest or factor is in the sum of $_____.

> C. For services and expenses from the start of the trial and until the date of this order, including the litigation of the amount of attorney's fee and a reasonable sum for the normally expected work in entry of judgment herein, the sum of $_____

This court retains jurisdiction of the case to enforce its orders and judgment in this matter, including its orders for the payment of the award of attorneys fees. Further, this court retains jurisdiction of the case to determine and enter an amended judgment regarding attorneys fees and expenses should there be any appeal of any order or judgment herein.

Let Judgment Be Entered Accordingly.

[court's usual date and signature lines]

§ 15.04   Form: application for common fund percentage award

[This form is based on the petition submitted by counsel in the case of *Banks v. City of Ocean Shores,* No. 99-2-00395-7 (Superior Court of Grays Harbor, Washington, 2002).]

CLASS COUNSEL'S PETITION FOR ATTORNEY FEE AWARD

INTRODUCTION

The efforts of plaintiffs' attorneys resulted in a common fund available for a class of persons broader than the plaintiffs. Plaintiffs attorneys thus were class counsel. So that all members of the class benefitted share in the expense of recovery, this petition is submitted.

The parties have submitted a settlement proposal that includes provision for a common fund attorney fee award to be set by the court. In reviewing class counsel's fee request, the Court acts as a fiduciary on behalf of the class members to assure that the attorney fee is reasonable. *Democratic Cent. Comm. v. Washington Metro. Area Transit Comm 'n,* 3 F.3d 1568, 1573 (D.C. Cir. 1993). Class counsel requests a common fund attorney fee award of 25 percent of the total refund amount ordered for the class.

In the courts of this state, attorney fees may be awarded if authorized by contract, statute or a recognized ground in equity. *Bowles v. Retirement Systems*, 121 Wn.2d 52,70, 847 P.2d 440 (1993). The common fund doctrine is one of the recognized equitable grounds for such an award.. Under the common fund rule, "a litigant or a lawyer who recovers a common fund for the benefit of persons other than himself or his client is entitled to a reasonable attorney's fee from the fund as a whole." *Boeing Co. v. Van Gemert,* 444 US 472,478, 100 S. Ct. 745, 62 L. Ed. 2d 676,68 1 (1 980). Common fund attorney fees today are most often determined using the percentage of recovery method. Absent special circumstances, the guidelines fee awards are in the range of 25 to 33   percent of the common fund amount. Here, class counsel only requests 25 percent, and counsel believes that the benchmark 25 percent fee is appropriate.

ARGUMENT IN SUPPORT OF TWENTY-FIVE PERCENT COMMON FUND ATTORNEY FEE AWARD

The attorney fee should be set using the percentage of recovery method.

Two approaches are generally used in determining attorney fee awards: the percentage of recovery method and the lodestar method. Under the percentage of recovery method, the attorney fee is calculated as a percentage of the amount recovered in the litigation. Under the lodestar approach, the fee is calculated from the hours spent by the attorneys working on the case. A leading decision on common fund attorney fee awards is *Bowles v. Retirement Systems,* 12 1 Wn.2d 52, 847 P.2d 440 (1993). That decision holds that the percentage of recovery approach is an appropriate method for determining the attorney fee in a common fund case, and explains how common fund benefit attorney fee awards should be calculated.

> While the lodestar method is generally preferred when calculating statutory attorney fees, the percentage of recovery approach is used in calculating fees under the common fund doctrine. *Arizona Citrus Growers*, 904 F.2d at 1311 ; *Blum v. Stenson,* 465 U.S. 886,900 n. 16,79 L. Ed. 2d 891, 104 S. Ct.1541 (1984). The primary explanation for this distinction is that statutory attorney fees are separately assessed against the defendant while common fund attorney fees are taken directly from the recovery obtained by the plaintiffs. In common fund cases, the size of the recovery constitutes a suitable measure of the attorneys' performance. See *In re GNC Shareholder Litig. : All Actions*, 668 F. Supp. 450,451-52 (W.D. Pa. 1987). In common fund cases, the "benchmark" percentage is 25 percent of the recovery obtained. *Arizona Citrus Growers,* 904 F.2d at 131 1 ; see also 3 NEWBERG ON CLASS ACTIONS § 14.03 (2d ed.1985) (20 to 30 percent is the usual common fund award). Under special circumstances, this figure can be adjusted upward or downward, or can be replaced with a lodestar calculation. *Arizona Citrus Growers*, 904 F.2d at 1311.

> *Bowles v. Retirement Systems,* 121 Wn.2d 52, at 72-73, 847 P.2d 440 (1993).

The modern trend is toward calculating common fund attorney fee awards by using the percentage of recovery approach. See, e.g., *In re NASDAQ Market-Makers Antitrust Litig.*, 187 F.R.D. 465 (S.D.N.Y. 1998); *Swedish Hosp. Corp. v. Shalala,* 1 F.3d 126 1 (D.C.Cir. 1993); COURT AWARDED ATTORNEY FEES, REPORT OF THE THIRD CIRCUIT TASK FORCE, 108 F.R.D. 237 (1986). The preference for the percentage of recovery approach is based on several factors.

First, a percentage fee better aligns the interest of the lawyer to the interest of the class because the lawyer gains only to the extent that the class gains. *In re Oracle Sec. Litig.*, 13 1 F.R.D. 688,694-95 (N.D. Cal. 1990). This alignment of interest avoids or limits a number of problems that plague hourly lodestar fee calculations. For example, it avoids the negative incentive inherent in the lodestar approach - i.e., encouraging attorneys to "spend as many hours as possible, billable to the firm's most expensive attorneys." *Swedish Hosp. Corp. v. Shalala*, 1 F.3d at 1271. Instead, the percentage fee is measured by the value of the lawyer's work will profitably contribute to the success of the litigation, and there is no artificial reward or penalty to skew this judgment. This approach better serves the interest of the class because"[it matters little to the class how much the attorney spends in time or money to reach a successful result." Id. at 1268.

Second, the percentage of recovery method is also more in line with the economics of a plaintiff litigation practice and how privately negotiated fees are determined when the lawyer assumes the risk of an adverse outcome. Contingent percentage fee arrangements are the norm in non-class action cases where the plaintiffs are financially unable to advance the full cost of undertaking litigation, and the same should be true in class actions where the plaintiffs are financially unable to advance the full cost of undertaking litigation.

> The object in awarding a reasonable attorney's fee, as we have been at pains to stress, is to give the lawyer what he would have gotten in the way of a fee in an arm's length negotiation, had one been feasible. . . . The class counsel are entitled to the fee they

> would have received had they handled a similar suit on a contingent fee basis, with a similar outcome, for a paying client.

> In re Continental Illinois Sec. Litig., 962 F.2d 566, 572 (7th Cir. 1992) (Posner, J.).

Society's experience in using fee percentages in non-class action cases .provides a meaningful comparison by which to judge the appropriateness of a contingent fee in the class action setting. An after-the-fact lodestar fee calculation cannot measure the risk and uncertainty of litigation any more than one can measure the "fairness" of betting odds after the horse race is over. Risk and uncertainty are often dominant elements in deciding whether to undertake a piece of litigation. Contingency percentage fees reflect this fact; lodestar calculations do not.

Third, the percentage approach also avoids the burdensome and sometimes unfathomable difficulties of trying to compute a proper lodestar fee. As at least one judge has noted:

> [A percentage fee] award is consistent with the new learning . . . announced by the Ninth Circuit in Paul, Johnson [886 F.2d at 2721 which . . . will . . . take us back to straight contingent fee awards bereft of largely judgmental and time wasting computations of lodestars and multipliers. These latter computations, no matter how conscientious, often seem to take on the character of so much Mumbo Jumbo. They do not guarantee a more fair result or a more expeditious disposition of litigation.

> In re Union Carbide Corp. Consumer Prod. Bus. Sec. Litig., 724 F. Supp. 160, 170 (S.D.N.Y. 1989). See also THIRD CIRCUIT TASK FORCE REPORT, 108 F.R.D. at 255 (the lodestar technique is a "cumbersome, enervating, and often surrealistic process of preparing and evaluating fee petitions.").

Because there are no objective standards to guide the lodestar process, it can easily produce inconsistent and unpredictable results. Thus, the lodestar method can end up requiring both the lawyers and the judge to spend considerable time and effort on attempting a fee analysis that provides little if any meaningful guidance in determining a reasonable fee.

Finally, the percentage of recovery method takes into account the fact that this case will not be over at the time the fee award is made. It is entirely possible that one side or the other will attempt to appeal the Court's final judgment. Class counsel will have to successfully fend off all such efforts to prevail in this case, and no one knows what this will take. This is much the same situation that lawyers and clients face at the beginning of any contingent fee case when they agree to a fee percentage in the face of tremendous uncertainties. The contingency percentage fee is widely used because it is easily understood and value based, and because it minimizes distorted incentives for attorneys. All of those reasons apply with equal force here.

25 percent was the agreed judgement of counsel and party at the start of the litigation as the amount necessary to induce counsel to undertake the case.

> Class counsel's attorney fee request is based on the fee arrangements negotiated between class counsel and the class representatives at the outset of this litigation. In the

> engagement letters that memorialize that fee agreement, class counsel and the class representatives agreed that a 25 percent fee was appropriate: We have agreed to undertake this action on a contingent fee basis. . . . We expect to request an award of the benchmark 25%. We believe that this percentage fairly reflects the litigation risks, the expected time and difficulty of the case, the legal expertise required and the amount in controversy. In agreeing to the terms of this engagement, you indicate that you concur with this judgment.
>
> See Declaration of William C. Severson, filed in this case.

These terms of engagement that were agreed to between class counsel and the class representatives are relevant because they reflect what the attorney and class representatives viewed as a reasonable fee percentage at the beginning of the lawsuit. The reasonableness of the fee should be judged by foresight rather than hindsight. In re NASDAQ Market-Makers Antitrust Litig., 187 F.R.D. at 488.

While the fee agreement between class counsel and the class representatives is not binding on the Court, it does reflect the honest judgment of those parties, giving consideration to the efforts, risks, uncertainties and anticipated burdens of the proposed litigation. Such front-end evaluations of a case are significant because more accurately than any other measurement, they reflect the risk that the attorney assumes at the outset of the litigation. See *Swedish Hosp. Corp. v. Shalala*, 1 F.3d at 1268.

A minimum benchmark percentage for a minimum common fund attorney fee award is 25 percent of the fund. See Bowles, supra. Class counsel believes that the minimum benchmark percentage award is appropriate in this case because there are no special circumstances that call for adjusting the fee percentage either upward or downward from the benchmark level.

An attorney fee award of 25 percent is a usual percentage rate

For a common fund benefit fee award, typical fee percentages usually fall into the range of 20 percent to 30 percent. See 4 NEWBERG ON CLASS ACTIONS 14:6 at 550 (4th ed. 2002). See also *Democratic Cent. Comm. v. Washington Metro. Area Transit Comm 'n,* 3 F.3d 1 568, 1 573 @.C. Cir. 1 993); *Swedish Hosp. Corp. v. Shalala,* 1 F.3d 1261 (D.C. Cir. 1993); *In re Continental Illinois Sec. Litig.*, 962 F.2d 566 (7th Cir. 1992); *Torrisi v. Tucson Elec. Power Co.*, 8 F.3d 1370 (9th Cir. 1993); *In re SmithKline Beckman Corp. Sec. Litig.*, 75 1 F. Supp. 525 (E.D. Pa. 1 990); *Brown v. Phillips Petroleum Co.*, 838 F.2d 451 (10th Cir. 1988); *Camden I Condominium Ass'n v. Dunkle,* 946 F.2d 768 (11th Cir. 1991). See also, *Litigation* (3rd ed. 1995), 524.12 1, p. 189. See also, Federal Judicial Center, *Empirical Study of Class Actions in Four Federal District Courts* (1996), p. 151 (graph showing 42 class actions with fee awards ranging from 26% to 31%); Federal Judicial Center, *Awarding Attorneys' Fees and Managing Fee Litigation* (1994), p. 68 ("Most district courts select a percentage in the 20% to 30% range, and the Ninth Circuit has indicated that 25% is the 'benchmark' award.").

Not surprisingly, these fee percentages awarded by the courts correspond to the fee percentages observed in private contingent fee litigation. Under non-class action fee agreements, the lawyer takes on the risk that he or she may receive little or nothing in return for a substantial investment of time and resources. Class counsel assumed those same risks here.

In undertaking to represent the class, counsel bound itself to vigorously pursue the litigation, regardless of how it unfolded, The risks were considerable. A reasonable fee "should always be based on risks. A greater risk justifies a higher percentage fee." *Allard v. First Interstate Bank,* 112 Wn.2d 145, 158,768 P.2d 420 (1989) Gore, J., dissenting). Here, the fee percentage in the engagement agreement between class counsel and the class representatives reflects the fact that at the outset, the parties saw no reason to depart from the minimum 25 percent fee percentage. Nothing in the subsequent history of the case should alter that conclusion.

The benchmark percentage may be adjusted "when special circumstances indicate that the percentage recovery would be either too small or too large in light of the hours devoted to the case or other relevant factors." *Six Mexican Workers v. Arizona Citrus Growers,* 904 F.2d 1 30 1, 1311 (9th Cir. 1990). The percentage approach, however, compensates the attorney for success, not for hours billed. This guiding principle should not be abandoned when evaluating whether the benchmark percentage should be adjusted.

Case law provides little guidance in determining when "special circumstances" might justify departure from the 25 percent benchmark. Most reported decisions on attorney fee awards are trial court decisions that reflect the conflicting opinions and prejudices of individual judges. Many of these decisions involve peculiar factual circumstances from which it is difficult to draw broadly applicable conclusions. While recognizing that there is great variation among individual decisions, several adjustment considerations emerge from a review of the case law.

It is only in huge cases that the percentage is reduced to less than 25 percent.

First, many decisions recognize that the 25 percent benchmark does not apply equally to all sizes of cases. Rather, smaller recoveries often receive higher percentage awards, while the fee percentage may be reduced in larger cases. See *In re SmithKline Beckrnan Corp. Sec. Litig.,* 75 1 F. Supp. at 534. As of the late 1990's, it appears that the 25 percent benchmark typically applies without a "size-of-recovery" adjustment to recoveries in the $1 to $50 million range. See *In re NASDAQ Market-Makers Antitrust Litig.,* 1 87 F.R.D. at 486. The recovery in this case is at the lower end of the range to which the 25 percent benchmark typically applies.

Class counsel exerted substantial effort.

A second adjustment factor often discussed in the decisions is the amount of effort involved in prosecuting the case. See, e.g., In re Crazy Eddie Sec. Litig., 824 F. Supp. at 326- 327; Bowling v. PJizer, Inc, 102 F.3d 777,780 (6th Cir. 1996). The concern underlying this adjustment factor is that a 25 percent fee may be excessive for a case that requires little attorney effort and where the attorney's investment of time and resources is relatively small. In analyzing this factor, courts typically compare the percentage fee award with the lodestar fee indicator to see if the risk multiplier appears excessive. In practice, courts differ widely on what constitutes an appropriate lodestar multiplier for purposes of this analysis.

See, In re Crazy Eddie Securities Litigation, 824 F.Supp. 320,326 which has noted that in the federal courts "'in recent years [lodestar] multipliers of between 3 and 4.5 have been common" Lodestar multipliers that are greater than 4 or 5 appear to attract judicial skepticism. See, e.g., In re NASDAQ Market-Makers Antitrust Litig., 187 F.R.D. at 488-89. Below the level of a 4 multiplier, a range of multipliers have been approved in individual cases. In considering whether an effort adjustment is appropriate, the question should be whether the history of the case indicates that reasonable, knowledgeable parties at its outset would have anticipated that a reduced fee percentage would be appropriate because of the expected ease or simplicity of the litigation. In other words, this factor should be used to police for situations in which a normal fee percentage would be excessive because the underlying case is clear and compelling, and unlikely to require typical level of effort to achieve a successful outcome. That is not the case here. This case was never viewed as easy. From the beginning class counsel expected that it would likely involve a substantial investment of time and resources. Nothing about the past or the expected future burden of pursuing this case calls for an adjustment to the benchmark fee percentage based on level of effort.

Class counsel's unadjusted lodestar fee to date is nearly $700,000. Based on an estimated total judgment value in this case of about $7,000,00), a 25 percent fee would to a lodestar multiplier of 2.5. This multiplier is well within the normal range.

Class counsel took a double risk in taking this case.

A third adjustment factor in evaluating a fee percentage is the level of risk assumed by class counsel. If the case is taken on a pure contingency, the risk is higher and deserving of a higher percentage fee. On the other hand, if counsel's compensation is only partially contingent, the level of risk decreases, as does the appropriate fee percentage. Here, class counsel undertook this case on a pure contingency. Moreover, this case involves a significant double contingency.

> Class counsel . . . have the case on a contingency. Moreover, it is a double contingency; first they must prevail on the class claims, and then they must find some way to collect what they win.

> *Torrisi v. Tucson Elec. Power Co.*, 8 F.3d 1370 (9th Cir. 1993) at 1376-77.

The double level of risk is present in this case. Class counsel's contingency involves both the risk of losing on the merits and the risk of nonpayment, even if successful. Contingent fee arrangements are only possible if the lawyer is rewarded for undertaking the contingency risk. Common fund fee awards must maintain the viability of bringing such actions on a contingency basis.

> I practiced law for 29 years and found the contingent fee the one outstanding custom of our judicial system which makes our system of justice far superior to England's. Without the contingent fee, the poor and working people of America would be deprived in civil cases of the ability to process their claims and great injustices would be effectuated.

Allard v. First Interstate Bank, 112 Wn.2d 145, 158,768 P.2d 998, 773 P.2d 42 (1989) (Dore, J., dissenting).

As a practical matter, this action could only be brought on a contingency basis - no individual plaintiff had a sufficient monetary stake to justify the costs and risks of the litigation. The percentage of recovery fee method, which provides a fair compensation for the risk of undertaking a contingency case, assures that plaintiffs will be able to obtain access to the judicial system in such circumstances.

<u>Other benefits are received by the class</u>

A fourth adjustment factor sometimes considered in common fund fee awards is the value of other benefits that the class obtains from the litigation beyond the amount of the common fund from which the fee is paid. The damages awarded the plaintiffs do not reflect the substantial additional benefit that class members received because the litigation forced the defendant to stop its unjustified practices. Such future benefits to the class are properly considered in judging the reasonableness of a common fund fee award.

CONCLUSION

The proposed 25 percent common fund fee award will equitably apportion the costs of this litigation to all of the class who benefit from its outcome. All such beneficiaries should contribute proportionally to the costs of the litigation. The proposed 25 percent attorney fee reflects both the minimum benchmark percentage for common fund fee awards and also the fee percentage established at the start of this litigation to attract counsel to undertake the effort and risk of this litigation. The proposed percentage meets all the tests for a percentage award. Class counsel respectfully requests that the court award the fee requested.

[Attorney's usual signature and date block]

Chapter 16   Using Experts in Proving or Attacking the Amount of Fee

§ 16.01   You need an expert on the fee amount

Improve your odds of a judgment declaring the "Reasonable Attorney Fee" in the case to be the amount your side wants it to be. Use expert witness testimony in legal fee disputes[174] to examine and testify on:

✓   Reasonableness of legal fee hourly charges,
✓   Reasonableness of number of hours on a project,
✓   Duplication / non-duplication of effort or efficient / inefficient practices,
✓   Standard of care and ethics in billing practices, and
✓   Reasonableness of law firm billing practices,

An attorney friend may be all that you can afford as an expert witness, in smaller cases. So even though an attorney friend has no special training or experience in examining attorney fee bills outside his/her own bills, ask for their opinion. An attorney expert of some calibre is better than not having any support to your own estimate of your own worth and your own testimony that your bills as reasonable.

But a true expert witness should be sought when large amounts are at stake. The pitfalls of using "the attorneys I know" and not using a true professional expert witness is illustrated well by the following quotation.

> Appellants submitted affidavits of three attorneys. The affidavit of Steven J. Schiffman, who practices in the Middle District of Pennsylvania, provided the following relevant information: 1) when a case is a high risk, he requests an hourly rate of $85 per hour plus a percentage of any award; 2) he sets fees differently in civil rights cases; 3) without an enhancer, plaintiffs would face greater difficulty in obtaining representation; and 4) because of the risk of nonpayment, he declined representing plaintiff Rode. The affidavit of Charles E. Schmidt, who also practices in the Middle District, provides the following relevant information: 1) his firm does not accept a contingency fee case unless it would generate a fee 50-100% over their normal hourly rate; 2) he is unaware of any experienced personal injury lawyer who would take a contingency fee case unless it generated significantly more than an hourly rate; and 3) without the presence of an enhanced fee, potential plaintiffs would have greater difficulty obtaining representation. The affidavit of Allen Levinthol, Director of the Dauphin County Bar Association, provides the following relevant information: 1) in Dauphin County, potential plaintiffs have difficulty obtaining representation for claims involving civil rights; and 2) this difficulty would be enhanced without the prospect of an enhanced fee.

---

[174] We discussed this briefly, and introduced the premise, in Chapter 14 of this Handbook.

[47]   Essentially, these affidavits only indicate how two attorneys treat contingency fee cases differently than hourly rate cases, and that without some kind of enhancement, potential plaintiffs would have difficulty attracting competent counsel in these types of cases. This evidence does not satisfy the criteria of Delaware Valley II. We note that it is not the number of affidavits submitted that is important, rather it is the content of the affidavits and the expertise of the affiant, with a proper foundation, to make the representations contained therein. *Counsel should seek to establish the necessity of a contingency multiplier in the same manner as he or she would seek to establish any fact which requires scientific, technical or specialized knowledge to understand -- through use of expert testimony. See Fed.R.Evid. 702-706. In fact, a single person, qualified as an expert and with the proper foundation, could produce testimony that would satisfy the four evidentiary requirements* of Delaware Valley II. Here, at a minimum, the affidavits fail to establish the first two requirements: how the relevant market treats contingency cases differently from hourly rate cases and the degree to which that market compensates for contingency. ....We therefore conclude that the district court did not abuse its discretion in denying appellants' request for a contingency multiplier.

Rode v. Dellarciprete, 892 F.2d 1177 (3d Cir. 01/04/1990)[Emphsis supplied.]

In small fee cases the cost of true independent expert witnesses on legal fees may not be economically justified.[175]   For those smaller cases, the testimony of the billing attorney alone may be all that can be afforded.[176]   Or a few hours of time from the attorney in an office down the street from you to be your expert witness may be all that you can afford. But once you get up over the $100,000 range of attorneys' fees in the case, the cost of expert testimony is usually less than the amount the award may be adjusted upward or downward by failure on your side to have a good expert witness. Hence, in most big fee cases there is an economic benefit to obtaining true expert testimony.

◀◗ **WARNING.** I have to give a disclaimer here. Part of my professional work (in Bucklin Of Counsel and at www.Bucklin.org) is testifying as an expert in legal fee disputes on what is a reasonable fee. You can assume that I am biased on the desirability of having an expert on your side.

Indeed, in settlement negotiations having an expert's opinion on the reasonable attorney fee amount can move settlement figures significantly. Without an expert opinion being disclosed the defense assumes that the plaintiff is not serious about recovering an amount for fees during the settlement. With the expert opinion confronting the defense

---

[175] Some jurisdictions e.g., North Dakota, NDCC 28-26-06 dictate that a prevailing party receive as costs "The fees of expert witnesses. The fees must be reasonable fees as determined by the court, plus actual expenses." If you are a prevailing party in such a state, and know you are going to get an award in some amount, the statutory mandate will more frequently make it economically advantageous to use an expert.

[176] In *Aquilla Southwest Pipeline, Inc. v. Harmony Exploration, Inc.*, 48 SW3d 225 (San Antonio, 2001) the attorney himself was the only person testifying as to fees. It was held sufficient without any real evidence of the attorney's qualifications as an expert. An attorney probably will always be allowed to testify as an expert on fees, as having some qualifications as an expert witness in the field — unless a Daubert-style challenge keeps out the testimony as "unreliable." (In the Aquilla case the Texas court pointed out there was no challenge to the evidence on a reasonable attorney's fee.)

attorney, the defense attorney must send it along to the insurer with a statement that if the plaintiff prevails then attorneys fees in the amount of the expert's opinion may increase the judgement as additional "hard damages" in the case.

Likewise, if the plaintiff has disclosed an expert witness on attorney fees in a large fee case but the defense indicates they will have no expert, plaintiffs will assume that the fee amount they are asking for is a "hard" number in the negotiations.

As a preliminary consideration, you need to determine whether it is a requirement that expert testimony is needed in the case. Where the jury is the fact finder of what is a reasonable fee, the answer is that you do need one. A jury is without the expertise to determine the standard of what the attorney should do as reasonable and what is a reasonable fee. Some of the states holding the jury to be the fact finder consistently also take the position that when the court substitutes for the jury as a fact finder, the judge also needs expert testimony and cannot simply use her own experience as "judicial notice" of what is a reasonable fee. For example see Cantu v Moore,[177] The court reversed an award of attorney's fees in part, finding that appellees failed to establish their entitlement to an award of conditional appellate attorney's fees. The only testimony regarding appellate attorney's fees was the testimony of a person who was not an attorney. No expert testimony was introduced to prove the amount of attorney's fees that would be reasonable & necessary for the appeals work. The court noted that evidence in the form of expert testimony is required to support an award of attorneys' fees.

On the other hand, if the judge is the fact finder of what is a reasonable fee, frequently the judge is said to be sufficiently qualified by nature of his/her job to be the necessary expert on the case before the court, on what was reasonably done and what the customary fee rate. Even if your state requires other evidence than the judge's personal observations, the judge's own observations will be sufficient if you and your adversary agree that the judge may decide on the basis of stipulated documents or evidence and briefs.

The general rule against an attorney being both a witness and an attorney in the same case is founded on experience and the practical difficulties involved in beating your own drum before the jury. The rules of ethics in all states forbid an attorney from being a witness in the case the attorney is litigating, with certain exceptions to the general prohibition. One of those exceptions is that the lawyer in the case testify regarding fees and services in the case. The exception is based only on expediency, as explained in the comments to the ABA Model Rule:

[177] Texas App., Case 04-01-00524-CV--- San Antonio ,2002, See also cases like *Lesikar v. Rappeport,* 33 S.W.3d 282, 308 (Tex. App.—Texarkana 2000, pet. denied); *Woollett v. Matyastik,* 23 S.W.3d 48, 52 (Tex. App.—Austin 2000, pet. denied)(Reversing award of $50,000 of fees. "A court does not have authority to adjudicate the reasonableness of attorney's fees on judicial knowledge without the benefit of evidence."); *Brown & Root U.S.A., Inc. v. Trevino,* 802 S.W.2d 13, 16 (Tex. App.—El Paso 1990, no writ).

Rule 3.7 Lawyer As Witness

(a) A lawyer shall not act as advocate at a trial in which the lawyer is likely to be a necessary witness unless:

. . . .

(2) the testimony relates to the nature and value of legal services rendered in the case.

. .

ABA Model Rules of Professional Conduct

Paragraph (a)(2) recognizes that where the testimony concerns the extent and value of legal services rendered in the action in which the testimony is offered, permitting the lawyers to testify avoids the need for a second trial with new counsel to resolve that issue. Moreover, in such a situation the judge has firsthand knowledge of the matter in issue; hence, there is less dependence on the adversary process to test the credibility of the testimony.

Comments to Rule 3.07, *Model Rules of Professional Conduct*

Although the ethics rules permit attorneys to testify concerning legal services in their case, it appears unseemly, especially if the two opposing lawyers each testify in contradictory terms about what the specific attorney's hourly charge is and whether it is "customary for a man of my fine reputation before the leaders of this community" or "sky-high and a consumer rip-off." The first problem of the claimant's attorney herself/himself testifying as an "expert" in a legal fee dispute is the appearance it creates for the judge or jury. The attorney appears to be engaging in unseemly "boasting" of what a great and experienced attorney he/she is and then engaging in self serving testimony on his fee being a "customary" fee rate in the community. Juries recognize the bias of the attorney. There are even ethics opinions in some states that say that although the rules of professional conduct for the state have an exception in the attorney-as-witness-rule to allow an attorney to testify on the amount and nature of his own attorney fees, it is poor practice to do so.

Second, the average attorney really has no satisfactory expert qualifications to evaluate his/her own work or the "customary" fees. Unless the attorney has been in the business of setting fees other than his/her own, it is the rare attorney who has taken the time to become an expert in what are the "customary" fees and services of attorneys outside of his/her own law firm.

The biggest problem arising when the claimant's attorney herself/himself is declared to be a testifying "expert" with an expert opinion is that an expert has to give a report and is subject to a deposition as an expert. If you are in federal court or your state rules follow the federal rules, the adverse defense attorney has the right to demand to see every document which the "expert" has considered in determining the value of services.

(B) Except as otherwise stipulated or directed by the court, this disclosure shall, with respect to a witness who is retained or specially employed to provide expert testimony . . . .be accompanied by a written report prepared and signed by the witness. The report shall contain *a complete statement of* all opinions to be expressed and the basis and reasons therefor; the data or other *information considered by the witness in forming the opinions....*"

Fed. R. Civ. Proc.,, Rule 26. [Emphasis supplied.]

In most states and the federal courts all "information considered by the witness" means "every document" including privileged and work product documents seen by the expert, even if it was not a basis for the opinion. The rationale is that if it was seen, at a minimum the item was considered as to whether it should or should not be part of the basis of an opinion. In short, in most jurisdictions, an expert has no privilege to withhold documents if they were seen during the course of the expert's work. So, if the expert on fees is the attorney in charge of the case, he/she may have to forget about the attorney-client privilege blocking anything from view of the adverse party.

§ 16.02   Hire your expert early

Often, experts on attorney fee disputes are not hired until an expert disclosure deadline is near. Waiting this long is usually a mistake. The practice that will pay off in a financially better result for you is to hire your expert as soon as you have a fee dispute.. Why? There are several reasons.

If you are on the prevailing side, you need to have the records that can only be built at the start of the case. A day's worth of consultation and advice will pay off in less attorney time spent at the end of the case trying to put the records house in order. At the start of the case, hire an expert for a consultation on how to have the records that will best support your fee request at the end of the case.

When the fees are ready to be disclosed in discovery, your expert can point out the strengths and weaknesses of your fee invoices and fee records.

Your expert can do the same for your opponent's case. Just as you need to know the strength and weaknesses of your own case you need to know those of opponent's case.

Your expert can help you draft discovery. Drafting interrogatories and requests for production regarding the reasonableness of a fee request is unknown territory for most lawyers. can be tricky. You may not always know what to ask for, much less how to ask for it. Experts can help you ask for what you need and avoid the requests that miss the mark and do not furnish you with the ammunition you need for your side of the battle.

Your expert can help you cross-examine the other side's expert. The opposing expert has spent years learning the topics and issues you are going to inquire about. You think you also know those issues simply because you are a lawyer (hence an expert on attorney fees, right?) You are wrong. Just being a lawyer is not being an expert on attorney fees. To have effective cross-examination of the other side's expert on fees, you can use your own your expert's advice about the weaknesses of the other expert's opinions and how best to exploit them. Find out what points the other expert should concede and how to undermine the expert's credibility in the case of refusal to do so.

Your expert can help you settle the case. A strong expert on the reasonableness of attorney fees can be the biggest asset you have in settling this portion of the case to your benefit. An articulate expert with impressive credentials and a well-based, well-reasoned opinion can make opposing counsel tell his/her client about the chances of taking the matter further.

If the case does not settle, your expert can help you win at trial.

To get most of these benefits, you must hire an expert and get that person involved early. Early on, tell your client about the benefits of hiring and using an expert on fees and how those benefits outweigh the expense. Point out that the extra cost of hiring an expert may result in a net savings.

§ 16.03　　Presenting the expert witness

The testimony of your expert witness on the value of a reasonable attorney's fee for work in the case comes at the end of your case. The judge is telling you to hurry up, and you are also ready to wrap up the case and get to final argument. As a result, attorneys often give inadequate consideration to both what the jury wants to hear about the attorney fees they are to award, and also what the jury needs to decide the issue of attorney fees. The attorney looking at attorney fee issues usually is only interested in the background of the expert, and what is the expert's conclusionary opinion of the reasonable value of attorney's fees in the case. The jury's interest is not so limited.

Actually the jury is curious about "why" the hourly rate of attorneys is what it is, and why it is "so high." The jury is curious about what the attorneys did before the trial. The jury wants to know more of the "what happened in this case before the trial" than the attorney does. What the attorneys did before the trial started needs to be explained as a story of what "happened to this case on the way to the courthouse." You as an attorney know the litigation procedure, but a jury does not. The jury wants to know enough of the story of what "happened to this case on the way to the courthouse" to make what can be perceived as an intelligent decision.

The choice between the fee amounts set out by the competing sides in the litigation is a process of choice familiar to the juror every time they have competing bids on an auto repair. Forced to choose between two competing dollar price bids, a juror wants to know six things from each of the two competitors on the bid. That is why the jury really wants to know six things from an expert on the subject of attorney's fees. These are the things your expert needs to explain, (and you need to furnish the questions that will allow the expert to make the explanation). Think of it like an auto repair estimate process. The jury is experienced in repair estimates. They expect an expert on repairs to tell them:

　　　1. What much is a reasonable cost?

The jury expects more. To determine credibility, they expect to hear all of the additifollowing four items.

　　　2. What makes you an expert on the subject?

3. What physical examination did you make of the items in this case?

4. What are the factors that should be considered?

5. How do those factors lead to your conclusion?

The jury needs something else. When they have competing bids for repairs they expect to hear the competitor tell them the following.

6. Why is the conclusion of the other expert wrong?

Think of telling the jury these six things through your expert's testimony. Do not just limit the expert's testimony to items numbers 1 and 2 above. Even if the judge is telling you to finish up your case quickly, meet the jury's expectations and tell them what they feel they should know to make an intelligent decision.

Beyond these six items, however, there are other items. I have outlined all these items in a form checklist for a direct examination of an expert witness on attorney fees. (§ 39.18 Form: Checklist for Direct Examination, Expert Witness on "Reasonable Attorney Fee.") That checklist gives you the idea of what your fees expert should be asked to explain to the jury. If the matter of attorney fees is being tried to a judge, the same outline can be used, but not so much emphasis needs to be made of explaining the list of factors involved in setting a reasonable fee, and why ethics are involved.

Before you start using the Checklist for Direct Examination that follows, consider the exhibits you would like to have in evidence. Consider having as exhibits, among other possibilities:

✓ If not already in evidence, the itemized fee bills of the billing attorneys.

✓ A "flow-chart" of the case, showing procedures such as consolidation of cases, motions for dismissal, et cetera, where work reasonablely had to be done, or (on the defense) the extraneous work "not on prevailing causes of action," or unnecessary procedures. That is best for a jury. For a judge you might want to instead use a line item list of all the procedures and work done. You need an exhibit visually telling the story of "how the case got here to trial and the work needed to get it here."

✓ The expert's mathematical-style spreadsheets or charts showing any calculations the expert has made of hours reasonably spent or not spent

✓ The expert's spreadsheet, or chart, showing what is a reasonable fee for each attorney involved in the fee award.

✓ A list of all the factors considered by the expert.

✓   The expert's spreadsheets, or charts, showing the calculations to get to the ultimate fee suggested by the expert.

✓   The expert's full report.

✓   The expert's biography.

If exhibits are going to be used, add them at an appropriate place in the following checklist.

§ 16.04   Form: checklist for direct examination of your expert

Direct Examination, Expert Witness on "Reasonable Attorney Fee"

Mr. Expert, what is your occupation?

Ultimate Opinion in Short Form while Jury is Fresh.

Did I ask you to prepare an opinion what is the amount of a reasonable attorney fee for the reasonable fees for [_____'s] attorneys in this case?

Have you prepared such an opinion?

What is your opinion of the amount of a reasonable attorney fee?
> [Federal Evidence Rule 705 (and the like state rules) allow the expert to give an opinion without first testifying to the underlying facts or data, unless the court requires otherwise. Dollar value opinions are specially well suited to an examination started by asking for the conclusion first, especially if in voir dire or opening statement you have alerted the jury that attorney fees will be in issue and what your expert will say is the reasonable value of the work done.]

Are all the opinions that you express today opinions to a reasonable degree of certainty?

Expert Qualifications.

In a little while, I'm going to ask you what you did and how you came to that conclusion, but right now let's start with what makes you an expert on the subject of attorney's fees. We would like to know what your qualifications are to give that opinion that a reasonable fee would be $_____..

Have you been admitted to practice law in some state?

What legal education have you had?

What publications have you written?

What professional organizations do you belong to?
> [This area of expert qualifications should be gone into in detail. If the expert has been admitted to special boards or professional organizations, bring those out. One way to prevent the jury getting the idea that expert is bragging is to say "Mr. Expert, I have a list here that says you have been a member of ....and....and...and .....; and...   Is that list at least a partial list of the professional organizations to which you have belonged?]

Using some of those organizations for examples, would you tell us why being in those organizations bears on the quality or scope of the opinions you can give us today?

What in your work experience helps you evaluate a reasonable attorney fee in this case?

[To prevent long speeches that bore the jury, you can break the response up by first having the expert simply list law firms or companies for which he/she has worked, and then you respond by asking the question a juror might ask about certain of the jobs in the list: "Why did your work experience at _____ help you in examining the work done by the attorneys in this case and deciding on a reasonable fee for the work? If you do not ask the expert that, if the expert has the chance and is not cut off by you, the expert should him/her self say things such as :"My work as a _____ gave me experience and training in looking at attorneys' work beyond my own, comparing one attorney's work with another attorney and seeing what was a reasonable amount of time to bill to a client to get various legal work done." The point is that the jury wants to know why a particular job gives your expert better experience in looking at attorneys fees and the value of them than the adverse expert has.]

What fields of law or expertise are involved in giving an opinion in this case?

[Usually, there will be an ['expert field number one" - a field of litigation or transaction law involved; plus the field of Attorney Fees and Expenses, plus the field of Legal Ethics. The expert's answer should include all of them.]

What training and experience have you had in [expert field number one]?

What training and experience have you had in Attorney Fees and Expenses?

What training and experience have you had in Legal Ethics?

Have you worked as an expert for plaintiffs or for defendants?

Are there principles that are used by experts in the field of Attorney Fees to determine what is a reasonable fee? What are they?

[Ordinarily the expert will explain that court rulings, the code of professional responsibility, and writers on the subject generally agree on what are the factors Involved. If the case is in state court, the eight usual factors can be listed; if in federal court, the twelve usual factors. Preferably a poster board style listing should be made for the jury at this point, for an visual outline of the "Factors Involved" testimony later in the examination of the expert.]

Mr. Expert, you mentioned the field of Legal Ethics. How does legal ethics get involved in what is a reasonable attorney fee?

[Ethics gets directly involved because the state ethics code for lawyers, called the Code of Professional Responsibility, lists the eight items that are the minimum factors that must be considered. (In federal court it can be explained as a list of items that are in the federal list of items that must be considered.) The courts have required time records and detailed billing and fees submissions based on the ethical principals that there should not be anything hidden from the court in the billing, and that the bills should be as detailed and honest and based on the same ethical principle of high degree of care as fee bills given to clients.]

Did you examine this case for all of those Factors Involved as you looked at what the attorneys representing [client's name] did in this case?

Examination Made in This Case.

Now let's move to the subject of what you did to determine a reasonable attorney fee for this case. We would like to know what you have physically observed in this case, and what those examinations and observations showed.

What was date of your first examination of any document or physical item in this case?
What did you do in that first examination?
What did your first examination disclose?

After your first examination what did you do?
[A chronological explanation of what the expert did is usually easiest for the jury to follow, and allows the jury to understand the depth of the expert's examination. So an examination like you would use for a medical doctor works well. "Tell us the general course of your examination, what you did, and what that examination disclosed" works well.]

What did that disclose to you?

Will you explain for us the general course of the litigation/transaction in this case and what legal proceedings were involved?
[Ordinarily this is a good place for the expert to give the story of "how the case got to the courtroom" where the jury now can see what the attorneys are doing. The jury needs to know what the attorneys had to do to bring the evidence into court and actually try the case. That is the purpose of the above question. This is also a chance for your expert to explain why certain work of the attorneys was/was not relevant to be part of the attorneys' fees to be awarded in this case.]

➴ **Warning.** If you are in the federal courts, where the Dubert standards apply, or in a state court jurisdiction with similar gatekeeping functions to be performed by the judge, you need to affirmatively show those factors, if they have not been established on the record before the trial. During the following "Factors" part of the direct examination; if the expert has furnished a "methodology" section in his/her report, you can use this methodology as a checklist of questions you need to ask to be sure that the opinion of the expert meets the Daubert criteria (or like state criteria for admissibility of expert opinions). E.g., As a part of your examination, did you use any publications or studies? Inject these questions as appropriate. For example, when customary hourly rate is discussed, you can have the expert discuss any statistical attorney wage rate information he/she relied on and why the information can be classified as reliable.

Factors Considered in the Opinion.

Time - Hours recorded and whether reasonable.

Mr. Expert, as we started talking with you today, you said your conclusion was that a reasonable fee amount for the attorneys representing [client's name] in this case is
$_____ .   What method did you use in arriving at that dollar figure?
[The expert should explain he/she used the method commonly used by experts to solve the problem: first, determining from the materials in the case, including the fee billings, what was the reasonable amount of time spent on the matter; second, determining a market value of the services of attorneys of like skill reasonably required for the matter; third, multiplying hours times hourly rate to find "lodestar amount"; fourth, examining the other Factors Involved to see if the lodestar amount should be raised or lowered to reach a "reasonable fee."]

What examination did you make of the number of hours attorneys _____ claimed for doing the work?
[It is wise to use an exhibit that if possible the jury can have in the jury room, with the dollar figures you want them to adopt, with the major items involved.]

[If the following are to be discussed by the expert, it would be wise to break up any long period of speech by the expert by you asking additional specifics such as the following.]

What did that examination show?

Was the billing increment used by the attorneys appropriate?

Did there appear to be any peculiar time periods or unusual days recorded as worked by the attorneys?

Did the time records appear to be reasonably accurate and contemporaneous to the items recorded?

Was there intermingling of items or block billing in the time records?

Were the billing entries vague or specific?

Did there appear to be overstaffing, unnecessary work, or duplication of effort?

What are the reasonable number of attorney hours for doing the work in this case?

Is what the _____ attorneys claim a reasonable number of hours?

Hourly rate per attorney

What is "The fee customarily charged in the locality for similar legal services" for each attorney for the kind of work they did in the case?

What is the basis of that opinion?

[If the expert relies on a published study, she should testify why the study is reliable. It is not enough to show that the study was done, or that it was published; why is the study reliable? Explanation should be made of why (the methodology, rates of error, and results of) these studies are reliable or need to be taken account of by an expert on reasonable attorney fees.]

Lodestar Number

Would you do the multiplication for us? Would you multiply the reasonable number of hours times the customary market rate per hour for attorneys of like skill.

Is that figure of $_____ called the "lodestar" amount?

I your opinion, in this case, should the lodestar amount you just showed us by the multiplication, be the same as your "reasonable fee amount" you gave us earlier?

> [Give the expert the chance to explain that the other factors were considered but they do/do not change the figure upward/downward. You are going to ask the expert why/why not below. The above question is your bridge for the jury to understand what process your expert used.]

Other factors considered beyond hours and hourly rates

You have told us earlier that there was a list of [eight twelve] factors to be considered. So far you have told us about the hours and dollars per hour and how that multiplies to a certain dollar figure. Would you now tell us the consideration you made of [each of these other factors in the list] and if that factor affects what is a reasonable attorney fee.

[It will be more interesting if you ask questions to bring out the expert's consideration of each of the following factors, instead of subjecting the jury to a 20 minute monologue by the expert.]

The novelty and difficulty of the questions involved, and the skill needed to perform the legal service properly.

The likelihood, if apparent to the client, that the acceptance of the particular employment will preclude other employment by the lawyer.

The results obtained.

The time limitations imposed by the client or by the circumstances.

The nature and length of the professional relationship with the client.

The experience, reputation, and ability of the lawyer or lawyers performing the services.

Whether the fee is fixed or contingent.

Paralegal work

Did the legal assistants appear to have been qualified through education, training, or work experience to perform substantive legal work?

Was the legal assistant work done identified and described in general nature?

Was the legal assistant work done was work that traditionally has been done by lawyers?

Were the work items done by legal assistants clerical or secretarial typing jobs?

Was the legal work the legal assistants did performed under the direction and supervision of an attorney?

What did you determine were the number of hours reasonably spent by the legal assistants?

What was the hourly rate being charged for the legal assistants?

Was the hourly rate charged withing a customary range for legal assistant work of like skill?

Did you add this into the previous calculation of a reasonable fee for the attorneys?. If not in that previous calculation, should we do that now?

Work after start of trial

Do you have an opinion what the attorney's fees should be for any work done after the date this trial started, for the following areas of work?

> [B through E below, as appropriate to your jurisdiction. Many, if not most jurisdictions, have the appeals court, not the original trier of fact, assess the amount of reasonable fee for items C through E. However, if the jury is setting the fee through trial, you need to get item B from the expert.]

What is your opinion and basis of it. Please tell the jury the work typically involved and how you come to your conclusions.

> [Here is a good place to use a chalkboard or posterboard showing the following. Let the expert fill in the answers to your questions on the following items as the direct examination proceeds.]
>
> A. From the time the attorneys started work until the start of the trial.$_____
>
> B. Trial, per day of trial $_____
>
> C. For work in the intermediate court of appeals, if an appeal occurs. $_____
>
> D. In the Supreme Court if writ allowing appeal is not granted. $_____
>
> E. In the Supreme Court if writ allowing appeal is granted. $_____

Adverse expert's opinion

We have heard / will hear testimony from [experts on other side] regarding their opinion on reasonable fees. I would like your opinion, and the basis of that opinion, regarding some of the same items they discussed/we have been told they will discuss.

You have said that the reasonable number of hours to do the work is _____hours. Are the number of hours that have been asserted by [the attorneys for the adversary or the adverse expert] as the number of reasonable hours an appropriate number?

Please explain the basis for your answer.

You have said that the customary fee for this type of work should be $___ per hour for Attorney Jones, $_____ per hour for Attorney Smith, [et cetera]. Are the dollar per hour figures that have been asserted by [the attorneys for the adversary or the adverse expert] customary fees for this type of work?

Please explain the basis for your answer.

Expenses of the attorney

Mr. Expert, did I ask you to prepare an opinion and give us your opinion what the reasonable costs for Plaintiff/Defendant 's attorneys in this case?

Have you prepared such an opinion?

What is the general conclusion in your opinion?

What is the basis of that opinion?

Should those expenses be added to the total for a reasonable attorney fee amount? Why?

Items to end the direct examination

[Consider what opinion or testimony you want to end on, as a high note. Generally speaking the expenses are a low interest item in the testimony. Generally you will want to ask a few questions to get back to the your expert's ultimate dollar value on the reasonable fee being put to the forefront again. If nothing else suggests itself to you, you can always fall back on the following reaffirmation.

Mr. Expert, you have told us today that in your opinion the amount of a reasonable fee for the attorneys representing [client's name] in this case is $_____. Is that an opinion to a reasonable degree of certainty?

§ 16.05　Tips on deposing the adverse fee expert

There are two general schools of thought regarding the deposing of adverse experts. A minority of excellent litigators are of the school of thought that most cases settle; therefore you should depose the expert just as you would cross-examine the expert at a trial. These litigators aim to get the adverse party to lose confidence in their expert and therefore shift the settlement value in the litigator's favor. The goal is to throw all your ammunition at the expert so that the expert's testimony is less relied upon by the other side in setting their expectations of trial and the settlement amount. This school of thought says that it is ok to *not* find out everything the adverse expert knows, if asking for everything causes a recitation showing how great the adverse expert really is. Doing a cross-examination for a deposition under this theory assumes that you have received a disclosure or report of the adverse expert; and you just build a cross-exam as you would for any other witness at trial.

The following deposition checklist does *not* follow that school of thought. There are two reasons. First, for that type of cross-examination-deposition, you prepare as you would for other types of expert cross-exams. (If you want ideas for areas to explore in that sort of cross-exam-style-deposition, you can get ideas from the following deposition checklist.) Second, most of you are in the majority school of thought that follows. You are looking for a deposition checklist that follows the conservative theory of a comprehensive deposition of the expert, to drain the expert dry of everything of use to you. So that is the style of deposition checklist we provide in this book.

The majority of attorneys advocate that a deposition of an expert should be unlike the cross examination of the same expert at trial. At a deposition, runs the theory of this school of thought, to be safe and protect yourself from nasty surprises, you want to learn everything the expert might say at trial. You want to pin him/her down to only one answer for any question you have. You want to eliminate any deviation or unexpected statement at trial. You want the adverse expert to open up and ramble with everything, including things you would try desperately to avoid being heard by the jury, so that the deposition eliminates any surprise at trial. Following this theory, your goals in a deposition are (1) to have the expert state every opinion he/she has, stating them so clearly that they cannot be changed by the expert at trial; (2) to have the expert state all the basis for each opinion, and disclaim that there is anything else that supports the opinion; (3) to discover evidence you can use for cross examination of the expert at trial; and (4) to find any evidence, materials, or studies your expert does not know about. The following deposition checklist adopts those goals.

This deposition checklist does not waste time on "the usual preliminaries." They add nothing to the deposition of an adverse attorney fees expert. E.g., if you are impeaching at the trial, the jury will discredit an attorney expert who claims pity because he/she never was cautioned by another attorney to think before answering. Plunge in and get to the substance. Avoid a beginning that is the usual patter of what a deposition is all about and the qualifications of the witness. Such patter merely makes an expert more comfortable on the witness stand. Establish control, not a conversation. (That is why the following checklist has the witness qualifications at the end, not the beginning.)

As you go through the deposition - be sure to have the expert completely explain any exhibits, spreadsheets, or data summaries he/she has prepared. You want to be able to prepare to attack it if it is used as a summary or demonstrative evidence. You also want your own expert to be able to read this deposition's transcript and be able to completely understand any exhibits, spreadsheets, or data summaries the adverse expert has prepared.

§ 16.06   Form: checklist for deposing the adversary's fee expert

Cross Examination, Expert Witness on "Reasonable Attorney Fee"

Files and Records

Did you bring to this deposition, as requested, all your files and records in this case? [Before the deposition make a request in the nature of our form § 8.5 Form: Notice of Items Adverse Expert is to Bring to Deposition.]

[Make sure your have a copy of everything that the expert has brought with him, even if he/she is not using it or says he/she has not considered it.]

Did you **not** bring any item that we requested you bring?

If witness withholds any documents: ask if he/she has "considered" it. [Either in determining what was relevant, in forming his opinion or in preparing for the deposition.]

Identify any withheld items with great particularity, even if he/she says he/she has not considered it. Not only ask what it is, who wrote it or received it, and its date; but also ask the expert to specify number of pages, color or black and white, typed or handwritten, stapled or loose, an original or photocopy, et cetera. Also for each withheld item, ask who else has seen the item.]

Are there any items not brought to the deposition that he/she has seen in preparing his analysis and opinions? (Even if he/she is not using the item now and does not now have it in his files.) [Notice this is not the same question as the earlier question whether the expert has brought all his files and records. E.g., an attorney may have shown him something that never was put into the expert's file.]

Now, as to anything withheld or not brought to the deposition, find out
>Where is it now? (Surprising how many times it was left in the hotel room deliberately or is now in the adverse attorney's briefcase!)
>Why did you not bring it here?
>Who told you not to bring it here?

Fee Contract in the Underlying Matter.

Has he/she seen the attorney - client fee contract of the attorney whose work is being evaluated for a "reasonable fee"

If he/she has not seen it, why not?

If a fee a contract does not exist, has the expert considered the state or ethics rules that require fee contract. [E.g., Texas Professional Code Rule 1.04 says:" © When the lawyer has not regularly represented the client, the basis or rate of the fee shall be communicated to the client, preferably in writing, before or within a reasonable time after commencing the representation."]

The Records of Time Expended in the Underlying Matter.

Has the expert *seen*:
- the actual time slips?
- a copy of the computer raw data records of time?
- a computer print out of the time entries?
- bills of the billing attorney whose work is being evaluated for a reasonable fee?

Has the expert received:
- copies or the actual time slips?
- a copy of the computer raw data records of time?
- a computer print out of the time entries?
- bills of the billing attorney whose work is being evaluated for a reasonable fee?

In attorney fee disputes, the hourly time sheets of the attorney under investigation is important. Be sure that you have every time record that was considered by the adverse expert.

Has he/she seen the actual time slips? (Get them!)

Once you have the physical time records or other records of work done, ask if anyone has explained those records to him. Get everything the expert was told. Importantly, if the expert was not told anything about the meaning of the written words (e.g., "Research") on a time record, obtain admissions that the expert does not know anything more about the words (E.g, what was researched, or whether the mode of research meant reading an entire book on constitutional law or just reading a court rule that a beginning lawyer should know, or doing a keyword search on Westlaw.)

Does the expert's own firm routinely record time the attorneys' work each day on matters?

Why or Why Not does his own firm record attorney's time?

What method does his firm use to record time?

In addition to the method, find out the actual computer program they use to record time? E.g., Time slips, Tabs3, Amicus Attorney, PCLaw.

Is the expert's own firm's computer time program one of the many in which you can activate a clock in stopwatch fashion? (That is, the user clicks the program to start the computer stopwatch, types a note describing what was done, clicks the stopwatch on an off for interruptions, and clicks the stopwatch at the end of the work. That is all the effort needed to have a bill slip is automatically generated in the firm's computer for that client and matter.)

Is the expert's firm's computer time program capable of recording time in 1/10 hour increments?

What time increment does the experts own firm use?

What time keeping method does the attorney firm (the billing firm"whose work is being evaluate for a reasonable fee use?

Does the expert know the exact program used by the billing firm?

Does the expert know if the billing firm's computer and billing program is capable of recording time in 1/10 hour increments? In minute increments?

Does the expert know if the billing firm uses the features of its computer billing program to "round up" the actual time in creating the attorney firm bills and computer print outs of the time entries the expert has seen?

Did the billing firm always use its computer program to time the work they are billing in this case?

Does the expert know if all the time billed for in this case was accurately recorded?

Opinions Are Now Final!

Is he/she prepared to express opinions in this case?

(Is there anything he/she wants (or expects) to do to express trial opinion, but he/she has not yet done? - testimony? investigation?)

Has the attorney retaining him asked him to do any more work on the case?

Nail down that with nothing more than he/she now has in the case, he/she can express his opinions in final form.

Nail down that if he/she receives no more information, his opinions will not change.

Description of Method Used and Work Done.

What did the expert personally do to be able to express an opinion?

Did she have any work done by others (in his office or outside her office) so that she could express her onions?

What data or materials have been inspected/reviewed?

Did she interview the party for whom she is testifying?

What other persons have been interviewed regarding the case?

Why did the expert interview them?

When and under what circumstances were they interviewed?

What did they say?

Have you considered what they said? Do you rely on what they said?

Did you refer to any publications while studying this case?

> Identify the publications and the parts you looked at for this case.

> What did they say that is relevant to your opinions in this case.

What independent investigation did she do?

What independent investigation did he/she do?
Of court proceedings in the case.
Of documents involved in the case.
Of law involved in the case.
Of parties or witnesses involved, or how they were involved.

Did the expert run some sampling, testing or verification process?

Did the expert just take the word of the attorney who hired him?

Did the expert just take the word of the for whom she is testifying?

List of Opinions and Basic Grounds.

List the expert's opinions, each separately and clearly stated. [Use the expert's terminology, not yours in listing the opinions.] Restate it back to the expert to get her confirmation that you have it listed correctly.

For each opinion ask: "What are the grounds of that opinion?."

The expert on reasonable attorney fees normally will have each of the first three opinions printed below.

(1) The total reasonable attorney fee for all work done until _____ is $_____
Grounds of the opinion:_____

(2) The time and labor required was _____hours.
Grounds of the opinion: _____

(3) The hourly fee customarily charged in the locality for similar legal services is $_____per hour.
Grounds of the opinion: _____

(4) _____
Grounds of the opinion:

(5) _____
Grounds of the opinion:

(6) _____
Grounds of the opinion:

(7) and so forth. If there are other opinions, add them to the list.

Standards.

Tell us the state or federal statutes, rules, law, or legal professional standards that apply in determining a reasonable attorney fee for this case?

List all applicable statutes, rules, law, or legal professional standards.

[Inquire as to each one] Why does / does not this standard apply in this case?

Are there any other standards that apply to determine a reasonable fee in this case?

There are no other rules or standards that apply (to limit him at trial).

Factors Involved

The expert probably used the usual eight (state) or twelve (federal) point list of factors in his opinion on why the amount he/she chose is a "reasonable fee." Whether or not he/she did, go over each one of the following usual factors Involved, and see what he/she did (or did not do) in adjusting one way or the other from the lodestar amount (hours expended multiplied by hourly rate) to a "reasonable fee" amount.

Factor: the time and labor required.

> What examination did you make of the number of hours the billing attorneys claimed for doing the work?
> > What did your examination of the number of hours worked by the attorneys show you?

> What was the billing increment used by the attorneys? (1/10 hour or something else]
> > What did you do to determine the billing increment?
> > Was the billing increment used by the attorneys appropriate?
> > Why was the billing increment appropriate?

Did there appear to be any peculiar time periods or unusual days recorded as worked by the attorneys?
What did that examination show?

What examination did you make of the time records to see if the attorneys were accurate and making the entry contemporaneous to the item recorded?
What did that examination show?

What examination did you make of time entries to see if there was intermingling of items or block billing in the time records?
What did that examination show?

What examination did you make of time entries to see if the billing entries were vague or specific?
What did that examination show?

Did anyone explain to you the time entries on the time records?
{Use some examples on this question.   E.g., "Were you told anything about the meaning of the vague written word "Research" on the billing record for 11/12/2004?"]

Obtain admission that the expert does not know anything more about the words on the time entry than anyone else would. (E.g, the expert does not known what was researched or whether it meant reading a book on constitutional law or just looking up a court rule that a beginning lawyer should know.)

What examination did you make to see if there was overstaffing, unnecessary work, or duplication of effort?
What did that examination show?

Factor: the novelty and difficulty of the questions involved.

Factor: the skill needed to perform the legal service properly.
Is the "skill needed "different than the "skill actually used"?

Factor: the fee customarily charged in the locality for similar legal services.

Statistics

What statistics exist on attorney fee rates in [____the state involved___]?

Pin him down that there are no other statistics that he/she knows about.

Then ask what the statistics show in regard to this case?

Exactly what data was used / in compiling the statistics, and how was the study conducted?

Then ask if he/she considers these statistics are reliable?

Why are these statistics reliable / not reliable?

Has he/she relied on these statistics in determining the hourly rate customarily charged in the locality for similar legal services?

Non-Statistical Data.

Are there any anecdotes or reports of individual items regarding attorney fee rates in [____the state involved____] that you have considered in determining the hourly rate customarily charged in the locality for similar legal services?

Is it a hearsay report? Do you ordinarily rely on hearsay?

Experience.

Has the expert used his own experience in determining the hourly rate customarily charged in the locality for similar legal services?

Is the experience limited to the expert's own fee bills?

If the expert claims experience of other attorney's hourly charges: How many times has the expert actually had the experience of looking at the fee bills of other attorneys?
How many times in your own experience in this last year have you even heard a hearsay report of what other attorneys than yourself were charging in the locality for similar legal services?

In the last year?
Who were they? Who were the attorneys?
What work were they doing?
How many times did they charge that rate and not some other rate?

In the year before that? In the year before that? [and so on]

Factor: the amount involved and the results obtained.

Factor: the time limitations imposed by the client or by the circumstances

Factor: the likelihood, if apparent to the client, that the acceptance of the particular employment will preclude other employment by the lawyer.

Factor: the nature and length of the professional relationship with the client.

Factor: the experience, reputation, and ability of the lawyer or lawyers performing the services.

Factor: whether the fee is fixed or contingent on results obtained or uncertainty of collection before the legal services have been rendered.

We have discussed these factors today (List to the expert the ones actually discussed).

❏   the time and labor required;

❏   the novelty and difficulty of the questions involved;

❏   the skill requisite to perform the legal service properly;

❏   the likelihood, if apparent to the client, that the acceptance of the particular employment will preclude other employment by the lawyer;

❏   the fee customarily charged in the locality for similar legal services;

❏   the amount involved and the results obtained;

❏   the time limitations imposed by the client or by the circumstances;

❏   the nature and length of the professional relationship with the client;

❏   the experience, reputation, and ability of the lawyers performing the services; and

❏   whether the fee is fixed or contingent.

❏   [Other factors that were discussed]_____

Are there any other factors you think should be considered in determining a reasonable attorneys fee in this case?

If the expert says there are other factors considered in determining the reasonableness of a fee, inquire "Why" he/she thinks it should be considered, and "How" it affects the valuation of a reasonable fee in this case.).

Ending Sweep of Opinions.

Are there any other "opinions" that you have regarding the attorney's fee bill, attorney's hours or time recording procedures, or the attorney's qualifications? [This is an attempt to limit him at trial to those expressed today.]

Do you have any criticisms regarding the attorney's fee bill, attorney's hours, or time recording procedures?

If the expert says he/she has no criticisms, then ask if he/she considers the attorneys hours and time records to be "perfect."

Qualifications of the witness.

In what fields of law does the expert consider himself an expert?
[Warning: How the expert, you, and the court define the field is critical. For example, if the matter involves a will contest before a probate court, the opinions of a lawyer who claims general civil litigation expertise may be ruled out on a Daubert gatekeeper style motion if the judge thinks the field is "probate law."]"

What are your qualifications in [____the specific field of law involved___]?

Did you bring your curriculum vita or list of qualifications?

Go over any item in the curriculum vita in which you have some possibility of limiting its relevance to the expert opinion in this case.

Go over any item in the curriculum vita in which the other side has the possibility of expanding at trial to show increased expert credibility.

Did you bring a list of all publications authored by you within the preceding ten years.

Do any of your published papers discuss items involved in this case?

Go over any item which is not relevant to the expert opinion and establish that indeed it does not have relevance.

Were you the author of any other publication or study that is relevant to your opinions in this case?

Did you bring a list of any other cases in which you testified as an expert at trial or by deposition within the preceding four years?

Go over this list to find information which will allow you get a transcript. [Names of cases, city or court, and attorneys.]

In these other cases did you give an opinion on attorney fees.

What was your opinion of the usual or customary hourly fee rate of attorneys in those cases?

Job experience is especially relevant in attorney fee opinion qualifications. Go over details of job descriptions.

Limit his qualifications.

     In what fields does he/she agree he/she is not an expert?

Lack of experience in this specific type of case, et cetera.

If the expert is relying on experience, the expert should explain:
How that experience leads to the conclusion he/she reached,
Why that experience is a sufficient basis for the opinion.

How was he/she contacted to come into the case?

Does he/she advertise? Where and when? [Get sufficient information so you can look up the ads before trial.]

Testifies to make money

What is he/she being paid? By hour? At trial?

How much paid to date?

Is he/she a friend of the attorney for whom he/she is testifying?

Items on which to end the examination.

Consider what opinion or testimony you want to end on, as a high note. There is an off-chance that the deposition will be used if the expert is not available to testify live in court. How do you want the deposition to end if the adverse side plays it in court? If nothing else suggests itself to you, you can always fall back on asking questions about the expert's own hourly rate and comparing it to the hourly fee requested in this case. If the experts rate is lower or higher than the billing attorney, it often can be suggested that either the billing attorney or the expert has an unduly high rate.

§ 16.07   Form: summarizing time spent in litigation

Experts on either side of the fight about the time reasonably expended in litigation by a prevailing attorney often see some advantage in summarizing the time spent by categories of work done. The following form is sometimes of use in making such summaries.

Summarization of Litigation Time Expenditure

Phase I - Discovery.
Phase 2 - Other Activities Intended to Move the Litigation to Resolution.
Phase 3 - Settlement.
Phase 4 - Trial.

Phase I - Discovery

> Phase I is directed toward those initial discovery activities which allow an initial assessment of the settlement value of the case and the likelihood of settlement. The activities normally include, but are not limited only to the initial file review, answer, special exceptions, interrogatories, requests for production, requests for admission, motions to compel when appropriate, motions to dismiss, receipt of plaintiffs' medical records, employment records or other records to support lost wage claims and the like.

ITEM   HOURS

Initial file review
Preparation of answer, cross complaints, special exceptions, etc.
Preparation of initial motions(e.g., motion to dismiss)
     Type of motion
     Court appearance
Legal research (preliminary issues)
Interrogatories/Requests for Production/Requests for Admission
     Routine
     Complex
Obtaining and reviewing records (medical/employment/ etc.)
Response to discovery requests,
Client contact
Initial depositions / preparation   (indicate identity of deponents)

TOTAL ATTORNEY FEES IN PHASE 1   Hours

Phase 2 - Other Activities Intended to Move the Litigation to Resolution

If the case cannot be settled fairly soon after the initial deposition or two, Phase II should consist of those meaningful activities which will tend to move the case toward resolution. Activities to be considered in Phase II include the insureds deposition, summary judgment motions if applicable, designations and depositions of expert witnesses, and inspection of the accident scene. and mediation or arbitration.

ITEM   HOURS
Other depositions / preparation (indicate identity of deponents)
Motion practice
      Type of motion
      Court appearance
Legal research issues
Experts, conference and preparation (medical, technical, other)

TOTAL ATTORNEY FEES IN PHASE 2   Hours

Phase 3 - Settlement.

Activities of Phase III do not consist only of mediation and other formal settlement conferences, but also includes drafting of documents intended solely as settlement offers or responses, telephone calls and letters to prepare the way for final resolution.

TOTAL ATTORNEY FEES IN PHASE 3   Hours

Phase 4 - Trial.

If the case is not resolved at mediation, the only recourse is to prepare for trial and try the case.

Estimated length of trial - days
Trial Preparation - consider time required for preparation of witness examination, motion in limine, trial briefs, legal research, voir dire, jury instructions, etc.

TOTAL ATTORNEY FEES IN PHASE 4   Hours

****

SUMMARY

Phase I - Discovery.
        Hours _____
Phase 2 - Other Activities Intended to Move the Litigation to Resolution.
        Hours _____
Phase 3 - Settlement.
        Hours _____
Phase 4 - Trial.
        Hours _____

Total Hours _____

Appendix A: References - the Ethics of Time-Based Billing by Attorneys

If you only have time for one, read one of those indicated with an *

Altman. · Adam C. Altman, "To Bill, or Not to Bill? Lawyers Who Wear Watches Almost Always Do, Although Ethical Lawyers Actually Think About It First," 11 Geo. J. Legal Ethics 203 (1998).

Chan. · Sonia Chan, "ABA Formal Opinion 93-379: Double Billing, Padding and Other Forms of Overbilling," 9 Geo. J. Legal Ethics 611 (1996).

Lerman. · Lisa G. Lerman, "Scenes from a Law Firm," 50 Rutgers L. Rev. 2153 (1998).

Lerman. · Lisa G. Lerman, "Gross Profits? Questions about Lawyer Billing Practices," 22 Hofstra L. Rev. 645 (1994).

*Lerman. · Lisa G. Lerman, "Blue Chip Bilking: Regulation of Billing and Expense Fraud by Lawyers," 12 Geo. J. Legal Ethics 205 (1999).

Mallen. · Ronald E. Mallen, "Guidelines or Landmines? Preserving the Tripartite Relationship," For the Defense, June 1998, at 9.

Richmond. · Douglas R. Richmond, "Professional Responsibility and the Bottom Line: The Ethics of Billing," 20 S. Ill. L. J. 261 (1996).

Ricker. · Darelene Ricker, "Greed, Ignorance, and Overbilling: Some Lawyers Have Given New Meaning to the Term 'Legal Fiction,'" 80 ABA J. 62 (1994).

Ross. · William G. Ross, "Kicking the Unethical Billing Habit," 50 Rutgers L. Rev. 2199 (1998).

Ross. · William G. Ross, "The Ethics of Hourly Billing by Attorneys," 44 Rutgers L. Rev. 1 (1991).

*Ross. · William G. Ross, The Honest Hour: The Ethics of Time-Based Billing by Attorneys. Carolina Academic Press (1996).

Rotunda. · Ronald D. Rotunda, "Moving from Billable Hours to Fixed Fees: Task-Based Fees and Legal Ethics," 47 U. Kan. L. Rev. 819 (1999).

Schratz. · James P. Schratz, "I Told You to Fire Nicholas Farber -- A Psychological and Sociological Analysis of Why Attorneys Overbill," 50 Rutgers L. Rev. 2211 (1998).

Syverud. · Kent D. Syverud, "The Ethics of Insurer Litigation Management Guidelines and Legal Audits," Ins. Def. Rptr., May 1, 1999, at 180.

Toothman. · John W. Toothman, Real Reform, 81 ABA J. 80 (1995). This award-winning essay calls for the replacement of time-based billing.

Watson. · Lee A. Watson, "Communication, Honesty, and Contract: Three Buzzwords for Maintaining Ethical Hourly Billing," 11 Geo. J. Legal Ethics 189 (1998).

Appendix B: Specimen Cases Awarding Paralegal Time

American Petroleum Institute v. United States, 52 F.3d 1113 (Fed. Cir. 1996). Award of paralegal fees was found to be reasonable as a component of attorneys fees. The court noted that in some instances a charge for services by a partner would be inappropriate if the work could have been performed by a paralegal or associate attorney.

Brandt v. Schal Associates, Inc., 960 F.2d 640 (7th Cir. 1992).

Buchanan v. U.S., 755 F.Supp. 319 (D.Or. 1990), aff'd 765 F.Supp. 642 (D.Or. 1991).

Chambless v. Masters, Mates & Pilots Pension Plan, 885 F.2d 1053 (2nd Cir. 1989), cert. den. 496 U.S. 905.

Computer Statistics, Inc. v. Blair 418 F.Supp. 1339 (S.D.Tex. 1976).

Consolo v. George, 58 F.3d 791 (1st Cir. 1995). The award for paralegal fees hinged not on whether such fees were recoverable as an element of attorney fees but, rather, on the court's evaluation of the work performed by the paralegal, its reasonableness and its productivity. The court award paralegal fees as a component of the lodestar calculations, but did not include fees for redundant tasks also performed by the attorneys or for tasks which were purely clerical in nature.

Guinn v. Dotson (1994) 23 Cal.App.4th 262. Held that an award of attorney fees that did not compensate for paralegal service time would not fully compensate the attorney. They further examined the legislative intent of attorney fee statutes and found considerable history to support the concept that the generic term "attorney fees" was intended to encompass paralegal fees, where the prevailing practice is to separately bill a client for paralegal service time.

Gullet v. Stanley Structures, 722 P.2d 619, 222 Mont. 365 (1986).

Harman v. Lyphomed, Inc., 787 F.Supp. 772 (N.D. Ill. 1992).

In re Continental Illinois Securities Litigation, 985 F.2d 867 (7th Cir. 1993). The Court of Appeal rejected lower court's computation of paralegal fee award based on the paralegal's wage plus a percentage of overhead. The matter was remanded for recomputation by the lower court. At 985 F.2d 867, the court again remanded the lower court's recomputation of paralegal fees noting that the lower court still did not fully understand the concept of computing paralegal fees to be included in award.

In re Grenoble Apartments. II, 145 Bankr. 43 (Bankr.D.S.D. 1992), vacated and remanded 152 B.R. 608 (D.S.D. 1993).

In re Sounds Distributing Corporation, 122 Bankr. 952 (W.D. PA 1991).

Little Rock School District. et al. v. Pulaski County Special School District #I, 959 F.2d 716 (8th Cir. 1992).

Maltzer v. Provident Life & Accident Ins. Co., 843 F.Supp. 692 (M.D. Fla. 1993).

Metro Data Systems, Inc. v. Duranao Systems, Inc., 597 F.Supp 244 (D.Ariz. 1984). The court refused to authorize compensation for lawyers performing services that could have been performed by a legal assistant.

Miller v. Alamo, 983 F.2d 856 (8th Cir. 1993).

Missouri v. Jenkins, 491 U.S. 274, 109 S.Ct. 2463, 105 L.Ed.2d 229 (1989). The U.S. Supreme Court held that in setting a reasonable attorney's fee under 28 U.S.C 1988, a legal fee may include a charge for legal assistant services at market rates rather than actual cost to the attorneys

New Mexico Citizens for Clean Air v. Espanola Mer., 72 F.3d 830 (IOth Cir. 1996).

Nichus v. Liberio, 973 F.2d 526 (7th Cir. 1992). The court held that while hours claimed for paralegals and law clerks are compensable, two of the individuals for whom paralegal time was claimed were not shown to be paralegals/law clerks by training or licensure.

Occidental Chemical Corporation v. The Power Authority of the State of New York, 786 F.Supp. 316 (W.D. NY 1992), aff'd at 990 F.2d 726 (2nd Cir. 1993).

Price v. Cole, 574 N.E.2d 403 (Mass.App.Ct. 1991).

Ross v. Buckeye Cellulose Corp., 764 F.Supp. 1543 (M.D.Ga. 1991).

Stewart v. Sullivan, 810 F.Supp. 1102 (D.Hawaii 1993). Paralegal fees were awarded at $65 per hour. The court excluded 2.5 hours because the paralegal was performing a ministerial tasks such as photocopying and hand deliveries.

Sundance v. Municipal Court (1987) 192 Cal.App.3d 268. The court noted that the award of attorney fees for paralegal fees has become common place in California.

U.S. Football League v. National Football League, 887 F.2d 408 (2nd Cir. 1989).

Wasson v. Secretary of Secretary of Dept. of Health and Human Services, 24 Cl.Ct. 482 (1991).

Appendix C: Excerpts from Role Models America

The type of time records submitted is a part of the consideration of a reasonable fee determination. *Role Models America, Inc. v. Brownlee*,[178] reiterates the established law on the subject of requirements for time billing records. Because the case describes so well the type of time records needed, and the consequences of a law firm's failure to have such time records, we quote liberally here for your use in pasting quotations into your own briefs..

Role Models America, Inc. v. Brownlee, 353 F.3d 962 (D.C.Cir. 01/13/2004)

[Excerpts only.]

[10] The opinion of the court was delivered by: Tatel, Circuit Judge

[11] In an earlier decision in this case, we ordered the Secretary of the Army to correct procedural errors he committed in disposing of excess military property, errors that deprived appellant, a non-profit organization, of an opportunity to compete for the property. For its work in securing that decision, appellant now seeks an award of attorneys' fees pursuant to the Equal Access to Justice Act. Because appellant has satisfied the statutory requirements for an award, we grant its application for fees. But because it has failed to justify the amount it seeks, we award significantly less than requested. * * * *I.

[15] Having secured the relief it sought, Role Models now requests, pursuant to the Equal Access to Justice Act, 28 U.S.C. § 2412 (2000) (EAJA), reimbursement for the attorneys' fees that it incurred in bringing the appeal. * * * *

[29] This brings us to the amount of fees to be awarded. The EAJA authorizes courts to award "reasonable attorney fees." 28 U.S.C. § 2412(d)(2)(A). Role Models seeks compensation for the work of two partners, one counsel, one associate, six legal assistants, one law clerk, two research librarians, and a legislative specialist. Their hourly rates range from $495 for the lead partner to $285 for the associate to $165 for the law clerk. According to Role Models, these fourteen individuals logged a total of 1058 hours

in connection with the appeal and with the preparation of its fee petition. Multiplying the appropriate rates and the number of hours, Role Models requests $342,741.25 in legal fees. It also seeks $12,773.44 for expenses, as well as leave to "supplement its Application to reflect the additional fees and expenses incurred while litigating its EAJA application." * * *

[38] Number of Hours

[39] Role Models, as mentioned, seeks reimbursement for 1058 hours of work. The government insists that 1058 hours is unreasonable, arguing that several of Role Models's attorneys appear to have repeated each other's work and adding that "[t]his case involved no discovery, did not require any travel, did not require interview of witnesses, or involve multiple pleadings." Appellees' Opp'n at 12. Defending its request, Role Models argues (essentially reiterating its justifications for a special-factor increase in the statutory cap) that the substantial number of hours is reasonable "[g]iven the time parameters and the complexity of the pertinent statutes and regulations." Appellant's Reply at 7-8. It also states that "the research and writing performed for the appeal was divided by factual and/or legal areas among the attorneys," and that "at no time were there parallel, full-time work efforts." Id. at 8 (internal quotation marks omitted).

[40] Role Models has the burden of establishing the reasonableness of its fee request, see, e.g., North, 59 F.3d at 189, and "[s]upporting documentation 'must be of sufficient detail and probative value to enable the court to determine with a high degree of

---

[178] 353 F.3d 962 (D.C.Cir., 2004)

certainty that such hours were actually and reasonably expended,' " In re Olson, 884 F.2d 1415, 1428 (D.C. Cir. 1989) (per curiam) (emphases omitted) (quoting United Slate, Tile & Composition Roofers v. G & M Roofing & Sheet Metal Co., 732 F.2d 495, 502 n.2 (6th Cir. 1984)). We agree with the government that the time records Role Models has offered permit no such certainty.

[41]   To begin with, many time records lump together multiple tasks, making it impossible to evaluate their reasonableness. See id. at 1428-29 ("[W]hen an attorney bill[s] for more than one task in a day, the court is left to approximate the amount of time which should be allocated to each task. With such inadequate descriptions the court cannot determine with a high degree of certainty, as it must, that the billings are reasonable." (footnote and internal quotation marks omitted)). For example, one entry indicates that on September 17 Role Models's lead lawyer spent 10.25 hours performing the following six tasks: "Telecon[ference] with R. Alexander; conference with J. Port, K. Dodd, C. Bonat regarding research; review research; draft brief; review bankruptcy materials; revise brief." Another entry indicates that on October 3 the associate spent 1.25 hours on the following four tasks: "Revise Lis Pendens filing; call bankruptcy attorney (G. Johnson) and leave message; call circuit court regarding procedure for Lis Pendens filing; finalize draft of Lis Pendens filing." Not only do similarly lumped entries appear throughout the time records, but the two we have mentioned include time spent on bankruptcy matters, which have nothing to do with this appeal. Although Role Models says it has deducted all time spent on bankruptcy matters, the lumping prevents us from verifying that it deducted the proper amount of time.

[42]   Many time records also lack adequate detail. See In re Sealed Case, 890 F.2d 451, 455 (D.C. Cir. 1989) (per curiam) ("[W]e note numerous instances of documentation and specification that do not adequately describe the legal work for which the client is being billed. This makes it impossible for the court to verify the reasonableness of the billings, either as to the necessity of the particular service or the amount of time expended on a given legal task."). The law clerk's time records, for instance, give an identical one-line entry, "[r]esearch and writing for appellate brief," on eight consecutive

weekdays: the clerk billed 8.25, 6.25, 7.25, 8.25, 7.25, 4, 8, and 4.25 hours on those days. Such generic entries are inadequate to meet a fee applicant's "heavy obligation to present well-documented claims." Kennecott Corp. v. EPA, 804 F.2d 763, 767 (D.C. Cir. 1986) (per curiam). Similarly inadequate are the numerous entries in which attorneys billed simply for "research" and "writing," or for time spent in teleconferences or meetings -- over one hundred in total -- the purposes of which are not provided. See In re Meese, 907 F.2d 1192, 1204 (D.C. Cir. 1990) (per curiam) (reducing an award because "[t]he time records maintained by the attorneys, paralegals and law clerks are replete with instances where no mention is made of the subject matter of a meeting, telephone conference or the work performed during hours billed"); Olson, 884 F.2d at 1428 ("[T]here are multitudinous billing entries, included among other entries for a particular day, that wholly fail to state, or to make any reference to the subject discussed at a conference, meeting or telephone conference.").

[43]   Attorneys also billed for time spent dealing with individuals whose roles in the case are never explained. For example, on March 27 one attorney charged over $2000 for time spent performing the following tasks: "Emails with K. Esters of CNS; telecons with R. Alexander; draft letter to Bresee; review public benefit conveyance regs." Who are Bresee and K. Esters? What is their connection to this case? What is CNS? Without answers to these questions, such time entries -- of which there are many examples throughout the time records -- are manifestly inadequate. See In re Donovan, 877 F.2d 982, 995 (D.C. Cir. 1989) (per curiam) ("[W]e are also compelled to deduct - charges incurred when attorneys held conferences and teleconferences with persons referenced as 'Geiser' and 'Wells.' The application fails to document who these individuals are or the nature of their relationship to the investigation; consequently, we cannot evaluate whether such fees were reasonably incurred.").

[44]   The shortcomings in the time records are particularly serious because we have no idea what it was about this case that required an investment of over 1000 hours -- nearly six months' worth of forty-hour weeks. Involving no discovery and presenting neither complex nor

contested facts, the case presented a straightforward challenge to an agency's failure to comply with its own regulations. Although Role Models rightly observes that its attorneys had to spend time familiarizing themselves with the case, we fail to see how this justifies such a significant number of hours. We appreciate that the attorneys made "substantial efforts - to produce the most polished brief possible, and to be meticulously prepared to respond to the Court's questions at oral argument." Appellant's Application at 10-11. But as we have said, "there is a point at which thorough and diligent litigation efforts become overkill." Okla. Aerotronics, Inc. v. United States, 943 F.2d 1344, 1347 (D.C. Cir. 1991).

[45]   "Duplication of effort is another basis on which [the] hours seem excessive." Davis County Solid Waste Mgmt. & Energy Recovery Special Serv. Dist. v. United States EPA, 169 F.3d 755, 761 (D.C. Cir. 1999) (per curiam). For example, on three separate occasions two individuals, one an associate charging over $200 an hour, billed time for filing the same brief. Similar unexplained duplication of work appears throughout the time records. More generally, Role Models has failed to explain why this relatively straightforward case required the efforts of three senior attorneys, each billing at least $400 per hour. Perhaps something about this case required so many lawyers expending so many hours. But because the time records contain so little information, we have no basis for concluding that hours that appear to be excessive and redundant are in fact anything other than excessive and redundant. See In re Espy (Townsend Fee Application), 346 F.3d 199, 204 (D.C. Cir. 2003) ("[I]nadequate documentation makes it impossible for the court to verify the reasonableness of the billings, either as to the necessity of the particular service or the amount of time expended on a given legal task." (internal quotation marks omitted)); see also Murray, 741 F.2d at 1427 ("[H]ours that are 'excessive, redundant, or otherwise unnecessary' must be excluded-" (quoting Henley v. Eckerhart, 461 U.S. 424, 434 (1983))).

[46]   The time records suffer from two additional defects. First, on a number of occasions one attorney's records indicate that he or she spent time meeting with another attorney, while the second attorney's records report no such meeting. For example, the associate reported that on February 13 she spent 4.5

hours on the following tasks: "Call Clerk's Office for D.C. Circuit regarding Bill of Costs' filing procedure; discuss with P.D. Richardson; read EAJA research." Yet Mr. Richardson billed no time discussing the case with the associate on that day. In fact, Mr. Richardson charged no time at all on February 13. Similarly, on July 16 Mr. Richardson billed for time spent on a "[t]eleconference with J.C. Port," but Mr. Port's time records, though including an entry for discussions with the law clerk, contain no reference to a teleconference with Mr. Richardson. Such unexplained inconsistencies appear throughout the time records.

[47]   Second, several time records include tasks that do not warrant reimbursement. For example, Role Models's lead attorney billed for time spent on a "telecon with Herald Mail reporter." In this circuit, the government cannot be charged for time spent in discussions with the press. See Am. Petroleum Inst. v. United States EPA, 72 F.3d 907, 913 (D.C. Cir. 1996) (citing Meese, 907 F.2d at 1203); Donovan, 877 F.2d at 993-94. Role Models's lead attorney also spent time after oral argument "review[ing] summary of argument," "review[ing] cases," and "[r]evis[ing] summary of argument," but Role Models has not explained how these tasks helped it prevail in its appeal. Furthermore, two lumped entries report unspecified amounts of time spent drafting and revising the firm's engagement letter with Role Models. The government should not have to pay for administrative matters relating to the formal relationship between Role Models and its attorneys. Also, a legal assistant logged two hours to "[v]isit Court of Appeals for the D.C. Circuit to obtain copy of Government's brief." Given that the government served its brief directly on Role Models's attorneys, it should not have to pay for this time. Nor should it have to reimburse Role Models for two hours that a partner spent "[c]ompleting application for admission to D.C. Circuit Bar" and fifteen minutes that the associate spent "[r]esearch[ing] admission to D.C. Circuit Bar [and] prepar[ing] application materials" for the partner. Not only do we assume that a Washington law firm offering itself as a specialist in Federal court litigation would treat the cost of joining the bar of this court as an expense of doing business not chargeable to clients -- much less to the Federal government -- but this partner did not even participate in the oral argument. Cf. Miller v. Alamo, 983 F.2d 856, 862 (8th Cir. 1993) ("The government

challenges the Millers' request for reimbursement of the $30 fee for having the Millers' attorney admitted to the Eighth Circuit Bar. We agree that [the relevant fee-shifting statute] should not be used to require the government to fund the enhancement of an attorney's versatility or capability."). Finally, as already mentioned, two individuals -- an associate and a legal assistant -- spent time filing each of Role Models's briefs. We do not understand why attorney or even legal assistant skills were required for this job. "[P]urely clerical or secretarial tasks should not be billed at a paralegal rate regardless of who performs them." Missouri v. Jenkins, 491 U.S. 274, 288 n.10 (1989); see also Meese, 907 F.2d at 1203 ("The court - deducts those charges by both paralegals and law clerks for such tasks as 'delivering' or 'picking up' various documents- In our view, such tasks are 'purely clerical or secretarial' and thus cannot be billed at paralegal or law clerk rates.").

 48]   In view of all this -- inadequate documentation, failure to justify the number of hours sought, inconsistencies, and improper billing entries -- we will allow reimbursement for only fifty percent of the attorney hours that Role Models requests. See Henley, 461 U.S. at 433 ("Where the documentation of hours is inadequate, the district court may reduce the award accordingly."). A fixed reduction is appropriate given the large number of entries that suffer from one or more of the deficiencies we have described. See, e.g., Copeland v. Marshall, 641 F.2d 880, 903 (D.C. Cir. 1980) (en banc) ("[T]he District Court Judge in this case -- recognizing, as he did, that some duplication or waste of effort had occurred -- did not err in simply reducing the proposed - fee by a reasonable amount without performing an item-by-item accounting."); see also Okla. Aerotronics, 943 F.2d at 1347 (affirming the district court's flat forty percent reduction in allowable hours). For the four attorneys we will therefore award fees for 410.25 hours, half the 820.5 requested. At the adjusted statutory rate of $143.25 per hour, this comes to $58,768.31. Because the law clerk's time records suffer from the same inadequacies that characterize the attorneys' time records, we will award fees for only half of his hours as well. Reducing the law clerk's hourly rates by twenty-five percent because of Role Models's failure to justify those rates, see supra page 11, we will award $8,881.41 for the clerk's time.

[49]   The government opposes any recovery for the legal assistants, arguing that a party may not recover fees for work done by non-attorneys. But we have previously affirmed a fee award that "includ[ed] paralegal time." Okla. Aerotronics, 943 F.2d at 1352; see also Olson, 884 F.2d at 1426 ("This Circuit 'holds that paralegals and law clerks are to be compensated at their market rates.' " (quoting Donovan, 877 F.2d at 993 n.20)). It is true, as the government points out, that in a subsequent decision we denied recovery for paralegal work and in doing so cited a Fifth Circuit decision deeming such time to be an "unrecoverable overhead expense." See Democratic Cent. Comm. v. Wash. Metro. Area Transit Comm'n, 12 F.3d 269, 272 (D.C. Cir. 1994) (per curiam) (citing Allen v. United States Steel Corp., 665 F.2d 689, 697 (5th Cir. 1982)). In that case, however, we denied reimbursement for paralegal fees because the purpose of the paralegal's work was "not sufficiently specified." Id. Here, by contrast, the legal assistants' time records, unlike the attorneys' and the law clerk's, provide adequate detail and show that these employees performed suitable tasks. We will therefore award reimbursement for the full number of hours requested for the legal assistants' time, with the exception of the two hours that a legal assistant spent visiting this court to pick up a brief and the time that a legal assistant spent on three separate occasions filing a brief. See supra page 16. As to the latter, the entries for two of the three occasions are lumped, leaving us unable to determine exactly how much time the legal assistant actually spent filing the brief. Because the single "unlumped" entry shows that the legal assistant spent 0.75 hours, we will use that figure for all three. Reducing the legal assistants' hourly rates by twenty-five percent because of Role Models's failure to justify those rates, see supra page 11, we will award $4,147.51 for the work of the six legal assistants.

[50]   The government argues that the EAJA does not permit the government to be charged for the work of the research librarians and the legislative specialist. We need not consider that issue, however, for we think Role Models has failed to overcome the assumption that "work done by librarians, clerical personnel and other support staff - [is] generally considered within the overhead component of a lawyer's fee." Olson, 884 F.2d at 1426-27. Role Models has not, for example, shown that law firms in

Washington customarily bill clients for such services, or even that its own attorneys customarily bill for them.

[51]   Expenses

[52]   Role Models seeks $12,773.44 for expenses, having properly excluded several categories -- such as messenger services and ground transportation -- that we have deemed non-reimbursable. See Mass. Fair Share v. Law Enforcement Assistance Admin., 776 F.2d 1066, 1069 (D.C. Cir. 1985) (per curiam). Role Models should also have excluded "overtime services," see, e.g., Michigan v. United States EPA, 254 F.3d 1087, 1096 (D.C. Cir. 2001), and we will deny recovery for those services. We will also deny recovery for search service expenses, document delivery services, and publications because Role Models has failed to explain what these categories comprise.

[53]   Although the rest of the expense categories are properly chargeable to the government, Role Models appears to ask for more than it incurred. For example, although its attorneys billed Role Models $9,448.89 for their use of Westlaw, Role Models requests $10,027.08. Similar discrepancies occur with Lexis expenses ($311.82 billed to Role Models v. $323.17 requested), copying charges ($1,678.06 billed to Role Models and not already reimbursed v. $1,716.34 requested), and search services expenses ($433.47 billed v. $578.07 requested). With each discrepancy we will award the lower, billed, amount (except for search services, which we have said we will deny entirely). The government urges us to deny any recovery for computer-research charges, but we decline to do so because such services presumably save money by making legal research more efficient. See Hirschey v. FERC, 777 F.2d 1, 6 (D.C. Cir. 1985) (finding that "a charge - for computer research is appropriate").

[54]   We will therefore award a total of $11,438.77 in expenses: $1,678.06 for copying plus $311.82 for Lexis plus $9,448.89 for Westlaw.

[55]   ****.

[56]   In highlighting the shortcomings of the time records submitted in this case and in reducing Role Models's fee request, we emphasize that we make no judgment either about the propriety of Role Models's decision to pay its attorneys for the services for which it now seeks reimbursement or about the attorneys' billing Role Models for those services. To begin with, the EAJA and relevant case law limit, or in some instances entirely prohibit, recovery for certain services that law firms routinely and properly bill clients. More important for purposes of our analysis here, law firms may well have understandings with clients and a level of trust that permit billing on the basis of time records like those at issue here. In awarding fees under the EAJA, however, we have a special responsibility to ensure that taxpayers are required to reimburse prevailing parties for only those fees and expenses actually needed to achieve the favorable result. In fulfilling that responsibility, "we are not prepared to hold that the willingness of a private client to pay a bill necessarily demonstrates that the charge was reasonable under the statutory definition and can therefore be automatically assessed against the government." Kennecott Corp., 804 F.2d at 767. That said, "we do not intend to tar [petitioner's law firm] - with any brush of over-billing or over-staffing as related to their relationship with this or any other client. We simply conclude that the petitioner has not sufficiently justified the degree of staffing - to bring it within the zone of reasonableness contemplated by Congress-" North, 59 F.3d at 193.

[57]   In sum, we will award Role Models $83,236: $58,768.31 in attorneys' fees plus $8,881.41 for the law clerk plus $4,147.51 for the legal assistants plus $11,438.77 for expenses. Role Models's request for leave to supplement its application is denied.

[58]   So ordered.

Appendix D: Excerpts from Henley v. Eckerhart

The United States Supreme Court of Henley v. Eckerhart has discussion which is helpful to understanding of the apportionment that should be made when the prevailing part has not been successful on all claims.   We print excerpts here as an aid for your quotations to the court.

U.S. Supreme Court
Henley v. Eckerhart, 461 U.S. 424 (1983)

[Excerpts only.]

Respondents, on behalf of all persons involuntarily confined in the forensic unit of a Missouri state hospital, brought suit in Federal District Court against petitioner hospital officials, challenging the constitutionality of treatment and conditions at the hospital. The District Court, after a trial, found constitutional violations in five of the six general areas of treatment. Subsequently, respondents filed a request for attorney's fees under the Civil Rights Attorney's Fees Awards Act of 1976, 42 U.S.C. 1988, which provides that in Federal civil rights actions "the court, in its discretion, may allow the prevailing party, other than the United States, a reasonable attorney's fee as part of the costs." After determining that respondents were prevailing parties under 1988 even though they had not succeeded on every claim, the District Court refused to eliminate from the attorney's fees award the hours spent by respondents' attorneys on the unsuccessful claims, finding that the significant extent of the relief clearly justified the award of a reasonable attorney's fee. The Court of Appeals affirmed.

Held:

* * * * But where the plaintiff achieved only limited success, the court should award only that amount of fees that is reasonable in relation to the results obtained.* * * *.

664 F.2d 294, vacated and remanded.

JUSTICE POWELL delivered the opinion of the Court.

Title 42 U.S.C. 1988 provides that in Federal civil rights actions "the court, in its discretion, may allow the prevailing party, other than the United

States, a reasonable attorney's fee as part of the costs." The issue in this case is whether a partially prevailing plaintiff may recover an attorney's fee for legal services on unsuccessful claims.

* * * *

The District Court first determined that respondents were prevailing parties under 42 U.S.C. 1988 even though they had not succeeded on every claim. It then refused to eliminate from the award hours spent on unsuccessful claims:

* * * * Finding that respondents "have obtained relief of significant import," id., at 231, the District Court awarded a fee of $133,332.25. This award differed from the fee request in two respects. First, the court reduced the number of hours claimed by one attorney by 30 percent to account for his inexperience [461 U.S. 424, 429] and failure to keep contemporaneous records. Second, the court declined to adopt an enhancement factor to increase the award. The Court of Appeals for the Eighth Circuit affirmed on the basis of the District Court's memorandum opinion and order. 664 F.2d 294 (1981). We granted certiorari, 455 U.S. 988 (1982), and now vacate and remand for further proceedings.

* * * * In this case petitioners contend that "an award of attorney's fees must be proportioned to be consistent with the extent to which a plaintiff has prevailed, and only time reasonably expended in support of successful claims should be compensated." Brief for Petitioners 24. Respondents agree that a plaintiff's success is relevant, but propose a less stringent standard focusing on "whether the time spent prosecuting [an unsuccessful] claim in any way contributed to the ultimate results achieved."

* * * *A plaintiff must be a "prevailing party" to recover an attorney's fee under 1988. The standard for making this threshold determination has been framed in various ways. A typical formulation is that "plaintiffs may be considered

`prevailing parties' for attorney's fees purposes if they succeed on any significant issue in litigation which achieves some of the benefit the parties sought in bringing suit." Nadeau v. Helgemoe, 581 F.2d 275, 278-279 (CA1 1978). This is a generous formulation that brings the plaintiff only across the statutory threshold. It remains for the district court to determine what fee is "reasonable."

The most useful starting point for determining the amount of a reasonable fee is the number of hours reasonably expended on the litigation multiplied by a reasonable hourly rate. This calculation provides an objective basis on which to make an initial estimate of the value of a lawyer's services. The party seeking an award of fees should submit evidence supporting the hours worked and rates claimed. Where the documentation of hours is inadequate, the district court may reduce the award accordingly. [461 U.S. 424, 434]

The district court also should exclude from this initial fee calculation hours that were not "reasonably expended." S. Rep. No. 94-1011, p. 6 (1976). Cases may be overstaffed, and the skill and experience of lawyers vary widely. Counsel for the prevailing party should make a good-faith effort to exclude from a fee request hours that are excessive, redundant, or otherwise unnecessary, just as a lawyer in private practice ethically is obligated to exclude such hours from his fee submission.

* * * *The product of reasonable hours times a reasonable rate does not end the inquiry. There remain other considerations that may lead the district court to adjust the fee upward or downward, including the important factor of the "results obtained." This factor is particularly crucial where a plaintiff is deemed "prevailing" even though he succeeded on only some of his claims for relief. In this situation two questions must be addressed. First, did the plaintiff fail to prevail on claims that were unrelated to the claims on which he succeeded? Second, did the plaintiff achieve a level of success that makes the hours reasonably expended a satisfactory basis for making a fee award?

In some cases a plaintiff may present in one lawsuit distinctly different claims for relief that are based on different facts and legal theories. In such a suit, even where the [461 U.S. 424, 435] claims are brought against the same defendants - often an institution and its officers, as in this case - counsel's work on one claim will be unrelated to his work on another claim. Accordingly, work on an unsuccessful claim cannot be deemed to have been "expended in pursuit of the ultimate result achieved." Davis v. County of Los Angeles, 8 E. P. D., at 5049. The congressional intent to limit awards to prevailing parties requires that these unrelated claims be treated as if they had been raised in separate lawsuits, and therefore no fee may be awarded for services on the unsuccessful claim. 10

* * * * If, on the other hand, a plaintiff has achieved only partial or limited success, the product of hours reasonably expended on the litigation as a whole times a reasonable hourly rate may be an excessive amount. This will be true even where the plaintiff's claims were interrelated, nonfrivolous, and raised in good faith. Congress has not authorized an award of fees whenever it was reasonable for a plaintiff to bring a lawsuit or whenever conscientious counsel tried the case with devotion and skill. Again, the most critical factor is the degree of success obtained.

Application of this principle is particularly important in complex civil rights litigation involving numerous challenges to institutional practices or conditions. This type of litigation is lengthy and demands many hours of lawyers' services. Although the plaintiff often may succeed in identifying some unlawful practices or conditions, the range of possible success is vast. That the plaintiff is a "prevailing party" therefore may say little about whether the expenditure of counsel's time was reasonable in relation to the success achieved. In this case, for example, the District Court's award of fees based on 2,557 hours worked may have been reasonable in light of the substantial relief obtained. But had respondents prevailed on only one of their six general claims, for example the claim that petitioners' visitation, mail, and telephone policies were overly restrictive, see n. 1, supra, a fee award based on the claimed hours clearly would have been excessive.

There is no precise rule or formula for making these determinations. The district court may attempt to identify specific hours that should be eliminated, or it may simply reduce [461 U.S. 424, 437] the award to account for the limited success.
* * * *. The applicant should exercise "billing judgment" with respect to hours worked, see supra, at 434, and should maintain billing time records in a manner that will enable a reviewing court to identify distinct claims. 12

* * * * A reduced fee award is appropriate if the relief, however significant, is limited in comparison to the scope of the litigation as a whole.

* * * * The judgment of the Court of Appeals is vacated, and the case is remanded for further proceedings consistent with this opinion.

Footnotes

* * * * [Footnote 3] The 12 factors are: (1) the time and labor required; (2) the novelty and difficulty of the questions; (3) the skill requisite to perform the legal service properly; (4) the preclusion of employment by the attorney due to acceptance of the case; (5) the customary fee; (6) whether the fee is fixed or contingent; (7) time limitations imposed by the client or the circumstances; (8) the amount involved and the results obtained; (9) the experience, reputation, and ability of the attorneys; (10) the "undesirability" of the case; (11) the nature and length of the professional relationship with the client; and (12) awards in similar cases. 488 F.2d, at 717-719. These factors derive directly from the American Bar Association Code of Professional Responsibility, Disciplinary Rule 2-106 (1980).

* * * * [Footnote 7] As we noted in Hanrahan v. Hampton, 446 U.S. 754, 758 , n. 4 (1980) (per curiam), "[t]he provision for counsel fees in 1988 was patterned upon the attorney's fees provisions contained in Titles II and VII of the Civil Rights Act of 1964, 42 U.S.C. 2000a-3(b) and 2000e-5(k), and 402 of the Voting Rights Act Amendments of 1975, 42 U.S.C. 1973l(e)." The legislative history of 1988 indicates that Congress intended that "the standards for awarding fees be generally the same as under the fee provisions of the 1964 Civil Rights Act." S. Rep. No. 94-1011, p. 4 (1976). The standards set forth in this opinion are generally applicable in all cases in which Congress has authorized an award of fees to a "prevailing party."

* * * * [Footnote 9] The district court also may consider other factors identified in Johnson v. Georgia Highway Express, Inc., 488 F.2d 714, 717-719 (CA5 1974), though it should note that many of these factors usually are subsumed within the initial calculation of hours reasonably expended at a reasonable hourly rate. See Copeland v. Marshall, 205 U.S. App. D.C. 390, 400, 641 F.2d 880, 890 (1980) (en banc).

* * * * [Footnote 12] We recognize that there is no certain method of determining when claims are "related" or "unrelated." Plaintiff's counsel, of course, is not required to record in great detail how each minute of his time was expended. But at least counsel should identify the general subject matter of his time expenditures. See Nadeau v. Helgemoe, 581 F.2d 275, 279 (CA1 1978) ("As for the future, we would not view with sympathy any claim that a district court abused its discretion in awarding unreasonably low attorney's fees in a suit in which plaintiffs were only partially successful if counsel's records do not provide a proper basis for determining how much time was spent on particular claims").

[Footnote 13] In addition, the District Court properly considered the reasonableness of the hours expended, and reduced the hours of one attorney by 30 percent to account for his inexperience and failure to keep contemporaneous time records.

[Footnote 14] The District Court expressly relied on Brown v. Bathke, 588 F.2d 634 (CA8 1978), a case we believe understates the significance of the results [461 U.S. 424, 439] obtained. In that case a fired schoolteacher had sought reinstatement, lost wages, $25,000 in damages, and expungement of derogatory material from her employment record. She obtained lost wages and the requested expungement, but not reinstatement or damages. The District Court awarded attorney's fees for the hours that it estimated the plaintiff's attorney had spent on the particular legal issue on which relief had been granted. The Eighth Circuit reversed. It stated that the results obtained may be considered, but that this factor should not "be given such weight that it reduces the fee awarded to a prevailing party below the `reasonable attorney's fee' authorized by the Act." Id., at 637. The court determined that the unsuccessful issues that had been raised by the plaintiff were not frivolous, and then remanded the case to the District Court. Id., at 638. Our holding today differs at least in emphasis from that of the Eighth Circuit in Brown. We hold that the extent of a plaintiff's success is a crucial factor that the district courts should consider carefully in determining the amount of fees to be awarded. * * * * In remanding the Eighth Circuit implied that the District Court should not withhold fees for work on unsuccessful claims unless those claims were frivolous. Today we hold otherwise.

CHIEF JUSTICE BURGER, concurring.

I read the Court's opinion as requiring that when a lawyer seeks to have his adversary pay the fees of the prevailing party, the lawyer must provide detailed records of the time and services for which fees are sought. It would be inconceivable that the prevailing party should not be required to establish at least as much to support a claim under 42 U.S.C. 1988 as a lawyer would be required to show if his own client challenged the fees. A district judge may not, in my view, authorize the payment of attorney's fees unless the attorney involved has established by clear and convincing evidence the time and effort claimed and shown that the time expended was necessary to achieve the results obtained.

A claim for legal services presented by the prevailing party to the losing party pursuant to 1988 presents quite a different situation from a bill that a lawyer presents to his own client. In the latter case, the attorney and client have presumably built up a relationship of mutual trust and respect; the client has confidence that this lawyer has exercised the appropriate "billing judgment," ante, at 434, and unless challenged by the client, the billing does not need the kind of extensive documentation necessary for a payment under 1988. That statute requires the losing party in a civil rights action to bear the cost of his adversary's attorney and there is, of course, no relationship of trust and confidence between the adverse parties. As a result, the party who seeks payment must keep records in sufficient detail that a neutral judge can make a fair evaluation of the time expended, the nature and need for the service, and the reasonable fees to be allowed.

In some cases a plaintiff may present in one lawsuit distinctly different claims for relief that are based on different facts and legal theories. In such a suit, even where the claims are brought against the same defendants - often an institution and its officers, as in this case - counsel's work on one claim will be unrelated to his work on another claim. Accordingly, work on an unsuccessful claim cannot be deemed to have been "expended in pursuit of the ultimate result achieved."

* * * * If, on the other hand, a plaintiff has achieved only partial or limited success, the product of hours reasonably expended on the litigation as a whole times a reasonable hourly rate may be an excessive amount. This will be true even where the plaintiff's claims were interrelated, nonfrivolous, and raised in good faith. Congress has not authorized an award of fees whenever it was reasonable for a plaintiff to bring a lawsuit or whenever conscientious counsel tried the case with devotion and skill. Again, the most critical factor is the degree of success obtained.

Application of this principle is particularly important in complex civil rights litigation involving numerous challenges to institutional practices or conditions. This type of litigation is lengthy and demands many hours of lawyers' services. Although the plaintiff often may succeed in identifying some unlawful practices or conditions, the range of possible success is vast. That the plaintiff is a "prevailing party" therefore may say little about whether the expenditure of counsel's time was reasonable in relation to the success achieved. In this case, for example, the District Court's award of fees based on 2,557 hours worked may have been reasonable in light of the substantial relief obtained. But had respondents prevailed on only one of their six general claims, for example the claim that petitioners' visitation, mail, and telephone policies were overly restrictive, see n. 1, supra, a fee award based on the claimed hours clearly would have been excessive.

There is no precise rule or formula for making these determinations. The district court may attempt to identify specific hours that should be eliminated, or it may simply reduce the award to account for the limited success. * * * *. The applicant should exercise "billing judgment" with respect to hours worked, see supra, at 434, and should maintain billing time records in a manner that will enable a reviewing court to identify distinct claims. * * * * A reduced fee award is appropriate if the relief, however significant, is limited in comparison to the scope of the litigation as a whole. [Emphasis supplied to the court's statement of an appropriate methodology.]

Appendix E: In re Bristol-Myers Squibb

In re Bristol-Myers Squibb
Slip Copy, 2005 WL 447189
S.D.N.Y.,2005.
Feb 24, 2005 (Approx. 4 pages)

Only the Westlaw citation is currently available.

United States District Court,
S.D. New York.
In re BRISTOL-MYERS SQUIBB SECURITIES
Litigation
No. 02 Civ. 2251(LAP).
Feb. 24, 2005.

OPINION AND ORDER

PRESKA, J.
*1 This Matter Pertains to All CasesLead
counsel for lead plaintiffs and the class ("Lead
Counsel") have petitioned for reimbursement of
their expenses incurred in this class action and
an allowance of fees in connection with the
settlement approved at a fairness hearing held
on November 9, 2004 (the "Fairness Hearing").
The fees and expenses requested by counsel
were set forth in the notice of said hearing, and
no objection was made by any Class Member.
[FN1]

FN1. "Class Member" refers to each entity and
person who purchased the common stock of
Bristol-Myers Squibb during the period October
19, 1999 through March 10, 2003.

Lead Counsel have obtained for the Class a
recovery of $300,000,000 (the "Settlement
Fund"), of which Lead Counsel seek an award
of 7.5%, net of
approved notice costs and expenses, and
reimbursement of litigation expenses in the
amount of $557,580.75. At the Fairness
Hearing, I reserved decision as to the fees and
allowances to be made to Lead Counsel. For
the reasons stated below, attorneys' fees are
awarded to Lead Counsel in the amount of 4%
of the Settlement Fund, or $11,937,696.78.

BACKGROUND

The history of this case is set forth in detail in
my April 1, 2004, Memorandum Opinion and
Order. See In re Bristol-Myers Squibb Sec.
Litig., 312 F.Supp.2d 549 (S.D.N.Y.2004). I
restate only those facts that are pertinent to
this motion. On September 19, 2001,
Bristol-Myers Squibb ("BMS" or the
"Company") announced a $2 billion equity
investment in ImClone pursuant to which the
Company agreed to co-market and develop
with ImClone the cancer treatment drug,
Erbitux. Compl. ¶ 157. [FN2] However, on
December 28, 2001, the Food and Drug
Administration ("FDA") informed ImClone, by
way of a "refusal-to-file" ("RTF") letter, that the
FDA would not review the Erbitux Biologics
Licence Application because the data
submitted by ImClone was insufficient to
support fast track approval at that time. Compl.
¶¶ 181, 187- 88. On March 21, 2002, this
action commenced with the filing of a class
action complaint asserting that various of the
Company's statements of optimism about the
ImClone investment were false and misleading
within the meaning of § 10(b) of the Securities
and Exchange Act of 1934.

FN2. "Compl." refers to the Consolidated Class
Action Complaint filed on April 11, 2003.

In April 2002, BMS issued its Form 10-K for the
year ending December 31, 2001, in which it
disclosed that certain of its domestic
wholesalers had built up excess inventory of
BMS' pharmaceutical products. Compl. ¶¶ 113,
123. Also during April, the SEC began an
informal inquiry into BMS' wholesaler inventory
buildup, which became a formal investigation in
August 2002. Compl. ¶¶ 127, 130. On April 11,
2002, various plaintiffs filed a class action
complaint alleging that the Company engaged
in "a systematic program of moving sales from
future periods [into the current period] in a
process of what is sometimes called 'channel
stuffing." ' April 11 Compl. ¶ 35. [FN3] In late
October 2002, the Company announced that,
based on the recent advice of its accountant,
PricewaterhouseCoopers LLP ("PwC"), the
Company expected to restate its financial
statements for certain prior periods. Compl. ¶
134; Grayer Decl. Ex. A at 48. [FN4] In a
stipulation signed on November 27, 2002, and

filed on December 5, 2002, the parties agreed that an amended consolidated complaint would be served two weeks after the Company restated its earnings.

FN3. "April 11 Compl." refers to the complaint filed on April 11, 2002, under the caption David Wilmer v. Bristol-Myers Squibb Company, et al., 02 Civ. 2827(LAP).

FN4. "Grayer Decl." refers to the Declaration of Elizabeth Grayer in Support of Motion to Dismiss the Consolidated Class Action Complaint with Prejudice filed on October 14, 2003.

*2 On March 10, 2003, BMS publicly announced the expected scope and substance of its restatement, which was formally contained in three amended public filings submitted to the SEC on March 19, 2003: a Form 10-K/A for the year ended December 31, 2001, and Forms 10-Q/A for the three-month periods ended March 31, 2002, and June 30, 2002, (collectively, the "Restatement"). Compl. ¶ 2.The parties entered into a stipulation and order on April 3, 2003, which modified the December 5 stipulation to give Lead Plaintiffs an opportunity to review the Company's amended 2002 10-Q filings. Accordingly, on April 11, 2003, Teachers' Retirement System of Louisiana, Louisiana State Employees' Retirement System, General Retirement System of the City of Detroit, and Fresno County Employees' Retirement Association (collectively, "Lead Plaintiffs") filed the Complaint. Defendants moved to dismiss the Complaint beginning on August 1, 2003. Pursuant to the Private Securities Litigation Reform Act of 1995 ("PSLRA"), 15 U.S.C. § 78u-4, discovery was stayed during the pendency of Defendants' motions to dismiss. Berger/Block Decl. ¶ 35. [FN5] On September 9, 2003, Lead Plaintiffs filed a single joint opposition to all pending motions to dismiss. Oral argument was held on March 29, 2004, and, on March 31, 2004, the motions to dismiss were granted, resulting in dismissal of the Complaint with prejudice.

FN5. "Berger/Block Decl." refers to the Joint Declaration of Daniel L. Berger and Jeffrey C. Block in Support of the Proposed Settlement, Plan of Allocation and Application for an Award of Attorneys' Fees and Reimbursement of Expenses filed on October 19, 2004.

Lead Plaintiffs filed a Notice of Appeal on April 28, 2004. While the appeal was pending, the parties engaged in settlement discussions which culminated in the Stipulation and Agreement of Settlement executed on July 29, 2004 (the "Stipulation"). Berger/Block Decl. ¶ 28. Just five days later, on August 4, 2004, the SEC announced the filing of a civil fraud action against BMS and the simultaneous settlement of that action. Berger/Block Decl. ¶ 31. Since that time, Lead Counsel and the SEC have worked cooperatively to distribute notices of settlement in both cases. Berger/Block Decl. ¶ 32.Lead Counsel seek an award of attorneys' in the amount of 7.5% of the $300,000,000 Settlement Fund, minus $1,000,000 in approved notice costs and $557,580,75 in expenses incurred by Plaintiffs' Counsel, or $22,383,181.44. The fees sought result from two negotiations between Lead Plaintiffs and their counsel. The first negotiation occurred in preparation for the execution of retainer agreements with certain of the Lead Plaintiffs. Berger/Block Decl. ¶ 48; Lead Pl. Decl. ¶ 14. [FN6] That agreement provided for a fee of 15% of the total recovery if such recovery was obtained upon either a decision on a motion to dismiss or prior to the commencement of discovery. Lead Pl. Decl. Ex. 1. Sometime after the Stipulation was entered, "Lead Plaintiffs and Lead Counsel revisited the retainer agreement in view of the fact that the Complaint had been dismissed with prejudice," and they agreed to reduce the attorneys' fees by half, to 7.5%. Lead Pl. Memo. at 23, [FN7] Lead Pl. Decl. ¶¶ 15-16, and Berger/Block Decl. ¶ 49. On October 19, 2004, Lead Counsel filed the present Motion for an Award of Attorneys' Fees and Reimbursement of Expenses.

FN6. "Lead Pl. Decl." refers to the Joint Declaration of William T. Reeves, Jr., Kevin Torres, Ronald Zajac and Roberto Pena in Support of the Proposed Settlement, Plan of Allocation and Award of Attorneys' Fees and Reimbursement of Expenses dated October 12, 2004, and filed on October 19, 2004.

FN7. "Lead Pl. Memo." refers to the Memorandum of Law in Support of Lead Plaintiffs' Motion for Entry of Judgment Approving Class Action Settlement and Plan of Allocation and Motion for an Award of Attorneys' Fees and Reimbursement of Expenses filed on October 19, 2004.

DISCUSSION

A. The Standard*3 Attorneys who create a common fund from which members of a class are compensated are entitled to "a reasonable fee--set by the court--to be taken from the fund." Goldberger v. Integrated Resources, Inc., 209 F.3d 43, 47 (2d Cir.2000) (internal citation omitted). Simple logic teaches that such a fee award depletes the amount by which the class is benefitted. See Mautner v. Hirsch, 32 F.3d 37, 40 (2d Cir.1994). Accordingly, I have a duty "to award fees with moderation and a jealous regard for the rights of those with an interest in the fund but who are not before the Court." Burger v. CPC Intern, Inc., 76 F.R.D. 183, 188 (S.D.N.Y.1977).

The Court of Appeals has sanctioned the lodestar and percentage methods for calculating reasonable attorneys' fees in class actions. Goldberger, 209 F.3d at 50. Under both methods, the following factors are used to determine what constitutes a reasonable fee: (1) the risks of pursuing a case; (2) the complexity and uniqueness of the litigation; (3) the quality of representation; (4) counsel's time and effort; (5) the requested fee in relation to the settlement; and (6) public policy considerations. Id.The lodestar method entails "scrutiniz[ing] the fee petition to ascertain the number of hours reasonably billed to the class and then multipl[ying] that figure by an appropriate hourly rate." Id . at 47 (citing Savoie v. Merchants Bank, 166 F.3d 456, 460 (2d Cir.1999)). The resulting lodestar may then be increased by applying a multiplier based on the factors enumerated above. Id.

The second method is the far simpler percentage method, by which the fee award is "some percentage of the fund created for the benefit of the class." Savoie, 166 F.3d at 460. In determining what percentage to award, courts consider the same factors used to gauge the appropriate multiplier for the lodestar. Goldberger, 209 F.3d at 47. The percentage is lowered frequently where the

common fund is large in order to avoid a perceived windfall for plaintiffs' counsel. Roberts v. Texaco, 979 F.Supp. 185, 195 (S . D.N.Y.1997).Typically, courts utilize the percentage method and then "cross-check" the adequacy of the resulting fee by applying the lodestar method. See Goldberger, 209 F.3d at 50. When used merely as a cross-check, the hours documented by counsel need not be thoroughly scrutinized, see id., a process that Judge McLaughlin in Goldberger likened to "resurrect[ing] the ghost of Ebenezer Scrooge, compelling district courts to engage in a gimlet-eyed review of line-item fee audits." Id. at 49. Courts typically reduce the percentage of the fee as the size of the recovery increases and utilize the lodestar method to confirm that the percentage amount does not award counsel an exorbitant hourly rate. See In re NASDAQ Market-Makers Antitrust Litig., 187 F .R.D. 465, 486, 489 n. 24 (S.D.N.Y.1998) (internal citations omitted).

B. Application

*4 The first, and most important, Goldberger factor is the risk in pursuing the case. See Goldberger, 209 F.3d at 54 (quoting City of Detroit v. Grinnell Corp., 495 F.2d at 448, 471 (2d Cir.1974)); see also Klein v. Salvi, No. 02 Civ. 1862, 2004 WL 596109, at *7 (S.D.N.Y. March 30, 2004) (internal citations omitted). From Lead Counsel's perspective, "[t]he most obvious risk is the appeal that was pending prior to the Settlement." Lead Pl. Memo. at 15. However, it is well-settled that the risk of the litigation must be measured as of when the case is filed. See Goldberger, 209 F.3d at 55 (citing DiFilippo v. Morizio, 759 F.2d 231, 234 (2d Cir.1985); In re Fine Paper Antitrust Litig., 751 F.2d 562, 583 (3d Cir.1984)). The risk that Lead Plaintiffs would not prevail on appeal after dismissal of the Complaint is, therefore, irrelevant to this inquiry. Lead Counsel claim to have faced just two risks at the inception of the case: (1) failure to prove Defendants' intent to commit fraud; and (2) difficulty in proving the amount of damages. Lead Pl. Memo. at 15. The only fact presented by Lead Counsel in support of these risks--that the Complaint was dismissed for failure to plead scienter adequately--is a byproduct of hindsight and, consequently, does not demonstrate that such a risk was present at the time of their filing of a complaint. Goldberger, 209 F.3d at 54; see Lead Pl. Memo. at 15. In any event, proving scienter is one of the "general hurdles" facing plaintiffs in almost every securities case, see Goldberger,

2099 F.3d at 54, except, perhaps, where a criminal conviction precedes the civil action. Thus, Lead Counsel have failed to set forth a single fact that was apparent prior to the commencement of the case that would demonstrate any unusual degree of risk in pursuing the action. To the contrary, the circumstances preceding the filing of the Complaint, set out below in the discussion of the complexities of this litigation, particularly the Company's restatement of its financials, support a finding that this case falls along the low end of the continuum of risk. See id.

Next, I consider the complexities and uniqueness of the litigation. Lead Counsel cite the necessity of proving the elements of securities fraud, the amount of damages, and the magnitude of the alleged fraud as evidence of the complexity of the litigation. See Lead Pl. Memo. at 31. Certainly, managing the large class of plaintiffs and reaching a $300 million settlement was not a simple task for Lead Counsel, but, in the realm of securities class actions, prosecution of this action was less complex than most. All of the alleged misstatements were easily found in the public record. The public expressions of optimism uttered by the Company and its officers provided the bases for the Erbitux claims and the financials laid bare the channel-stuffing claims. Similarly, the claims were precipitated by public events. The FDA's issuance of the RTF letter predated the Erbitux claims, and the restatement preceded the channel-stuffing allegations. Lead Counsel merely drafted complaints setting out roughly chronologically the material in the public record and alleging Defendants' knowledge and scienter. Neither the facts nor the legal and accounting theories were complicated. Among securities class actions, this case as a whole was neither unique nor complex. Compare In re Visa Check/Mastermoney Litig., 297 F.Supp.2d 503, 523 (E.D.N.Y.2003) (finding magnitude and complexities of case "enormous"), aff'd, Wal-Mart Stores, Inc. v. Visa U.S.A., Inc., No. 04-0344, 04-1055, 04-1052, 04-0514, 2005 WL 15056 (2d Cir. Jan 04, 2005); In re Sumitomo Copper Litigation, 74 F.Supp.2d 393, 395 (S.D.N.Y.1999) (case involved "almost overwhelming magnitude and complexity"); In re NASDAQ, 187 F.R.D. at 474, 488 (finding that "liability in this case requires proof of an unusually complex conspiracy involving 37 Defendants and a 'checkerboard' of fact situations and disparate periods for each of 1,659 different securities" and that "the issues

were novel and difficult requiring a challenge to a long-standing industry practice and the exercise of skill and imagination.").*5 The quality of representation in this case is not in dispute and in light of the relatively low level of complexity of the matter, neither favors nor disfavors counsels' fee application.

The fourth Goldberger factor is the time and effort expended by counsel. Pursuant to the PSLRA, discovery was stayed during the pendency of the motions to dismiss that resulted in dismissal of the case with prejudice. Berger/Block Decl. ¶ 35. Although Lead Counsel responded to Defendants' motions to dismiss and engaged in post-settlement confirmatory discovery, Lead Pl. Memo. at 14, this case is distinguishable from those relied on by Lead Counsel in support of a large fee award. See Lead Pl. Memo. at 26. For example, Plaintiffs' counsel In re Sumitomo Copper Litigation, engaged in an investigation that involved the review and analysis of eleven million pages of documents, some seven million of which were in Japanese, located in London, Hong Kong, and Tokyo, and consulted extensively with more than ten experts over a period of more than three years without any governmental assistance. 74 F.Supp.2d at 395. Similarly, counsel in NASDAQ expended great effort in the necessary analysis of a complex conspiracy involving 37 defendants and 1,659 different securities. See 187 F.R.D. at 474, 488.

Here, Lead Counsel's pre-Complaint investigation consisted of: (1) interviewing dozens of witnesses familiar with the facts underlying the Complaint; (2) reviewing BMS' public filings and disclosures, press coverage, and market analyst reports; (3) analyzing the events and transactions alleged in the Complaint; (4) consulting with forensic accounting experts; and (5) retaining and consulting with a damages expert. See Lead Pl. Memo. at 14. Although Lead Counsel, together with certain Plaintiffs' Counsel, reviewed over 2.3 million pages of documents in confirmatory discovery, Lead Pl. Memo. at 14, clearly, the record here is lacking the kind of detailed accounting analysis and impressive documentary volume that was present in In re Sumitomo Copper Litigation or the documentary volume and sophisticated analysis present in NASDAQ. Of course, confirmatory discovery occurred after settlement was agreed to and, while post-settlement confirmatory discovery can serve important purposes, it has "created a temptation for lawyers to run up the number of hours for which they can be paid." See Goldberger, 209 F.3d at 48. Given the timing and circumstances of this settlement, Lead Counsel have not satisfied their burden of persuading me that confirmatory discovery in this case was not make-work.

While Lead Counsel certainly expended considerable time and effort in reaching the settlement agreement set forth in the Stipulation, it is not thirty times more difficult to settle a thirty million dollar case as it is to settle a one million dollar case. See id. (quoting Union Carbide, 724 F.Supp. at 166). "A lawyer's fee should not be likened to a case of salvage, where reward is given to the successful finder, often with little regard to how much or how little effort the finder expended." Klein, 2004 WL 596109, at *11. The sequence of events in this case suggests that Lead Counsel's time and effort, while worthy, does not constitute the sort of extraordinary effort that might merit a large percentage fee award (particularly here, where the Settlement Fund out of which Lead Counsel will be paid contains almost $300,000,000). That the Complaint had been dismissed with prejudice and, while the appeal was pending, the parties reached a settlement agreement that was executed just five days before filing and simultaneous settlement of the SEC action suggests that it was the Company's desire, prompted by the SEC, to put its house in order that caused the settlement, not any action on the part of Lead Counsel.

*6 Finally, I consider whether public policy favors Lead Counsel's requested fee award. See id. Although in the abstract a 4.3 multiplier would not fall outside the spectrum of multipliers that have been deemed reasonable in cases relied upon by Lead Counsel, see Lead Pl. Memo at 29 (citing Maley v. Del Global Techs. Corp., 186 F.Supp.2d 358, 371 (S.D.N.Y.2002) (4.65 multiplier); Roberts, 979 F.Supp. at 198 (5.5 multiplier); Weiss v. Mercedes-Benz of N.A., Inc., 899 F.Supp. 1297, 1304 (D.N.J.1995) (9.3 multiplier)), fee awards should be assessed based on the unique circumstances of each case. See Goldberger, 109 F.3d at 52.

Lead Counsel correctly argue that public policy supports granting attorneys fees that are sufficient to encourage plaintiffs' counsel to bring securities class actions that supplement the efforts of the SEC. See Lead Pl. Memo. at 33 (citing Bateman Eichler Hill Richards, Inc. v. Berner, 472 U.S. 299, 310 (1985)). However, attorneys' fees that amount to more than four times the unscrutinized lodestar figure would provide far more than sufficient encouragement to plaintiffs' counsel, indeed, would provide a windfall, where there appears, at the commencement of the litigation, no more than the usual risk of non-recovery. The unique facts of this case support that view, given the timing of both the Complaint and the Stipulation. Lead Counsel suggest that refusing to grant their requested 7.5% fee [FN8] would amount to punishment that deters future such lawsuits, thereby stifling the purpose of securities laws and leaving harms without redress. Lead Pl. Memo. at 33. If reducing attorneys' fees to an amount that is reasonable in relation to the distinctive procedural history and the economics of this case amounts to punishment, "I am confident there will be many attempts to self-inflict similar punishment in future cases." See In re Visa Check/Mastermoney Litig., 297 F.Supp.2d at 525.

FN8. As noted above, the 7.5% fee is the result of renegotiations with Lead Plaintiffs following dismissal of the Complaint. Contrary to Lead Counsel's argument, that the fact that the 7.5% fee was negotiated with institutional Lead Plaintiffs, see Lead Pl. Memo at 22-23, should not and, here, does not, lead to the conclusion that this percentage is presumptively fair. Despite the improvements intended by the PSLRA, "plaintiffs in common fund cases [generally remain] mere 'figureheads,' and the real reason for bringing such actions [remains] 'the quest for attorneys' fees.' " Goldberger, 209 F.3d at 53 (quoting Ralph K. Wittler, Paying Lawyers, Empowering Prosecutors, and Protecting Managers: Raising the Cost of Capital in America, 42 Duke L.J. 945, 984 (1993) and citing to PSLRA). As Judge McLaughlin noted in Goldberger, neither the defendants nor the plaintiffs themselves have any incentive to expend resources to object to a fee request: "Defendants, once the settlement amount has been agreed to, have little interest in how it is distributed and thus no incentive to oppose the fee. Indeed, the same dynamic creates incentives for collusion--the temptation for the lawyers to agree to a less than optimal settlement 'in exchange for red-carpet treatment on fees.' And the class members--the intended beneficiaries of the

suit--rarely object. Why should they? They
have no real incentive to mount a challenge
that would result in only a 'minuscule' pro rata
gain from a fee reduction." Goldberger, 209
F.3d at 52-53 (internal citations omitted). The
general rule recognized by Judge McLaughlin
holds true here where no one has opposed the
fee request, and thus the fact that Lead
Plaintiffs negotiated a 7.5% fee is not
persuasive.

The lodestar figure in this case is
$5,192,155.10. That a fee award of
$11,937,696.78 results in a quite reasonable
multiplier of 2.29 further convinces me that this
award is reasonable. See In re Cendant Corp.
PRIDES Litig., 243 F.3d 722, 742 (3d Cir.2001)
(finding that a survey of cases with megafunds
over $100 million shows that lodestar
multipliers of 1.35 to 2.99 are common).Having
considered all of the factors set forth in
Goldberger and having cross-checked the
resulting fee by way of the lodestar method, I
find that a fee of $11,937,696.78 to be paid out
of the Settlement Fund is reasonable.

Lead Counsel's motion for reimbursement of
expenses in the amount of $557,580.75, to be
paid out of the Settlement Fund as well, is also
granted.

CONCLUSION

For the reasons set forth above, Lead Plaintiffs'
Motion for Attorneys Fees
and Reimbursement of Expenses is granted, to
the extent noted in the
foregoing Opinion and Order.

SO ORDERED

S.D.N.Y.,2005.
In re Bristol-Myers Squibb
2005 WL 447189 (S.D.N.Y.)
END OF DOCUMENT

Appendix F: Hooveen v. Exxon Mobil Corp, Order on Attorney Fee

Hooven v. Exxon Mobil Corp., No. 00-5071 (E.D.Pa. 02/14/2005)

[1] IN THE UNITED STATES DISTRICT COURT FOR THE EASTERN DISTRICT OF PENNSYLVANIA

[2] Civil Action No. 00-5071

[3] 2005.EPA.0000203< http://www.versuslaw.com>

[4] February 14, 2005

[5] JOE HOOVEN ET AL., PLAINTIFF
v.
EXXON MOBIL CORPORATION AND MOBIL CORPORATION EMPLOYEE SEVERANCE PLAN, DEFENDANTS

[6] The opinion of the court was delivered by: Rufe, J.

[7] MEMORANDUM OPINION AND ORDER

[8] Before the Court are Plaintiffs' Motions for a Determination of Attorneys' Fees and Expenses and for an Award of Prejudgment and Post-judgment Interest.*fn1 This follows the Court's March 31, 2004 ruling that Defendants breached a unilateral contract called the Change in Control Plan Summary Plan Description ("SPD") with Plaintiffs.

[9] I. Background*fn2

[10] In 1999, Exxon and Mobil were preparing for a merger. The merger was expected to result in the loss of approximately 9,000 to 12,000 jobs. As an incentive to

employees to remain with Mobil pending the merger despite the uncertainty of employment in the merged company ("Exxon Mobil"), Mobil included a program of enhanced severance benefits for employees in the Change in Control Plan ("CIC Plan"). To explain the CIC Plan to employees, Mobil developed a SPD and distributed it to employees, including Plaintiffs, in August 1999.

[11] Most relevant to this case, the CIC Plan contained a severance benefit eligibility exception with respect to divestitures affecting tier four employees, such as Plaintiffs.*fn3 Specifically, it stated that tier four employees who were offered comparable employment with the purchaser or successor after divestiture would not receive enhanced severance benefits. However, the SPD distributed to employees did not accurately reflect this provision. Instead, the SPD implied that tier four employees would receive an enhanced severance package if they did not receive an offer of employment from Exxon Mobil after the merger. The SPD did not contain an exception for divestiture.

[12] After the change in control on November 30, 1999, Mobil divested Plaintiffs' entire division (the Mid-Atlantic Marketing Assets Division) to Tosco Corporation.*fn4 At a meeting on December 2, 1999, Mobil informed Plaintiffs that: 1) they would not be offered jobs with Exxon Mobil; 2) they were all being offered comparable employment at Tosco; and 3) as tier four employees who had been offered equivalent employment pursuant to a divestiture, they would not be receiving severance benefits under the CIC Plan.

[13] Believing they were entitled to enhanced severance benefits under the SPD, Plaintiffs filed this lawsuit advancing claims for breach of fiduciary duty, equitable estoppel, common law breach of contract, and reporting and disclosure violations under the Employee Retirement Income Security Act of 1974 ("ERISA"). Plaintiffs succeeded on the common law breach of contract claims. (Count III of their complaint).

[14] Under ERISA, companies have an affirmative obligation to inform employees of their rights through written plan documents.*fn5 The SPD, a required document, is the primary informational document issued to plan beneficiaries to inform them of their rights and obligations.*fn6 The contents of the SPD and the language used to communicate the contents are carefully proscribed by statute and regulation.*fn7 Of particular importance here, ERISA requires that the SPD must contain a description of any circumstances that may result in disqualification, ineligibility, denial, or loss of benefits.*fn8 The Third Circuit has ruled that where there is a conflict between a plan document and a summary plan description, the summary plan description governs.*fn9 In this case, because of discrepancies between it and the CIC Plan, the Court found that the SPD governed Plaintiffs' situation.

[15] The SPD formed a unilateral contract, which was accepted when the Plaintiffs chose to stay on through the uncertainties of the change in control rather than seeking other employment. The Third Circuit has directed the courts to apply Federal common law contract principles to claims for plan benefits.*fn10 Accordingly, Plaintiffs were not required to prove reliance upon the SPD in order to enforce their claim for severance benefits.*fn11 The Court found absolutely no indication in the text of the SPD that tier four employees who were terminated from Mobil but offered comparable employment after divestiture would be ineligible for enhanced severance benefits. A provision in the CIC Plan precluded Mobil from amending the terms of the Plan within two years of the change in control, so the errata to the SPD, issued after the change in control, did not change the Plaintiffs' rights under the original SPD. Therefore, the Court found that Defendants were in breach of contract and ordered Defendants to provide Plaintiffs with enhanced severance benefits in accordance with the terms of the SPD.*fn12

[16] II. Attorneys' Fees

[17] A. Fees under the CIC Plan

[18] Plaintiffs claim that the CIC Plan compels Defendants to pay Plaintiffs reasonable attorneys' fees and expenses. They further argue that the payments by each Plaintiff of 33 a% of his or her recovery incurred under the contingency fee agreement between each Plaintiff and counsel were reasonable fees to incur in the matter and should be fully reimbursed by Defendants. Plaintiffs rely upon this language in the CIC Plan:

[19] The Company shall pay to each Eligible Employee all reasonable legal fees and expenses incurred by such Eligible Employee in pursuing any claim under the Plan in which such Eligible Employee prevails in any material respect.

[20] Defendants respond that: 1) any claim for fees must be pursued with the CIC Plan Administrator before petitioning the Court; 2) the CIC Plan is only required to pay attorneys' fees for claims under the administrative claims procedure, not for claims pursued through a lawsuit; 3) Plaintiffs did not advance a claim for denial of benefits under the CIC Plan, so Plaintiffs have not prevailed on a claim under the CIC Plan, as required for an award of attorneys' fees; and 4) should the Court award attorneys' fees, it should: a) calculate a reasonable fee using the lodestar method rather than the percentage of recovery method; and b) limit fees to time spent on Count III of the Complaint (the only Count on which Plaintiffs succeeded).

[21] First, the Court finds that it would be futile for Plaintiffs to pursue attorneys' fees with the CIC Plan Administrator, and will not require them to do so.*fn13 Second, the Court finds nothing in the CIC Plan which limits the term "claim" to an administrative claim. The plain meaning of the term "claim" includes claims made in Federal court.*fn14 Third, Plaintiffs prevailed on a claim for breach of contract, where a unilateral contract was formed by Plaintiffs' implied acceptance of the SPD through remaining in the company's employ pending the change in control. The discrepancy between the CIC Plan and the SPD was an important factor in the Court's ruling. The Court ordered Defendants to provide severance benefits to Plaintiffs in accordance with the SPD. Because the SPD summarizes the CIC Plan, the Court finds that Plaintiffs prevailed on a claim under the CIC Plan and are

contractually entitled to reasonable attorneys' fees.

[22]   Plaintiffs ask the Court to award attorneys' fees based on the contingency fee agreements between Plaintiffs' and their counsel. Defendants ask the Court to award attorneys' fees based on the lodestar method, and suggest that the Court should further reduce the award by granting fees only for time spent litigating the one successful claim.

[23]   The Court will first address Defendants' request that attorneys' fees only be awarded for time spent litigating Count III. The plain language of the CIC Plan obligates the Defendants to pay all reasonable fees incurred in pursuing a claim in which the employee prevails in any material respect. Where a plaintiff is deemed prevailing although he succeeded on only some claims for relief, the court must address two questions: 1) did plaintiff fail to prevail on claims that were unrelated to claims on which he succeeded; and 2) did plaintiff achieve a level of success that makes the hours expended a satisfactory basis for a fee award?*fn15

[24]   Here, the four counts in the Complaint were pled as alternative theories of the case, and they were all related claims. Furthermore, although Plaintiffs prevailed only on the theory set forth in Count III, the Court awarded them the full amount of the enhanced severance benefits they sought.*fn16 Since the remedy was fully favorable to Plaintiffs, and Plaintiffs prevailed in a "material respect,"*fn17 the Court will not limit attorneys' fees to the actual time spent litigating Count III. Such a limitation is also not anticipated by the attorneys' fees provision of the CIC Plan. Furthermore, it is quite apparent that such parsing of claims would be impossible given the nature of the litigation in this matter.*fn18

[25]   The Court turns now to the final question: whether it is appropriate to award attorneys' fees based on the contingency fee agreements between Plaintiffs and their counsel.*fn19 If so, these agreements to pay counsel 33a% of any recovery achieved would yield 58approximately $2 million in attorneys' fees, based on an estimated recovery for Plaintiffs in the amount of $6 million.*fn20 In

contrast, a calculation of fees using the lodestar method would yield approximately $1.24 million in fees by Plaintiffs' estimate.*fn21 The contingency fee requested is approximately 61% higher than counsel's fees would be based on a lodestar calculation. The Court recognizes that the CIC Plan language regarding attorneys' fees manifests a compensatory rationale: to compensate beneficiaries for monetary outlays they would not have had to make but for Defendant's breach of the contract. Since it is undisputed that the Plaintiffs incurred fees in the amount of 33a% of their recovery, the Court must decide whether the sum incurred was reasonable.

[26]   This Court has wide discretion in awarding reasonable attorneys' fees.*fn22 The starting point for calculating "reasonable" attorneys' fees in a case is the product of the number of hours reasonably expended on the litigation and a reasonable hourly rate (the lodestar figure).*fn23 In addition, the computation of attorneys' fees may reflect two additional factors: the contingent nature of success and the quality of the attorneys' work.*fn24 When considering the contingent nature of success, the Court must consider: 1) the probability or likelihood of success viewed at the time of filing the suit; 2) the probability of the defendant's liability; 3) whether the case is asserted under well-settled law or is advancing a novel theory; 4) whether damages will be easy or difficult to prove; 5) risks assumed by counsel in developing the case, including the number of hours of labor risked without guarantee of remuneration, costs to the firm of processing motions, taking depositions, etc., and the development of prior expertise; and 6) the delay in receipt of payment for services rendered.*fn25 The Court may also adjust upward or downward from the lodestar figure based on the quality of counsel's work, which can be assessed by examining: 1) the results obtained for the plaintiffs in comparison with the best possible recovery; 2) the overall benefit conferred on the plaintiffs; and 3) counsel's professional methods.*fn26

[27]   Turning first to the number of hours spent in litigation, the Court has reviewed time records submitted by Plaintiffs' counsel,*fn27 which document over 6000 hours of work on this case.*fn28 The total was reduced by 62 hours, which counsel felt were unnecessary to achieving success for their client.*fn29

Defendants take issue with the number of hours spent in this litigation, arguing that the hours claimed by counsel are grossly excessive, unreasonable, and duplicative, and also that many of the hours charged were spent on issues of law on which the Plaintiffs did not ultimately prevail. The Court has already addressed the latter issue. As to the allegedly excessive nature of the hours billed, the Court disagrees with Defendants.

[28]   For work to be included in a calculation of attorneys' fees, it must be useful and of the type ordinarily necessary to secure the final result.*fn30 This case involved fifty-two named plaintiffs, and counsel were required to address discovery requests directed at each plaintiff. The case also involved extensive motion practice and unsettled issues of law. Submitting and responding to motions, especially on unsettled or novel issues of law, can be time consuming and involve extensive research. Even experienced attorneys must engage in many hours of research when confronted with unsettled issues of law. Furthermore, it was not unreasonable to sometimes assign more than one attorney to work on similar tasks in this case.*fn31 The Court notes that this case involved an eight day trial, during which both Plaintiffs and Defendants had multiple attorneys in the courtroom, and counsel for both sides were extremely well prepared. The Court has no doubt that counsel's representation of the fifty-two plaintiffs in this matter consumed a great deal of time fact finding, taking and defending depositions, producing and reviewing other discovery, performing legal research, drafting motions and briefs, preparing Plaintiffs' case for trial, appearing in court, and other tasks. The Court has reviewed Plaintiffs' detailed documentation of time spent by counsel on each of these tasks and others, and the Court does not find the time spent to be excessive or the staffing to be unnecessarily redundant.

[29]   Next, the Court must make a finding as to prevailing market rates to determine whether Plaintiffs' fee request is reasonable.*fn32 Counsel set different hourly rates for paralegals, associates, and partners, and the rates for associates and partners increased with years of experience.*fn33 Plaintiffs submitted documentation to prove that the hourly rates suggested are consistent with

prevailing market rates in the community.*fn34 The Court finds that the suggested hourly rates are reasonable and consistent with the market rates in the Philadelphia region.

[30]   Defendants have not alleged that the hourly rates Plaintiffs' counsel suggest are inconsistent with current local rates, but they argue that the Court should calculate the lodestar using the hourly rates in effect when the time was spent, not counsel's current hourly rates.*fn35 The Third Circuit has explicitly disapproved such a practice: "When attorney's fees are awarded, the current market rate must be used. The current market rate is the rate at the time of the fee petition, not the rate at the time the services were performed."*fn36 The Court finds that Plaintiffs correctly used their current, reasonable billing rates when calculating the lodestar figure. Therefore, the Court finds that Plaintiffs' lodestar calculation of $1,244,690.00 is reasonable.

[31]   Plaintiffs' counsel have also provided detailed documentation of costs incurred, broken down by type of expense (e.g. costs of court reporters, transcripts, electronic research of legal issues, photocopying, postage, travel, etc.). The Defendants have not disputed the evidence regarding the costs Plaintiffs' counsel incurred, nor have they suggested that the documented costs are not of the type normally charged to fee-paying clients in the Philadelphia region. The Court finds that the costs incurred are not excessive, and are of the type typically passed on to clients in this region.*fn37 Accordingly, Plaintiffs' request for costs in the amount of $89,091.72 is reasonable.

[32]   Plaintiffs ask the Court to increase the lodestar figure to approximately $2 million (which represents 33a% of Plaintiffs' approximately $6 million recovery). This represents a 61% increase over the lodestar amount. Therefore, the Court must consider whether two additional considerations, the contingent nature of success and the quality of counsel's work, warrant such an enhancement.*fn38

[33]   As noted above, the Plaintiffs entered into a contingency fee agreement with counsel.

In advancing Plaintiffs' claims, counsel have documented over 6000 hours of legal work, all performed without guarantee of remuneration. Counsel have also incurred almost $90,000 in costs for the case, including the costs of court reporters, transcripts, electronic legal research, travel and copies, again without guarantee of remuneration. Furthermore, this case was filed in October 2000, meaning that Plaintiffs' counsel worked on this matter for over four years without any payment for services rendered. They agreed to represent fifty-two plaintiffs in this complex case involving unsettled questions of law, and the probability of success was by no means certain. Although all of these factors support awarding a fee enhancement, the Court acknowledges that these contingencies may be generously compensated by an award of fees based on the lodestar figure, since such an award incorporates: 1) higher rates for more experienced attorneys; 2) charges for additional hours spent researching and briefing unsettled areas of law; and 3) current hourly rates for work performed in the past.*fn39

[34]   Turning to the quality of counsel's work, the Court finds that Plaintiffs derived significant benefit from the lawsuit, receiving approximately $6 million in severance pay among the fifty-two of them. In a difficult case,*fn40 counsel attained a judgment for the full value of the enhanced severance benefits to which Plaintiffs believed they were entitled under the SPD. Throughout this litigation, the Court has been impressed by the quality of counsel's work. The Court finds that the quality and effectiveness of counsel's representation of the fifty-two plaintiffs in this case warrants fees exceeding the level of compensation provided based on the lodestar calculation. This factor thus supports an enhancement of fees. The enhancement requested, a multiplier of approximately 1.61, seems fair and reasonable considering both the quality of counsel's work and the compensatory rationale of the CIC Plan's fee-shifting provision. Accordingly, the Court finds that the requested fee amount, 33a% of the Plaintiffs' recovery, is fair and reasonable and awards Plaintiffs the full amount of attorneys' fees incurred.

[35]   B. Fees Under ERISA

[36]   Plaintiffs have also filed a Motion for Att orneys' Fees under the fee shifting provisions of ERISA. In this Motion, they ask the Court to calculate fees using the lodestar method, and to enhance the lodestar figure to cover the full amount Plaintiffs owe their counsel under their contingency fee agreements. They also ask for costs.

[37]   There is no presumption in favor of granting attorneys' fees to a successful plaintiff in an ERISA suit, absent exceptional circumstances.*fn41 ERISA authorizes the Court, in its discretion, to award prevailing plan beneficiaries reasonable attorneys' fees and costs.*fn42 The Third Circuit has articulated a five factor test for the Court to consider: 1) the offending party's culpability or bad faith; 2) the ability of the offending party to satisfy an award of attorneys' fees; 3) the deterrent effect of an award of attorneys' fees against the offending party; 4) the benefit conferred on members of the Plan as a whole; 5) and the relative merits of the parties' positions.*fn43

[38]   Applying these factors to this case, the Court finds they do not support an award of attorneys' fees under ERISA.*fn44 First, the Court does not find that Defendants are culpable, nor that their actions involved bad faith. ERISA required Defendants to fully disclose any coverage exclusions in the SPD, but Defendants failed to incorporate the exclusion applying to tier four employees in the case of divestiture. During the trial in this matter, the Court reviewed the many draft versions of this provision of the SPD. The Court concluded that Defendants were taking care to represent the CIC terms correctly in the SPD but made an error in judgment at the end of the editing process in an effort to make the ineligibility provision clearer. Further, Defendants published the correct information on Mobil's intranet site. The Court found that Mobil did not intentionally deceive its employees; rather it had made the mistake of inartful drafting. Clearly, there was no bad faith, and simple negligence is not enough to establish "culpable" behavior.*fn45 Therefore, this factor does not weigh in favor of attorneys' fees.

[39]   The second factor, Defendants' ability to satisfy the award of attorneys' fees, clearly weighs in favor of an award of fees.

[40]   Factor three examines the deterrent effect of an award of attorneys' fees. Under the CIC Plan, Plaintiffs were clearly ineligible for enhanced severance benefits. However, the last version of the SPD was unintentionally misleading as to ineligibility of divested tier four employees. As noted above, the Court did not find a corporate philosophy of non-disclosure or culpable behavior; rather Defendants made an error in judgment at the last stages of drafting the SPD. Though ultimately unsuccessful, Defendants clearly made a good-faith effort to ensure that the SPD correctly summarized the CIC Plan. The Court finds that an award of attorneys' fees would not have a significant deterrent effect given the facts of this case. Therefore, factor three weighs against an award of attorneys' fees.

[41]   Fourth, the Court looks at the benefit conferred on other Plan members by the Court's judgment. The CIC Plan's terms could be modified at the discretion of the company starting in December 2001. The errata Exxon Mobil issued to fix the discrepancy between the CIC Plan and the SPD (issued before the filing of this lawsuit) would have become effective on that date. Furthermore, the SPD/ CIC Plan discrepancy at issue in this case affected only a subset of CIC Plan beneficiaries-consisting of tier four employees who were offered jobs with an acquiring company after a divestiture related to the Exxon Mobil merger-which subset included the fifty-two Plaintiffs.*fn46 All other Mobil employees who were terminated after the merger with Exxon (approximately 2500 employees) were eligible for enhanced severance benefits under the terms of both the CIC Plan and the SPD, so the holding of the Court in this case would not affect their rights. For these reasons, the Court cannot conclude that its decision creates benefits for CIC Plan members as a whole. This factor weighs against an award of attorneys' fees.

[42]   Finally, the Court considers the relative merits of the parties' positions. Plaintiffs received a favorable decision on Count III, but Defendants received a favorable decision on Counts I, II, and IV. Plaintiffs' position on Count III was by no means a matter of well-settled law. The issue was a close one, and Defendants' position was reasonable and not frivolous.*fn47 Again, this factor does not support a finding of attorneys' fees.

[43]   Having found that the only factor that weighs in Plaintiffs' favor is Defendant's ability to pay, the Court finds Plaintiffs are not entitled to attorneys' fees under ERISA.

[44]   III. Prejudgment and Post-Judgment Interest

[45]   The award of prejudgment interest to Plaintiffs is within the Court's discretion and should be based on considerations of fairness.*fn48 Generally, such awards are used to make a plaintiff whole when he has been denied use of money that is his.*fn49 The Court finds that considerations of fairness require an award of prejudgment interest in this case and awards such interest, calculated at the statutory Federal post-judgment interest rate*fn50 from December 2, 1999, the date Defendants constructively terminated Plaintiffs.*fn51 The Court also awards Plaintiffs post-judgment interest pursuant to 28 U.S.C. § 1961.*fn52

[46]   AND NOW, this 14th day of February, 2005, upon consideration of Plaintiffs' Motion for Determination of Attorneys' Fees and Expenses and an Award of Prejudgment and Post-Judgment Interest [Doc. # 129], Defendants' Response thereto [Doc. # 133], and Plaintiffs' Reply [Doc. # 139] and upon consideration of Plaintiffs' Motion for an Award of Attorneys' Fees and Costs Under ERISA [Doc. # 144] and Defendants' Response thereto [Doc. # 149], and for the reasons set forth in the attached Memorandum Opinion, it is ORDERED as follows:

[47]   1. Plaintiffs' Motion for Prejudgment Interest is GRANTED. Defendants are ORDERED to include a payment of pre-judgment interest in their calculation of Plaintiffs' severance benefits, calculated from December 2, 1999 through March 31, 2004, at the rate set forth in 28 U.S.C. § 1961;

[48]   2. Plaintiffs' Motion for Post-Judgment interest is GRANTED. Defendants are ORDERED to include a payment of post-judgment interest in their calculation of Plaintiffs' severance benefits, calculated from

April 1, 2004 until the date of payment, at the rate set forth in 28 U.S.C. § 1961;

[49]   3. Plaintiffs' Motion for Attorneys' Fees under the terms of the CIC Plan is GRANTED. Defendants are ORDERED to pay Plaintiffs' counsel an attorneys' fee in the amount of 33a% of the total benefit paid to Plaintiffs. Defendants are also ORDERED to pay Plaintiffs' counsel costs in the amount of $89,091.72.

[50]   4. Plaintiffs' Motion for Attorneys' Fees under ERISA is DENIED. IT IS SO ORDERED.

[51]   CYNTHIA M. RUFE, J.

Opinion Footnotes

----

[52]   *fn1 Plaintiffs have filed two Motions for Attorneys' Fees: one pursuant to the contractual provisions of the CIC Plan ("CIC Plan Motion"), and the other pursuant to fee-shifting provisions of ERISA ("ERISA Motion").

[53]   *fn2 Additional factual details and legal analysis are found in the Court's March 31, 2004 Memorandum Opinion and Order.

[54]   *fn3 The text of the CIC Plan was not distributed to employees but was available to employees upon request.

[55]   *fn4 The divestiture of this division was required by the FTC. The FTC also advised that Exxon and Mobil should make employees in the divested business available to the buyer, which they did. Tosco was not under any obligation to hire the former Mobil employees, but the Chairman of Tosco offered jobs to all employees of Mobil's Mid-Atlantic Marketing Assets Division at comparable or improved salaries and benefits.

[56]   *fn5 Curtis-Wright Corp. v. Schoonejongen, 514 U.S. 73, 83 (1995).

[57]   *fn6 Local 56, United Food and Comm. Workers Union v. Campbell Soup Co., 898 F. Supp. 1118, 1130 (D.N.J. 1995).

[58]   *fn7 29 U.S.C. §§ 1021-24; 29 C.F.R. § 2520.102-3(1).

[59]   *fn8 29 U.S.C. § 1022(b).

[60]   *fn9 Burstein v. Ret. Account Plan for Employees of Allegheny Health Educ. and Research Fund, 334 F.3d 365, 378 (3d Cir. 2003).

[61]   *fn10 Id. at 381.

[62]   *fn11 Id.

[63]   *fn12 Plaintiffs did not succeed on their claims for breach of fiduciary duty or equitable estoppel because they did not prove detrimental reliance on the SPD.

[64]   *fn13 The Court has previously addressed this argument on the merits and found that Plaintiffs were not required to pursue their underlying claims with the plan administrator because the administrative review process would have been futile in this matter. Mem. Op. and Order dated March 31, 2004, at 45.

[65]   *fn14 It is well established that the Court is not authorized to construe a contract in such a way as to modify the plain meaning of its words, under the guise of interpretation. Mellon Bank, N.A. v. Aetna Bus. Credit, Inc. 619 F.2d 1001, 1010 (3d Cir. 1980).

[66]   *fn15 See Henley v. Eckerhart, 461 U.S. 424, 434 (1983).

[67]   *fn16 Id.

[68] *fn17 Maher v. Gagne, 448 U.S. 122, 127 (1980)(holding that a party prevails if it has won substantially the relief originally sought in its pleadings).

[69] *fn18 See Gorini v. AMP, Inc., No. 03-2052, 2004 WL 2809997, at *3 (3d Cir. Dec. 8, 2004) (when much of counsel's time is spent litigating case as a whole, and claims involve a common core of facts and/or related legal theories, it may be difficult to divide hours spent on a claim-by-claim basis; instead, district court should focus on the significance of overall relief obtained by the plaintiff in relation to hours reasonably spent on litigation); see also Henley, 461 U.S. at 435.

[70] *fn19 The Third Circuit favors the use of contingency fees in cases involving a common fund, and the lodestar method in cases involving fee shifting statutes. In re Prudential Ins. Co. of Am. Sales Practices Litig., 148 F.3d 283, 333 (3d Cir. 1998). This case involves neither a common fund nor a fee shifting statute, but rather a contract term providing that Defendants will pay all reasonable attorneys' fees and expenses incurred by prevailing employees. As the fees will be paid by Defendants and not by Plaintiffs from a common fund, the situation is more akin to a statutory fee shifting case. However, unlike statutory fee-shifting, contractual fee-shifting is not subject to the prohibition on contingency enhancements to the lodestar calculation of fees. See City of Burlington v. Dague, 505 U.S. 557, 565 (1992)(holding that Federal fee-shifting statutes do not permit enhancement of fee award beyond lodestar amount to reflect fact that a party agreed to pay on a contingency-fee basis).

[71] *fn20 Pls.' CIC Plan Reply at 10.

[72] *fn21 Defendants' contentions regarding this figure are discussed in detail below.

[73] *fn22 See Lindy Bros. Builders, Inc. of Philadelphia v. Am. Radiator & Standard Sanitary Corp., 540 F.2d 102, 115 (3d Cir. 1976) (award of reasonable attorneys' fees is within the district court's discretion); Nationwide Energy Corp. v. Kleiser, No. 84-3517, 1987 WL

10655, at *2-3 (E.D. Pa. May 7, 1987) (holding that when contracts provide for payment of reasonable attorneys' fees and litigation expenses, the court has equitable control over what constitutes a reasonable recovery for attorneys' fees and expenses).

[74] *fn23 Lindy Bros. Builders, Inc., 540 F.2d at 108.

[75] *fn24 Id. at 112-115. See also Merola v. Atlantic Richfield Co., 493 F.2d 292, 297 (3d Cir. 1974) (holding that in enforcing a contractual agreement to pay reasonable attorneys' fees, courts should apply Lindy standards to determine amount of award. The lodestar factors-time spent and reasonable hourly rates-produce the market value of attorneys' services, and the contingency and quality factors "permit the district judge the needed flexibility to tailor the award to the actual performance of counsel.")

[76] *fn25 Lindy Bros. Builders, Inc., 540 F.2d at 117.

[77] *fn26 Id. at 117-118.

[78] *fn27 Guernsey Aff. and attachs. 1-3.

[79] *fn28 Plaintiffs' counsel have provided the Court with what appear to be contemporaneously documented time records. These records include the identity of the attorney or paralegal, the date, the activity, and the time spent on the activity tracked in 1/10 hour increments. Guernsey Aff. attach. 1. The time keeping records submitted to the court are as detailed as those kept by counsel who are billing clients at an hourly rate. In addition to these detailed records, Plaintiffs have submitted summary charts and affidavits regarding the time spent on various tasks. Guernsey Aff. and attach. 2.

[80] *fn29 Guernsey Aff.

[81] *fn30 Planned Parenthood of Cent. N.J. v. Att. Gen. of State of N.J., 297 F.3d 253, 266 (3d Cir. 2002).

[82]   *fn31 Id. at 272 (upholding district court's finding that the magnitude and complexity of the case mandated the help of numerous attorneys for both sides, and holding that attorneys working on similar tasks is not per se duplicative since careful preparation often requires collaboration and rehearsal).

[83]   *fn32 Burney v. Housing Auth. of Beaver County, 735 F.2d 113, 116 (3d Cir. 1984).

[84]   *fn33 The firm calculated the lodestar using the following billing rates: $120 per hour for paralegals, $195 to $240 per hour for associates, depending on experience, and $285 and $380 per hour for the two partners. Another partner in the firm charged $545 per hour for his work, but only spent about ten hours on the case. Guernsey Aff. In calculating the lodestar amount, Plaintiffs multiplied the number of hours each attorney or paralegal spent on the case by the hourly billing rate for that individual, and then added these products together to produce the lodestar sum. Pls.' ERISA Mot. at 12. But cf. In re RiteAid Corp. Sec. Litig., No. 03-2914, 2005 WL 159464 (3d Cir. Jan. 26, 2005) (reversing finding that attorneys' fees were reasonable where district court failed to use "blended billing rate")(this case is not binding on the Court, since it involved a fee petition from a common fund in a class action suit, but it is advisory).

[85]   *fn34 Pls.' ERISA Mot., Ex. B, C, D. Exhibit B is an affidavit from an attorney at another local firm, in which the affiant attests that the rates and costs requested by Plaintiffs' counsel are consistent with what other local firms charge clients for ERISA litigation. The comparison figures provided in Exhibit C and D contain information about the 2003 hourly rates for comparable law firms and Community Legal Services, Inc.

[86]   *fn35 Defs.' ERISA Mem. at 10.

[87]   *fn36 Lanni v. New Jersey, 259 F.3d 146, 149 (3d Cir. 2001); see also Missouri v. Jenkins by Agyei, 491 U.S. 274, 283-284 (1989) (finding that application of current rather than historic hourly rates is an appropriate adjustment for delay in payment of attorneys' fees).

[88]   *fn37 See Planned Parenthood of Cent. N.J., 297 F.3d at 267 (reasonable attorneys' fees include award of reasonable out-of-pocket expenses normally charged to a fee-paying client in the course of providing legal services).

[89]   *fn38 Merola, 493 F.2d at 297.

[90]   *fn39 See City of Burlington, 505 U.S. at 562-563 (enhancement of attorneys' fees for contingency is unnecessary as higher hourly rates for more experienced counsel and higher number of hours worked to overcome the uncertainty of outcome already compensate attorneys adequately).

[91]   *fn40 Defendants themselves emphasize the uncertainty of Plaintiffs' success in their response to Plaintiffs' fee request: "the issue [of validity of a Federal common law contract claim based on an SPD] is so close that after the parties each submitted briefs regarding the impact of the Burstein decision, the Court held extensive argument in chambers regarding the issue." Defs.' ERISA Mem. at 9.

[92]   *fn41 McPherson v. Employees' Pension Plan of Am. Re-Ins. Co., Inc., 33 F.3d 253, 254 (3d Cir. 1994).

[93]   *fn42 Id.

[94]   *fn43 Id. (citing Ursic v. Bethlehem Mines, 719 F.2d 670, 673 (3d Cir. 1983)).

[95]   *fn44 The Court notes, as a preliminary matter, that Plaintiffs prevailed not on an ERISA claim, but on a common law breach of contract claim related to their ERISA claims.

[96]   *fn45 McPherson, 33 F.3d at 257.

[97]   *fn46 The Court has heard no evidence as to whether there were other tier four

employees, besides the fifty-two Plaintiffs, who were subject to divestiture.

[98]   *fn47 Home for Crippled Children v. Prudential Ins. Co. of Am., 590 F. Supp. 1490, 1508 (W.D. Pa. 1984).

[99]   *fn48 Ambromovage v. United Mine Workers of Am., 726 F.2d 972, 981-982 (3d Cir. 1984).

[100]   *fn49 Id. at 982.

[101]   *fn50 28 U.S.C. §1961.

[102]   *fn51 See, e.g. Thomas v. Bd. of Tr. of Int'l Union of Operating Eng'rs, Local 542, Pension Fund, No. 97-CV-2426, 1998 WL 334627, at *13 (E.D. Pa. June 24, 1998) (awarding prejudgment interest calculated at Federal statutory post-judgment interest rate).

[103]   *fn52 Defendants argue that Plaintiffs did not obtain a "money judgment" against Defendants, because ERISA limits recovery to equitable relief. Defs.' CIC Plan Resp. at 13. This argument is simply incorrect. The Court found that Defendants were in breach of their contract with Plaintiffs under Federal common law, and awarded Plaintiffs the severance benefits owed to them under the contract. The Court awarded approximately $6 million in monetary damages to Plaintiffs. Mem. Op. and Order dated March 31, 2004.

LaVergne, TN USA
02 September 2009
156733LV00002B/71/A